The Politics of Denial

The Politics of Denial

Michael A. Milburn
Sheree D. Conrad

The MIT Press
Cambridge, Massachusetts
London, England

This book was set in Sabon by Graphic Composition, Inc., Athens, Georgia on the Miles 33 System.

Printed and bound in the United States of America.

Library of Congress Cataloging-in-Publication Data

Milburn, Michael A.
  The politics of denial / Michael A. Milburn, Sheree D. Conrad
  p.   cm.
  Includes bibliographical references and index.
  ISBN 0-262-13330-X (hardcover)
  1. Political psychology. 2. Political socialization. 3. Child rearing. 4. Parent and child. I. Conrad, Sheree D. II. Title.
JA74.5.M55   1996
320′.01′9—dc20   96-16100
                                                                          CIP

This book is dedicated to my parents,
Thomas Milburn and JoAnne Milburn
—M.A.M.
and to the memory of
David R. Mariani
—S.D.C.

Contents

Acknowledgments

This book would not have been possible without the help, advice, and support of a number of people. We want to thank our agent, Elizabeth Ziemska, for her support and enthusiasm, for believing in the project from the beginning, and for her very valuable suggestions about the content. We also want to thank Amy Pierce at the MIT Press, who brought great enthusiasm and commitment to the project and helped us to write a much better book.

The research of several of our students at the University of Massachusetts/Boston contributed tremendously to this volume, particularly Fabio Sala, Sheryl Carberry, Ron Levine, Anne McGrail, Patricia Casimira, and James Hopper.

Both Michael Lustig and Eric Webster worked tirelessly to gather primary materials for the text. They contributed insight and understanding to the research they did for this book, and it would never have been finished on time without their help. Thanks also to several other student assistants, Tomas Kavaliauskas, Suzanne D'Allessandro, Don Masterson, and Tom Gilmore, for their help with research on the book. Natalie Zacek did extensive research for chapter 7, and Johanna Milburn researched material for chapter 9.

Michael Laurie read early drafts of several chapters and provided valuable feedback. Marshall Cohen, Kathy Kraft, and Dianne Horgan read the entire manuscript and gave very important suggestions for changes, Peter Milburn provided important research assistance for chapter 9, Sheila Brownlow made an important contribution to chapter 6, and Cara Morris made an important contribution to chapter 9. Thanks for their help to Douglas Hodgkin, Simon Jackman, Brad Jones, Scott Keeter, Taeku Lee, Bill Kubik, Robert Yale Shapiro, Eric R. A. N. Smith, and other members of POR, the public opinion research Internet discussion group. We also want to thank our colleagues, Dennis Byrnes and Don Kalick, for their ongoing support.

Sheree Conrad gives thanks to Elizabeth O'Neill, Mary Kohák, Nancy Corbin, and Sheila Purdy for their love and support and also to her family, Thelma Dukes, and Diane, Steven, Alissa, Abby, and Aimée Bourque.

Michael Milburn thanks his daughters, Allison, Johanna, and Abby, for their support and forbearance during this project. His wife, Deborah Kelley-Milburn, deserves a special mention. Not many scholars have the extreme good fortune to be married to a highly skilled Harvard University reference librarian and expert on electronic databases and the Internet. Luckily for Dr. Milburn, he is one of those fortunate scholars. In many, many ways, this book would not have been completed without her. It probably would never have been started, either.

Material from *Spare the Child* by Philip Greven, Jr., copyright © 1990 by Philip Greven, Jr., is reprinted by permission of Alfred A. Knopf, Inc. Excerpts from *For Your Own Good* by Alice Miller, translated by Hildegarde and Hunter Hannum, translation copyright © 1983 by Alice Miller, are reprinted by permission of Farrar, Straus & Giroux, Inc., and by Faber & Faber, Ltd. Excerpts from the article "The Killing Trail" by H. G. Bissinger, which originally appeared in *Vanity Fair,* are reprinted with permission of William Morris Agency, Inc., as agent for H. G. Bissinger, © 1995 by H. G. Bissinger. Material from *The Ego and the Mechanisms of Defense* by Anna Freud, © 1966, is reprinted by permission from International Universities Press, Inc.

Introduction: What's Missing from This Picture?

In the early days of Operation Desert Storm, the networks played incessantly, often to gleeful commentary, an image straight out of a video game: a "smart bomb" zeroing in on a two-dimensional target. Many Americans were fascinated with the weapon and, admittedly, proud of its precision and the technological prowess it represented. Desert Storm was the "good war," the war to make us feel good about America again. Once it began, dissent was almost nonexistent; public opinion polls showed an approval rate of around 90 percent. The news media served as the war's cheerleaders, only much later raising such questions as the United States' role in helping create Saddam's war machine and the number of Iraqi civilians killed as a result of U.S. actions. Unpleasant truths.

The media are not alone in omitting or obscuring disturbing reality; governments and the military also frequently do so. For more than a year after the morning of March 16, 1968—when U.S. troops outside the village of My Lai massacred, raped, and maimed upwards of four hundred unresisting women, infants, and elderly—the Army managed to cover up the atrocity. When the story of Charlie Company finally hit the media, thirty men were charged but only one was convicted. Lieutenant William Calley, Jr., served four and a half months in military prison. Four and a half months for four hundred murders.

Much of what is eerily inexplicable in occurrences like My Lai, things that don't quite add up or make sense in the media and politics are the end product of a process of denial. *Denial*, a psychological defense mechanism, is an unconscious mental maneuver that cancels out or obscures painful reality. We hear no evil, see no evil, and hence feel no pain or confusion. We don't have to confront or change things that don't exist;

we don't have to examine our motives, intentions, and actions, or those of our government. In a 1994 *New York Times Magazine* article, Tim O'Brien summed up the denial of My Lai, then and now: "Evil has no place, it seems, in our national mythology. We erase it. We use ellipses. We salute ourselves and take pride in America the White Knight, America the Lone Ranger, America's sleek laser-guided weaponry beating up on Saddam and his legion of devils" (p. 52).

We are all capable of failing to see or hear the pain and evil around us or—when it becomes glaringly apparent and the evening news shows us corpses tumbling from the back of a dump truck into a mass grave in Rwanda—of failing to appreciate the emotional significance of what we see, of connecting the image with reality, of *feeling*. We dare not feel the pain or face the potential for evil within us. How many of us could say, with Tim O'Brien, "I more or less understand what happened on that day in March 1968, how it happened, the wickedness that soaks into your blood and heats up and starts to sizzle. I know the boil that precedes butchery"? (p. 53).

Our failure to confront the pain and evil within us, individually and in our national history, guarantees that we will whitewash our motives and justify our actions by vilifying "the enemy." And we will act out the violence and tragedy all over again—or do nothing to stop it.

The denial that affects our perception of important events like Desert Storm and My Lai also influences attitudes toward important political issues. It affects the political process by letting candidates manipulate voters with "hot-button" issues that are irrelevant to public policy at best, and destructive at worst. One such hot-button issue is support for the death penalty, which is currently very high in America. As more and more states reinstitute capital punishment, politicians do not hesitate to push the button, in spite of evidence that the death penalty fails to deter crime. A recent survey of American police chiefs found that they did not believe it reduces homicides. Moreover, there are hundreds of documented cases of innocent people wrongly convicted in capital cases.[1]

What purpose, then, does the death penalty serve? Supporting it and implementing it allow people to act out the anger, rage, and helplessness that many of us carry around and to direct these emotions at a target that is clearly and undeniably "evil." The death penalty lets us participate in retribution, retribution for the pain we have suffered but do not attribute to its correct source—our childhood.

The entertainment media too play an important role in the interaction between individual denial and the political process. The action-adventure genre, with its melodramatic presentation of good and evil, satisfies the public need for a target the hero can justifiably eliminate, often in grotesquely violent ways. The news media and their emphasis on the dramatic presentation of news events simply extend this view of the world. Thus Saddam Hussein becomes the next Hitler, a man so unquestionably malevolent that any amount of force or cost in civilian lives is justified to eliminate him.

Denial as a Way of Life: Politics in America

This book is based on a fundamental tenet of political psychology: that childhood experiences can affect the way we view the world and the political perceptions and understanding we develop. In the following chapters, we argue that we fail to see or hear evil because doing so is too painful and challenges the very basis of our assumptions about the world and ourselves. At times, denial is useful; it allows us to withstand traumatic experiences and go on functioning, often quite effectively. This is the positive side of denial. But it also exacts a price. If we deny reality, if we don't feel the pain of what is happening in Bosnia or in the house next door, we don't act, even in the small ways available to us, to change those realities. Instead, we may construct alternatives to reality, fantasy-worlds that further betray our perception of what is really occurring.

Nations, in fact, operate on the basis of such shared reconstructions of reality much of the time. This collective fantasy life is both revealed in politics and supported and maintained by it; our official life as a nation is built on a shared denial of painful realities and the suffering they engender. As children, we learn in our families to deny reality, to repress feelings, and to construct imaginary worlds. As adults, we deny aspects of contemporary reality that remind us of the emotional pain we suffered in childhood: the rage, the helplessness, and the sadness.

Feminists in the 1960s reminded us that the personal is political; the other piece of this realization is that the political is personal. On the national and international levels we work out emotions and dilemmas originating in childhood, at the same time denying that these emotions and dilemmas ever existed. In the process, we set up the conditions in which the next generation will suffer exactly the same pain.

The Origin of Denial

Political psychologists have long theorized a connection between the experiences of childhood and adult social and political behavior. It doesn't require an overly elaborate or implausible argument to make the point that we tend to become the kind of adults we are encouraged to be and allowed to be by our parents, siblings, culture, and historical era. Certainly, individuals make their own choices as they become adults and may end up far from their parents' geographical area, culture, social class, or political beliefs. Social and political beliefs are not, however, based solely on reason, on the free choices we make as adults. Some component of our seemingly rational views on issues such as military spending, abortion, gay rights, the death penalty, and so on, is emotional—and emotions are often carried over into adulthood from childhood experiences.

As long ago as 1950, a group of researchers who began studying anti-Semitism in Germany in the 1930s and had to flee from the Nazis theorized that unacceptable childhood emotions are transformed in adulthood into prejudice, hatred, and violence. According to Adorno and his colleagues (1950), rigid and punitive child rearing fosters anger toward parents, anger that can be neither expressed nor acknowledged for fear of parental reprisals. The child denies the reality about his or her parents—their rigidity, their punitiveness—and idealizes them, often holding them up as models. At the same time, the child has to split off and deny those aspects of the self the parents scorn—childishness, selfishness, sexuality, and, primarily, anger and aggressive impulses toward the parents. That "bad self" is attributed unconsciously, through the defense mechanism of *projection,* to others, usually members of minority groups in the society, who are then despised as evil, inferior, and dangerous.

Not surprisingly, once people come to believe that a particular group—African Americans, women, gays—are bad, they find it acceptable to take out their rage against these convenient scapegoats. Psychologists refer to this process as *displacement*. It is made possible initially by two defensive maneuvers: denial and repression of feeling. When children deny that their parents are harsh, even abusive, they repress their anger toward them, as well as their fear and sadness. Once they are no longer burdened with an accurate perception of what is going on around and within them, they can act out their rage and feelings of helplessness by picking on someone weaker.

More recently, Alice Miller, a European psychoanalyst, found that such treatment of children is not rare but is widely accepted in Western culture (1983). The humiliation and control of children in the name of child rearing is so common that it has become invisible.

However, neither Adorno and his colleagues nor Alice Miller point out that child rearing does not happen in a vacuum. The way we treat our children is a reflection of who we are and what we as a society believe. Our social and political attitudes, our institutions, and our child rearing practices produce the next generation of citizens who, through their social institutions and political behavior, in turn create the world their children will live in. No political scientist we know of has yet described how residual childhood emotion is displaced onto the political world to create the social and political beliefs and structures that will dictate what are considered acceptable emotions for the next generation.

Researchers interested in the development of political attitudes, an area called *political socialization,* have tended to focus on the family, the schools, and the mass media as major sources of political information. One study found that the average correlation, or match, between parents' and their children's attitudes on political issues was fairly low.[2] One of the highest correlations obtained was for partisanship; that is, identification with a particular political party. While political scientists recognize that there is a strong tendency for children to adopt the same party membership as their parents, they tend to attribute this correlation to what parents explicitly teach their children about politics rather than to lessons transmitted implicitly in the way they treat children. Most political studies ignore or minimize the relationship between personality and politics and pay very little attention to the possible effects of parenting style on the development of political attitudes.

We believe, however, that childhood experiences are a critical influence—along with education and parents' political opinions—on an individual's political orientation. The following example illustrates this process.

Gary, a lawyer working in Chicago, is the youngest of three brothers and was born when his father was 40 years old. Even though the three brothers grew up in the same family, their childhood experiences were quite different. Differences in their adult political attitudes appear to reflect the ways their father treated them.

    Gary's father, Sergei, was the son of Russian immigrants and grew up on the south side of Philadelphia. His early life was not easy; for a time, his father put him and his sister in separate foster homes to save money. Sergei harbored considerable resentment toward his father, in part because, until he was 18 years old, he had to give him his entire paycheck. When he was a teenager, he once got into a fight with his father on a carpentry job and was so angry he walked off the site and went home. Because he didn't even have five cents for trolley fare, the walk home took him all day.

    Sergei was never able to afford a college education, but he did obtain his high school equivalency certificate and worked as a machinist. During the 1930s he became a leftist and joined the Communist party. In the 1950s, he was blacklisted because he refused to sign the loyalty oath that was then required. Eventually he developed a drinking problem, which apparently affected his parenting. He had no hesitation in using his belt to discipline the two older boys when he felt they had misbehaved.

    Gary's experience, however, was quite different. He recalls one time at the age of seven when he had done something wrong, and his brother Tom urged their father to punish him. Sergei took Gary into the bedroom and took off his belt. Instead of using it on Gary, he told the boy that he was going to hit the bed with his belt and that Gary should yell loudly at each blow. They went through this charade for a while, then went out and let Tom in on the joke.

    This incident occurred at a good time in Sergei's life. His drinking was no longer a problem, and he was employed. He decided not to physically punish his sons any more, because hitting them was accomplishing nothing for the boys and made him feel bad about himself. The older boys always felt that Gary got off too easily.

    The differences in the political attitudes of the three boys seem to reflect the way they were treated. All of them attended college and so had similar educational backgrounds and attainments. Steve and Tom, however, are politically conservative, whereas Gary is fairly liberal. The two older boys were Reagan Democrats during the 1980s, carrying on their father's party identification but holding conservative views on social issues. Tom even holds some underlying racist attitudes that are consistent with the punitive way in which the two older boys were raised.

Gary's story is just one case; by itself, it cannot support sweeping conclusions about the relationship between child rearing and adult political attitudes. Our research with a much larger sample of individuals, however, confirms that residual childhood emotion does influence adult political attitudes.

We describe this research in chapter 3, after defining the concept of denial and describing its origins in chapter 1 and detailing the negative effects of denial on mental and physical health (as well as on thinking) in chapter 2. We go on in chapter 4 to explain how our model accounts for the rise of the Religious Right, its political attitudes, and some of the recent extreme acts of violence against abortion providers and gays. In chapter 5, we analyze the contributions of denial to current public opinion on issues such as punishment in the schools and prisons and immigration. Chapter 6 discusses the denial employed by political leaders to seduce their followers into a shared *folie à deux.* Chapter 7 looks at the literature on the legacy of American slavery and the way the pain and indignity experienced by slaves has been denied by whites, allowing them to scapegoat blacks and blame them for crime, welfare abuses, and other social ills. In chapter 8, we address extreme outcomes of the denial of childhood pain and rage as embodied in governmental violence and genocide. In chapter 9, we discuss the role of denial in the destruction of the environment. Finally, in chapter 10 we present some tentative proposals for alleviating the effects of denial on politics.

The argument of this book is based on empirical evidence from research we and others have conducted. In several chapters (most notably chapters 7 and 8) we extend our model of residual childhood emotions to explain historical events. We are both trained as social and political psychologists, not as historians, so these chapters are of necessity somewhat speculative. It is our hope that the ideas raised in these chapters will provoke debate among social scientists and lead to further research.

We see denial operating at both ends of the political spectrum; Republicans and Democrats alike engage in it. At times it is shared denial, as occurred when both parties failed to confront the savings and loan disaster in the 1988 elections; at other times their denial takes distinct forms that are characteristic of ideological differences. Conservatives have a tendency to deny the evidence of others' suffering as well as feelings of weakness within themselves, while liberals are more likely to deny external evil—such as genocide in Bosnia—and their own aggressive feelings.

Denial is woven into the fabric of American social and political life, in our shared national mythology and our social and political institutions. Its support by the media and Hollywood make it so pervasive that we neither notice nor question it. Yet it takes its toll on our physical health, our mental health, our ability to think clearly, and the legacy we hand on to the next generation. By fostering a fantasy world that creates an absolute split between good and evil, denial prevents us from entertaining any but the most simplistic solutions to our problems. In the end, it leaves us stranded in a public world that is naive, banal, and eerily askew and offers us nothing but superficialities, sentimentality, and melodrama.

We do not argue that childhood experiences explain all of an individual's political attitudes and beliefs; but we do present evidence that they exert a significant effect on his or her politics, an influence that social scientists and citizens alike have tended to ignore. Everyone wants to believe that the attitudes we hold are a result of a rational deliberative process based on "the facts." It can be disturbing to confront the possibility that certain emotional experiences in childhood may exert influence that, subsequently, distorts public life. Yet this uncomfortable possibility must be examined for the United States to confront successfully many important issues of public policy.

As individuals and as a nation we use denial to avoid unpleasant realities, often by lying to others and to ourselves about the true nature of reality. But denial is also achieved by the more subtle process of minimization. Howard Zinn, in *The People's History of the United States* (1995), gives a clear example of the way in which some historians have glorified Columbus's voyage to the New World while minimizing some of the negative effects of his achievement. The late Samuel Eliot Morison, a prominent Harvard historian, acknowledged Columbus's genocide of indigenous peoples and actually used that term; but he then passed over that reality quickly to focus on Columbus's seamanship. Zinn points out that "Outright lying or quiet omission takes the risk of discovery which, when made, might arouse the reader to rebel against the writer. To state the facts, however, and then to bury them in a mass of other information, is to say to the reader with a certain infectious calm: yes, mass murder took place, but it's not that important—it should weigh very little in our final judgments; it should affect very little what we do in the world." Zinn continues: "To emphasize the heroism of Columbus and his successors as navigators and discoverers, and to deemphasize their genocide, is not a technical necessity, but an ideological choice. It serves, unwittingly, to justify what was done" (p. 8).

Facing unpleasant truths is a necessary step in healing and in the growth of human potential. Denial and minimization of facts such as Columbus's genocide have ideological implications, it is true; but the argument we make in this volume is that there are important psychological reasons for such denial. Until those psychological issues are faced, a simple recitation of the facts will be largely ineffective in promoting change.

In the last five years or so, we have seen a popular backlash against exploration of one's childhood experiences and emotions, which in essence argues, "Give it a rest. Quit blaming your parents or society for your problems and grow up. Take responsibility for your own life." This argument minimizes the importance of childhood experience and the emotions it engenders even when it seems to acknowledge the reality of childhood suffering by then quickly obscuring it and accusing the victims of whining.

We heartily subscribe to the view that adults are responsible for their own behavior. Notice, however, that this implies that parents—who were surely adults—were also responsible for their behavior while their children were growing up. Parents who drank; who hit each other; who beat, raped, or neglected their children; or who treated them with contempt are in fact responsible for the negative consequences that their children suffer in adulthood.

Unfortunately, parents who behave in these ways frequently suffered the same or worse treatment at the hands of their own parents. Even though parents are responsible for their own behavior, they can hardly be blamed for raising children in the only way they know. We believe that all parents do the best they can, given the way they themselves were raised and the limitations of their culture and circumstances. Most parents do the best they can, but many do a terrible job.

The sad truth is that one can't go back and relive childhood with parents who now know better than to treat their children the way their own parents treated them. The even sadder truth is that, for many people, any attempt to get their parents to change or even acknowledge what they did is fruitless. Parents may never acknowledge their behavior or apologize for it. And they may never behave any differently. Many adults are left, then, with the responsibility to get help and change their own lives without the help or approval of their parents and, often, without the foundation of love and nurturing that all human children need.

It is true that blaming one's parents and resenting them for their failures are counterproductive and even unbecoming. Nevertheless, as a practical matter, the only way to get over an abusive childhood and go on to a different life is to acknowledge what happened in childhood and experience the painful emotions. This is a strictly practical matter, not a moral one. Individuals who wish to change must first experience the anger, fear, helplessness, and grief of childhood. They must also recognize and acknowledge that their parents did a less-than-perfect job of raising them.

We believe that only the truth will set us free, as individuals and as a nation, from the unintended consequences of the distressing experiences so many of us suffered in our childhoods.

Finally, we should warn against two possible misinterpretations of our data. It would be an oversimplification to claim that there are just two kinds of people: those who are in denial and those who are not. In fact, the use of denial as a way of processing information has to be viewed on a continuum. Just as people vary in their political attitudes from extremely conservative to extremely liberal, individuals vary from those who continually use denial, on the one extreme, to those who rarely employ it, on the other. What we document in this volume are the costs of the pervasive use of denial to both ourselves and our society.

An equally gross simplification of our findings would be to conclude that individuals spanked in childhood invariably become conservatives who hold punitive political attitudes. There are, in fact, many influences on public opinion.[3] Adult political attitudes reflect a combination of factors such as socioeconomic status, age, gender, and education, as well as childhood experience. What has become clear to us through our research, however, is that childhood experiences—particularly those involving harsh discipline and punishment—exert a destructive influence that social scientists typically ignore. Such childhood experiences appear to contribute to a climate of mean-spiritedness and punitiveness among the electorate and to make some citizens and groups vulnerable to the influence of divisive and punitive politicians.

1

Hear No Evil, See No Evil

According to legend, when King Boabdil, the last Moorish king, received word that his capital city of Alhama was about to be lost, he burned the letter containing the news and beheaded the messenger. Sigmund Freud cited this extreme example of political denial in a 1936 letter to a colleague. By destroying both the disturbing news and its bearer, he said, the king at least temporarily negated the unpleasant reality—the downfall of his city. Freud pointed out that, "[One] determinant of this behavior of the King was his need to combat a feeling of powerlessness. By burning the letters and having the messenger killed he was still trying to show his absolute power."[1]

Modern political leaders and their constituents are no less willing than King Boabdil to ignore evidence rather than face troubling political realities. Understanding the history and process of denial as a psychological mechanism is essential to a comprehensive understanding of current public opinion, political leaders, and events.

The Origin of the Concept of Denial

Sigmund Freud first used the concept of *denial* in 1923, when he maintained that little boys would rather believe they had actually seen a penis on a female than face the possibility that little girls have been castrated and they might be, too.[2] Since then, the term has been used more broadly and has become indistinguishable from other defense mechanisms, such as repression and dissociation. In colloquial use today, denial is sometimes applied even more loosely. When people accuse those who disagree with them of being "in denial," the term loses its meaning and becomes simply a generalized indictment of those who hold different views. It is important, therefore, to trace the origin and meaning of the concept before we explore the pervasiveness of denial in our culture and its political and social consequences.

It was Sigmund Freud's daughter and successor, the child analyst Anna Freud, who described the mechanism of denial in detail and later modified and expanded the term. Her *The Ego and the Mechanisms of Defense* (1946, 1966) became the classic source on *defense mechanisms,* the unconscious operations we use to ward off anxiety.[3]

It is important to understand the positive role of denial as a survival mechanism for children. Adults have a variety of ways of coping with threats from the external world; they can avoid dangerous or humiliating situations and, in some cases, change external circumstances or defend themselves by physical force. Anna Freud pointed out that these options are not readily available to small children. Their only recourse is to blot out mentally whatever in the external world disturbs or frightens them. This is her original, basic sense of the term denial. Freud described the ways children use fantasy to support and maintain their denial of reality by transforming unpleasant facts into their opposites. She referred to this process as "denial in fantasy." In her therapy with children she encountered a number of young boys who feared their fathers and transformed them, in fantasy, into animals.

A seven-year-old boy whom I analyzed used to amuse himself with the following fantasy. He owned a tame lion, which terrified everyone else and loved nobody but him. It came when he called it and followed him like a little dog, wherever he went. He looked after the lion, saw to its food and its comfort in general, and in the evening made a bed for it in his own room. As is usual in daydreams carried on from day to day, the main fantasy became the basis of a number of agreeable episodes. For example, there was a particular daydream in which he went to a fancy-dress ball and told all the people that the lion, which he brought with him, was only a friend in disguise. ... He delighted in imagining how terrified the people would be if they guessed his secret. At the same time he felt that there was no real reason for their anxiety, for the lion was harmless so long as he kept it under control. (p. 73)

At an age when boys, according to psychoanalytic theory, see their fathers as a hated and feared rival for their mother's affection, this little boy transformed the dangerous rival into a large wild animal, one that was completely under his control and was devoted to protecting him. His original anxiety about what his father might do to him appears in the fantasy only in the form of other people's terror of his lion.

Freud points out that stories of wild animals who protect and aid human children abound in folklore and fairy tales and that an expansion of the theme appears in such children's stories as *Little Lord Fauntleroy*. Here, a child succeeds where everyone else has failed in capturing the heart of a bad-tempered, evil old man. "Finally, the old man, whom no one else can control and who *cannot control himself* [our italics], submits to the influence and control of the little child and is even induced to do all sorts of good deeds for other people." In these stories and tales, "the method by which objective unpleasure and objective anxiety are avoided is very simple. The child's ego refuses to become aware of some disagreeable reality. First of all it turns its back on it, denies it, and in imagination reverses the unwelcome facts. Thus the 'evil' father becomes in fantasy the protective animal, while the helpless child becomes the master of powerful father substitutes" (pp. 78, 79).

The seven-year-old boy who fantasized that he owned a tame lion unwittingly confirmed her interpretation. One day Anna Freud went out to greet her small patient in the waiting room she shared with her father. At that moment, Sigmund Freud walked through the area. The little boy nodded to Anna Freud and, indicating her father, commented, "also a sort of lion" (Freud and Sandler 1985).

It is important to note that the denial Anna Freud described in these children occurred in conjunction with strong emotions the children could not tolerate—anger and jealousy toward the father they saw as competing for their mother's attention and fear of the revenge he might exact for their desire to have the mother to themselves. Denial is an equally important coping mechanism for children whose parents really do hurt them and for those who simply fear that they might. Later theorists argue that a key element in denial is the person's inability to deal with or tolerate a particular emotion, whether it is shame, anxiety, grief, or anger.[4]

Along with denial in fantasy, children employ denial in word and action to protect themselves from external threats of physical harm or humiliation. At a certain age, children love to receive such grownup gifts as a purse, a tool belt, or some other badge of maturity. They sometimes insist on carrying the object with them everywhere and become upset if it is lost or they are prevented, for example, from wearing the tool belt to the dinner table or even to bed. According to the child's logic, if I have a purse or tool belt, I'm not a little kid, I'm an adult. Adults promote this denial when they tell a child, "You're Daddy's big helper." Adults also encourage denial in word and action, by, for example, telling a child, "You do not hate Grandma. What a thing to say. Go give her a kiss." Denying the child's real feelings, they insist that he or she act out their exact opposite.

Anna Freud points out (1946, 1966), however, that denial in word and action is more difficult for children to sustain than denial in fantasy: "Dramatization of fantasies in word and act requires a stage in the outside world. So [the child's] employment of this mechanism is conditioned externally by the extent to which those around him will fall in with his dramatization" (p. 91). Unfortunately, as we will see in later chapters, adults are sometimes all too ready to accede to the denial political leaders engage in through *their* words and actions.

When King Boabdil burned the letter carrying news of the downfall of Alhama and beheaded the messenger, he was using denial in action to protect his illusion of omnipotence. Analyst Anita Eckstaedt (1989), in citing Freud's example of Boabdil, carries it further. In her view, denial is always the negation of some sort of loss: in the king's case, the loss of a city, of power, and of feelings of omnipotence; in other cases, the loss of a loved one or a cherished illusion. Denial often allows people to substitute other, less painful emotions—such as indignation, anger, and resentment—for the grief and mourning associated with the loss. It is not that the kingdom has fallen, but merely that an annoying messenger was spreading false news.

Eckstaedt goes on to argue that one of the chief ways people maintain their denial is by seducing others into a *folie à deux,* a shared denial of reality. A distorted view of the world is easier to support and maintain if others believe in it too. This, we believe, is a key mechanism for understanding how denial and distortion of reality are passed from one generation to the next within families, as well as for understanding how political leaders such as Hitler appeal to their followers. (We take this up in more detail in chapter 6.)

As children grow older, they find it more difficult to do away with reality entirely and may acknowledge a troubling fact but deny the feelings associated with it. This is what is called *denial of affect* (emotion). Adults engage in this type of denial quite often. For example, before survivors of sexual or physical abuse begin the process of healing, they frequently say things like, "Yes, I was abused, but it didn't really affect me," or "Sure, my father beat me, but it made me a better person."

Clearly the capacity for denial of both external reality and emotion developed in childhood continues into adulthood. The implications for politics are that adults, both ordinary citizens and political leaders, can simply deny threatening aspects of reality—like ethnic cleansing in Bosnia—or deny the feelings they evoke. The problem with denial, however, is that it delays recognition of a problem or a crisis until it becomes severe: even when the facts are indisputable, the denial of feelings reduces empathy for the suffering of others—thereby eliminating an important motivation for addressing the problem.

Anna Freud argues (Freud and Sandler 1985) that denial in adulthood is far more rigid and entrenched than it is in childhood. Children may deny some reality one moment and acknowledge it the next, but "in the adult, [denial] would be much more fixed . . . if the adult builds a great part of his life on denial, he has to do it very firmly." As a consequence, "people who use denial a great deal in adult life are very threatened by reality, if they are confronted by the reality directly." Later in her life Anna Freud believed that "in the politician or in the bigot or in someone in whom we would say there is a distorted ego, one can see the use of denial. I mean the sort of polemical, mob-rousing politician. The denial goes over into lying and falsification" (pp. 351–53).

Causes of Denial

Denial as a Reaction to Trauma

Denial is a common reaction to traumatic experiences such as natural disasters, war, torture, or childhood abuse. Psychoanalyst Dinora Pines (1986) describes two women patients who were survivors of Auschwitz. After World War II, both women put together relatively normal lives that included jobs, husbands, and children. But denial permeated their lives; neither had ever talked about her experiences in the death camp with her children. Both women found their marriages unfulfilling. The departure of their youngest children from home precipitated feelings of such intense loss—resulting in one case in a suicide attempt—that they sought treatment.

In a recent controlled study, Stephen Dollinger and Phoebe Cramer (1990) measured the use of denial and other defense mechanisms by twenty-seven boys aged ten to thirteen who were playing soccer in rural Illinois when lightning struck the field. All the players, plus most of the children and adults watching from the sidelines, were knocked down; one boy, who was hit directly, died. The use of denial by boys who witnessed the lightning strike was noticeably higher than among boys of the same age who had not experienced a trauma. Those who had the highest scores on measures of denial and other defense mechanisms were rated by child psychologists as showing less overt emotional upset. Their parents reported, however, that they experienced frequent sleep disturbances and physical complaints. It would seem that denial protected these children emotionally from the initial impact of a horrifying event, while perhaps allowing them time to assimilate it. The sleep and health problems attest to the fact that simply denying a disturbing event does not eliminate its psychological impact.

Instruction in Denial: "Normal" Child Rearing

While remarkable instances of denial can be observed in adults and children who experience an acute trauma, perhaps the most common source of denial is family interactions that are taken for granted as normal. There is reason to believe that, for many children, everyday child rearing is more traumatic than we suppose and is, in fact, built upon explicit instruction in denying both external reality and the child's feelings.

Poisonous Pedagogy   Alice Miller (1983) has written about what she calls *poisonous pedagogy*, the philosophy that has formed the basis of child rearing in the West for the last two hundred years. This widespread philosophy is based on the following assumptions: (a) that even in infancy children are willful; (b) that this willfulness is both insulting to the adult and dangerous, because it is evidence of fundamentally antisocial tendencies that, if not ruthlessly quelled, will result in disastrous consequences for the child's later character; (c) that the solution is to "break the child's will," to teach children unquestioning obedience to the will of adults as early as possible, preferably when they are still too young to notice or understand what is being done; and (d) that doing so frequently requires the most strenuous and manipulative means, often including physical punishment. Key to our discussion is Miller's further claim that parents and society, even today, believe they are breaking the child's will for his or her own good, out of love. According to Miller, the true motives behind punitive child rearing, as well as the true nature of its effects, are shrouded in denial. (As we show in chapter 3 and throughout this book, this childhood training in denial has damaging political and social consequences.)

Miller quotes extensively from child-rearing manuals of the last two centuries. The primary tool they recommend for breaking a child's will is physical punishment, usually whipping until the child is ready to beg for forgiveness and becomes ready to accept further parental direction. If the punishment is administered in a "loving" way, these manuals allege, the child will remember the friendly manner of the adult while losing the memory of the beating. Long passages from these guides also demonstrate how to break children's will by shaming them.

What is particularly disturbing are the passages Miller cites that instruct parents in teaching children to acquire self-control, for example, by requiring them to remain silent for long periods or inducing them to go hungry, or endure uncomfortable heat or cold. What this amounts to is teaching children to deny their feelings and their basic bodily needs.

This denial of feeling is central to Miller's concept of poisonous pedagogy. She cites, for example, a 1748 *Essay on the Education and Instruction of Children*, which advises parents to instruct the child in restraining his emotional reactions, then to have another person give the child an undeserved scolding (p. 26). If the child reacts emotionally, the author suggests punishing him or her "lovingly" and repeating the test.

The most chilling passage Miller found urges parents to teach their children to endure physical abuse and deny the pain as they experience it: "If after the chastisement the pain last for a time, it is unnatural to forbid weeping and groaning at once. But if the chastised use these annoying sounds as a means of revenge, then the first step is to distract them by assigning little tasks or activities. If this does not help, it is permissible to forbid the weeping and to punish them if it persists, until it finally ceases after the new chastisement" (pp. 24–25).

There are several revealing aspects of this passage. First, the eighteenth-century author, J. B. Basedow, characterizes a beaten child's crying as "annoying sounds," a description remarkably lacking in empathy. According to Eckstaedt, denial serves to short-circuit grief by substituting resentment and indignation. This may explain Basedow's curious choice of words; the crying of a child could appear annoying if the adult denied the child's pain and anguish (and memories of his or her own grief when subjected to such treatment in childhood) and substituted indignation at the child's behavior. How many times have we heard a parent say, "Oh, come on—you're not hurt. If you don't stop that crying now, I'll give you something to cry about!"?

Second, Basedow speaks of the child using "these annoying sounds as a means of revenge"; again, it is an amazing interpretation, a motive one might more reasonably ascribe to an adult. Presumably, a child who has just been beaten by a beloved parent cries because he or she is in pain, not out of a deliberate attempt to exact revenge. The author's comment is an example of another defense mechanism, *projection,* in which a person attributes his or her own feelings or motives to another. In this case, Basedow seems to be projecting his own anger and desire for revenge onto the hypothetical child.

The cruel practices that Miller cites from child-rearing manuals of another time may appear as mere shocking vestiges of the distant past. Yet the truth is that physical punishment is still widely used and approved of in our society. Some child-rearing manuals continue to insist that children must be taught to deny their emotions. James Dobson, a psychologist whose books on child rearing have sold over a million copies, believes children should be allowed to cry after a spanking for only a short time. In the 1992 revision of his *Dare to Discipline,* he instructs parents that "As long as tears represent a genuine release of emotion, they should be permitted to fall. But crying quickly changes from inner sobbing to an exterior weapon. It becomes a tool of protest to punish the enemy. Real crying usually lasts two minutes or less, but may continue for five. After that point, the child is merely complaining, and the change can be recognized in the tone and intensity of his voice. I would require him to stop the protest crying, usually by offering him a little more of whatever caused the original tears" (p. 70).

Dobson, like the eighteenth-century authors Miller cites, seems to see child rearing as a battle to establish control. He writes that one three-year-old girl had "hopelessly beaten her [mother] in a contest of wills, and the child had become a tyrant and dictator." He goes on to assert that this mother was being "challenged, mocked, and defied by her daughter," who didn't wish to take a nap (pp. 4–5). Advice to use verbal abuse, humiliation, and the withdrawal of love from children as additional means of breaking the child's will and exacting unquestioning obedience is even more common.

The use of physical punishment in child rearing has always been high and continues to be today. In a nationally representative sample of the general population, 3 percent of parents reported that they had kicked, bit, or punched their children, and 1 percent reported beating up their children at least once in the previous year. These figures imply that at least 1.4 million children are physically abused each year. In 1993, the Department of Health and Human Services reported 2.9 million cases of abuse and neglect, four times the number in 1976. Today, the number one cause of death among children under four years old is abuse by parents or other caregivers. What's more, 84 percent of parents have reported regularly using less severe types of physical punishment on children.[5]

Opinion surveys indicate that a considerable percentage of the U.S. population consider physical punishment normal and acceptable (Davis and Smith, 1991, 1994). In 1968 the Harris survey organization asked adults whether they approved of "a parent spanking his or her child assuming the child is healthy and over one year old"; 92 percent of the sample agreed. More recently, an annual poll administered by the National Opinion Research Center at the University of Chicago, has asked, "Do you strongly agree, agree, disagree, or strongly disagree that it is sometimes necessary to discipline a child with a good, hard spanking?" Support for spanking remained extremely high between 1986 and 1994, with 73 percent supporting it in 1994. During that period the percentage disagreeing with the need to spank children has increased somewhat, growing from 16.5 percent in 1986 to 26.6 percent in 1994 (Davis and Smith 1994). (see figure 1.1).

These data are consistent with the recollections of a national sample of adults about their own childhood punishment. In 1988, the Harris survey

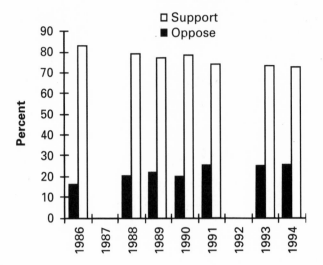

Figure 1.1.
Opinion on spanking from the National Opinion Research Center's General Social Survey.

asked 1,250 adults, "When you were growing up as a child, how often did your parents or guardian hit, spank, or physically discipline you when you misbehaved? Would you say very often, often, occasionally or never?" Over 85 percent of the sample reported being physically disciplined. In a systematic sample of mothers in a hospital waiting room and a private pediatrician's office, Socolar and Stein (1995) found that 42 percent of the mothers had spanked their child in the past week; 19 percent thought spanking a child less than a year old was acceptable; and 74 percent believed it appropriate for a child between 1 and 3 years old.

Although many national medical organizations have issued statements emphasizing the negative consequences of physical punishment, the majority of health-care professionals continue to support its use.[6] The physical punishment of children, we believe, remains acceptable because parents deny the very nature of what they are doing, their motives for doing it, and the consequences of this behavior for their children's emotional well-being and behavior. Research in psychology has demonstrated that physical punishment produces a variety of negative consequences, including—as we document in the following chapters—a cycle of intergenerational transmission of abuse and violence.

Not long ago, we encountered a striking example of the extent to which parents simply do not grasp the reality of what they are doing to their children. One day, Jenny, the eight-year-old daughter of a friend of ours, was playing at the house of a neighborhood friend. Their play was interrupted when the friend's four-year-old brother refused a request from his father and the father began to spank him. Having never experienced physical punishment herself, Jenny was at once fascinated and shocked. She asked the father, "Why are you hitting Billy?" The father, with the natural assurance of an adult explaining adult matters to a child responded, "Oh, I'm not hitting him, I'm spanking him." Jenny stared at him, placed her hands on her hips, and shot back, "Looks like *hitting* to me." The father was so taken aback, he stopped spanking his son.

The adults in the story of "The Emperor's New Clothes" convinced themselves that the emperor did in fact have fancy new robes, even though they were unable to see them. It took a child to persuade them that they were making a false distinction ("There are robes that can be seen, and there are robes that are invisible"). Jenny made exactly this point to her friend's father: the distinction between an adult "hitting a child" and an adult "spanking a child" is a false one. In either case, a many times larger and stronger person is causing physical pain to a child—pain that adults often considerably underestimate. The tremendous difference in size between adults and children is easy for adults to forget; nor do they recognize the emotional pain, as well as the helplessness and humiliation, experienced by children when someone they love hurts them.

We wish we could report that the father realized the error of his ways as a result of his conversation with Jenny. Unfortunately, this is not the case. Adults have many defense mechanisms that interfere with their capacity to change their beliefs and behavior, particularly those related to a subject as emotionally loaded as how to raise their children.

Why Use Physical Punishment?

The centuries-old religious justification for the use of physical punishment was given psychological support by Freudian developmental theory. Freud believed that punitive child rearing facilitated the process of moral development through "identification with the aggressor." He reasoned that a child harshly punished by parents would fantasize about retaliating against them. Since the child realizes, however, that these fantasies would bring even harsher punishment if acted upon, he or she would try to repress the feelings of rebellion. This repression can only be accomplished, Freud suggested, if the child identifies with the parent and internalizes the parents' moral values.[7]

Today, this justification is discredited among most psychologists. Research suggests that children learn to behave the way their parents treat them, rather than internalizing parents' moral values. A classic study of boys who engage in antisocial behavior by the eminent behavioral psychologists Bandura and Walters (1959) found that those who were physically punished by their fathers were less likely to engage in aggressive behavior inside their homes but more likely to be aggressive outside them—away from their fathers. This finding led Bandura to formulate his social learning theory, which emphasizes the process of *observational learning,* learning behaviors through seeing them modeled by others.

Parents often use physical punishment because it is easier than making other changes. One mother in a parents' group of two-year-olds claimed that she needed to spank her child frequently because he kept getting into the knickknacks on her living room coffee table. She refused to consider the alternative of placing the knickknacks out of reach for a year or two— and so preventing the negative interactions with her child—because she felt she shouldn't have to change her life to accommodate her son.

Even though most parents recognize the dangers of certain things in a child's environment, such as electrical outlets, and try to make them childproof, many feel that children should respect property, be careful of their parent's nice things, and so on. The fact is that young children are no more likely to make a distinction between a Hummel figurine and a toy than a dog is likely to distinguish between the old slippers you've given it to chew and your new leather pumps. This points to another reason for the use of physical punishment: many parents have expectations of children based on their interactions with adults and interpret certain misbehaviors on the part of children—spilling or breaking things, taking a toy away from another child—as deliberately destructive or malicious.

For many years, we have asked students in our classes whether physical punishment should be used in raising children. While the percentage saying "Yes" has gone down over the past several years, many still support its use. When we ask them what kind of situation requires physical punishment, students often give the example of a small child running into the street. They argue that for the "child's own good" it is necessary to spank him or her to prevent the more serious injury that might occur if the child ran into the street and was hit by a car. This is particularly important, they argue, for children between, say, two and three, who might not understand the danger.

We then ask students whether, after punishing the child for running into the street, they would feel comfortable leaving their unsupervised child to play in front of the house. Students invariably answer "Of course not! That wouldn't be safe." "Then why," we ask, "did you use physical punishment in the first place?" If physically punishing children does not teach them to avoid the street, why do it? Young children are just that, *young*. They need someone watching them, keeping them from harm and making sure their environment is safe. Physical punishment simply doesn't teach what the parent desires to teach; in fact, it may actually increase the likelihood that a child will run into the street. Research on pedestrian safety sponsored by the American Automobile Association Foundation (Embry and Malfetti 1982) demonstrates that young children who are nagged and spanked for running into the street will go there more often than those who are not punished.

What physical punishment really does in this situation is allow parents to deal with their own feelings, albeit in a less than constructive way. Imagining one's child being hit by a car produces considerable fear in most parents. Punishing their child is a way of saying "Don't do that to me!" But when this feeling is expressed through spanking, children have a hard time hearing the parents' fear and possible grief; they understand only their parents' rage, and the pain of being hit.

When drug companies manufacture a drug to treat a specific illness, they typically list the known side effects of the medication. Of course, using this term is a way of obscuring and minimizing the fact that the drug has many different effects, one of which is the intended consequence of treating the targeted disease or its symptoms. Other consequences—

for example, headaches, dizziness, nausea—are also effects of the drug but not ones to which the manufacturing company wishes to call attention. Using physical punishment on children is very similar. There is a wide range of effects, one of which (stopping the unwanted behavior) is the desirable one. What so many people overlook are the additional negative consequences, consequences to children's emotional health, self-esteem, and relationships within the family.

The Consequences of Physical Punishment

Physical Punishment Is not Always Successful in Changing Behavior
Often the punished behavior is suppressed but reemerges in a different situation when the parent is not present. To be effective in changing another person's behavior, the use of force generally requires surveillance, particularly with children. When parents punish them for engaging in a behavior the parents want to stop, children often learn not to engage in it when Mommy and Daddy are around. If the behavior has its own intrinsic rewards, however—for example, eating cookies before dinner—they are likely to do it when parents are not present. As reported earlier, Bandura and Walters noted this same pattern of behavior when fathers physically punished their sons for violent behavior.

Physical Punishment Teaches Children to Be Violent and to Accept Violence as a Part of Life
What message is communicated to children who are physically punished by their parents? Simply put, it tells them that it is acceptable to use violence against people to change their behavior, particularly if they are smaller and weaker than oneself. It should not surprise us to learn that studies find physical punishment a good predictor of later aggressiveness. Longitudinal studies of children and the effect of parental discipline demonstrate the same effects Bandura and Walters observed. The Cambridge–Somerville Youth Study evaluated boys between the ages of 5 and 9 and followed them into their forties.[8] The researchers found that adult criminality, including violent crime, was predicted by a history of corporal punishment and parental aggressiveness, as well as by an absence of supervision and parental affection. This finding has been documented by

other studies as well: using violence to teach nonviolence doesn't work and has many other negative consequences.

Unfortunately, a substantial proportion of the American public has not made the connection between what they are trying to teach a child and the means they use. A national survey of 1,012 participants done for *Parents Magazine* by the Roper Center (1987) found that 41 percent of respondents thought it appropriate to spank a child who deliberately hurts another child.

Physical Punishment Creates Fear and Anger in the Child

When someone causes us physical pain, our immediate reaction is anger and sometimes fear. Adults recognize this and, as a society, have instituted legal sanctions against assault. The emotional response of a small child to being hit is no different; if anything, given the difference in size between children and adults, physical punishment is that much more frightening. Most parents desire relationships of love, trust, and respect with their children, but using physical punishment undermines the emotional quality of the parent/child relationship. All children want the love and approval of their parents; even abused children express love for their parents. Physically punishing a child, however, adds a layer of negative feelings toward the parents. Bandura and Walters found that the boys who were physically punished for engaging in violent behavior expressed much higher levels of hostility toward their fathers than did boys who were not physically punished.

These emotions have serious consequences. A 1985 survey of over six thousand families (Straus and Kantor 1994) found that adolescents physically punished by their parents are at higher risk for depression and self-destructive behaviors such as suicide and alcohol abuse, as well as the outwardly destructive behaviors of child and spousal abuse.

Physical Punishment Teaches the Wrong Moral Lesson

Psychologists like Lawrence Kohlberg who study moral development have identified different types of reasons people give at various levels of moral development to explain why engaging in a particular behavior is wrong. For example, should a man steal a drug to save his dying wife if he doesn't have the money to buy it? While concern for others' feelings or adherence to some universal ethical principle (e.g., the sanctity of human life) reflects a high level of moral reasoning, in Kohlberg's view, the lowest level of reasoning equates moral behavior with avoiding punishment.

Very young children, for example, assume that a behavior is morally acceptable if it is rewarded and morally reprehensible if it is punished. They believe that might defines right. By relying on the use of physical punishment, parents teach their children to respond only to external controls on their behavior, rather than to develop an internalized set of moral standards, a conscience. In adulthood, such individuals may have no qualms about doing something wrong if they can get away with it; conversely, they may avoid behaviors that were punished in childhood, such as asking questions or expressing disagreement. A number of research studies have documented the negative effect of physical punishment on moral reasoning.[9]

Physical Punishment Can Actually Increase Misbehavior

A child who does not receive enough positive attention from his or her parents may begin to misbehave in order to get the parents' attention. Even though the child is punished, he or she may prefer negative interaction to no interaction at all.

Physical Punishment Reduces Children's Self-Esteem and Potential for Future Success

The frequent use of physical punishment results in lowered self-esteem.[10] Why would parents knowingly risk creating low self-esteem in their children when there are positive alternatives?

Physical Punishment Can Lead to More Serious Physical Abuse

Physical punishment may seem to be an effective way to stop children's misbehavior. What this means is that the parents' behavior in physically punishing children can be rewarding for parents, because they have obtained, at least temporarily, what they want. Psychologists have demonstrated very conclusively, however, what happens to a behavior that is rewarded: it tends to increase in frequency. Consequently, the use or threat of physical punishment may increase. Once parents have crossed the line of using physical force against a child and have found it rewarding, they may come to rely on it.

A second psychological principle that bears on the use of physical punishment is *habituation*. People tend to become accustomed to the same level of stimulation. This is a familiar effect in many everyday occurrences. For example, we probably notice that there is a hum in a fluorescent light when we first walk into a room. After a while, though, we realize we have stopped noticing the hum even though it continues. The same process can operate for children and the way they are disciplined. If parents routinely yell at them for misbehaving, children will tend to become habituated to their parents' yelling, and it will have less effect on their behavior. The parents may then decide they need to use more extreme discipline, such as spanking, to "get the child's attention." If children are routinely spanked, they may habituate to that level of punishment as well. Because adults often underestimate their own strength, particularly when they are angry, they may forget that they outweigh children by a hundred or more pounds. At such times, what is intended as a mild push might result in a child being thrown against a wall and, tragically, even killed or seriously injured.

Conclusion

We have seen that the majority of parents in America approve of the use of physical punishment with children. What is still considered normal child rearing is heavily dependent on the use of physical force to break children's will and coerce them into obedience. At the same time, parents lie to their children, telling them that the punishment is for "your own good"—in other words, that it is a sign of the parents' love and care. In this way, parents promote the child's tendency to deny the frightening reality of physical punishment and the emotions it creates.

The anger, fear, helplessness, and humiliation children experience when they are assaulted by their parents does not disappear as they grow up. We will see in chapter 3 that these denied emotions persevere into adulthood and may fuel punitive political and social attitudes. Nor is denial without its personal costs. In the next chapter, we examine some of these costs of denial.

2

"No, really, I'm fine"

Anyone who has read *Gone with the Wind* or seen the film is familiar with Scarlett O'Hara's famous line, "I won't think of it now." Whether it was Rhett leaving her or the loss of Tara, she dealt with any unpleasant reality by using denial. In the long run, it cost her dearly. Denial may allow a person to cope successfully over the short term, but evidence from numerous studies shows that the long-term consequences of denial are dangerous. People who deny traumas they have experienced and the pain associated with them or who block out the truth about their childhood or present circumstances pay a price in impairment of mental and physical health, ability to cope with new stresses, and even the ability to think clearly.

Although denial is usually considered a "primitive" defense mechanism, used primarily in early childhood and greatly attenuated by adolescence, researchers have found evidence that it is also used by adults in a wide range of contexts. Scientific research studies confirm, for example, that denial is characteristic of heavy drinkers and that alcoholics typically deny the extent of their alcohol consumption. Nor is it just alcoholics who deny their problem; society joins in that denial. Research has shown that even medical providers underdiagnose alcoholism.[1] Denial is also a common reaction to the death of a loved one and to one's own disability or impending death.[2]

A 1994 study by Thomas Haywood and Linda Grossman compared the use of denial by accused child molesters and normal adults. They found that accused molesters who denied charges against them also tended to engage in denial and minimization on tests of psychopathology. Moreover, their verbal reports of the strength of their sexual interest in children failed to match physiological measures of arousal in response to pictures of children.

The Function of Denial

The psychoanalytic concept of denial assumes that anxiety about a given thought or action motivates a person to deny having the thought or contemplating the action. Bernstein (1984) tested this hypothesis experimentally. He first presented the idea of having sex with their mothers to one group of men by giving them the sentence, "I would like to have sex with my mother." He speculated that thinking about incest would arouse guilt and anxiety because of the social taboo against it. He then asked the men how often they thought of their mother naked. Compared to a group of men who had not been presented with the idea of incest—Bernstein gave this group the sentence, "I would like to have tea with a friend"—the men in the first group reported thinking about their mother being naked significantly less often. They also claimed to respect their mothers more and to have seen them naked less often than the second group. This result is precisely what the theory of denial would predict. Because of cultural socialization prohibiting that behavior, individuals primed with the idea of incest would consider the possibility and would react to it with guilt and anxiety, which would activate the process of denial. Their protestations against anything related to that behavior even extended to claiming that they *never* thought about their mother being without her clothes.

This example demonstrates how denial is used as a defensive strategy to unconsciously protect against the emotional pain associated with unpleasant reality. Either the disturbing reality itself or the emotion it arouses may be denied. What are the effects of the persistent use of denial?

The Effects of Denial

Evidence is accumulating that individuals who use denial as a habitual way of approaching the world run a number of risks: negative consequences to their health, thinking, and emotional well-being, as well as intergenerational transmission of abuse. By not facing the emotional pain that produced the self-protective reaction of denial in childhood, a person risks passing on that pain to his or her children. For the children, addiction, antisocial behavior, or (as we see in a later chapter) punitive political attitudes may result.

Denial and Physical Health

Denial plays a role in a whole range of diseases that may develop as a result of, or be aggravated by, unhealthy behaviors. The unhealthy practices associated with many such diseases are well known. Most adults are aware that unsafe sexual practices increase the risk of HIV infection and that smoking places one at higher risk for heart and lung disease. Why, then, do so many people continue to engage in behaviors that are life threatening? Denial may play an important role. Weinstein (1984), for example, found that students perceived their peers as potentially at risk for a heart attack but believed they themselves were unlikely ever to have one. Moreover, they saw no relationship between the likelihood of suffering a heart attack and their own risky behaviors, such as smoking, eating red meat, or failing to exercise.

Aside from the role it plays in allowing people to continue indulging in self-destructive behaviors, denial is implicated in several categories of disease. Recent research has identified cases in which the risk of developing a particular physical illness, the likelihood of dying from it, or both seem directly linked to the person's denial of external reality or denial of emotions. In fact, the two often go together.

There appears to be a relationship between denial and emotional expression. People who tend to deny such unpleasant realities as symptoms of illness are also likely to be less emotionally expressive. This doesn't mean they don't feel anger, fear, or sadness, but simply that they are less likely to acknowledge or express such emotions. Clearly, being high in denial has important consequences for a person's health.

Denial, Emotionality, and Heart Disease   Dimsdale and Hackett (1982), for example, interviewed patients at Massachusetts General Hospital suspected of having heart disease. They conducted their interviews before patients received angiograms and classified patients as either low in denial (very worried) or high in denial (not worried at all). The latter sometimes even claimed that their hospitalizations were due to some "bureaucratic misunderstanding or misdiagnosis"). The high-denial patients who did not report feelings of tension or depression in fact had higher levels of heart disease than those low in denial.

In another study, Shaw and his colleagues used a measure of denial developed by Hackett and Cassem (1974) to look at the recovery of heart-attack patients. They found that patients higher in denial gained significantly less information in the cardiac rehabilitation program. This is of considerable potential importance, as other studies have shown that a high level of information, in combination with other factors, is an important factor in recovery from a heart attack.

One of the reasons physicians and nurses traditionally have not challenged patients' denial about their heart disease is the belief that denial protects patients from emotional distress, anxiety, and the possible physiological consequences of stress. Despite some evidence that denial does protect some patients from anxiety and its physiological concomitants, on the whole research does not support the practice of colluding with heart patients to deny their situation. There is, in fact, little evidence that denial reduces emotional distress among such patients.[3]

A number of research studies have found evidence, however, to suggest that denial may be adaptive in the short term, though maladaptive over the long term. For example, Levine and his colleagues (1987) interviewed hospital patients who had had a heart attack and followed them for a year after discharge. They found a curious mixed result: on the one hand, patients who scored high on a measure of denial spent less time in the intensive care unit and had fewer instances of arrhythmia during that time. On the other hand, those same people were less compliant with doctors' instructions over time, adapted to their situation less well, and were hospitalized more frequently during the following year.

Another group of researchers (Stern et al. 1976) earlier found that heart-attack patients high in denial failed to follow instructions while in the hospital and were more likely to return to their jobs and continue to work than patients low in denial. Taken together, the results suggest that patients high in denial, though they appear to function better, may return to previous activity levels in defiance of medical instructions, jeopardizing their long-term recovery.

The price of avoiding emotional distress for patients high in denial appears in some cases to be a shorter life. In a study of 367 heart-attack victims, Havik and Maeland (1988) found that patients who showed a high level of denial about the impact of illness on their lives did in fact report less emotional distress. At the same time, their rate of survival was lower than patients with lower levels of denial who reported more distress.

For certain individuals, denial may be a habitual coping strategy that is associated with higher levels of physiological reactivity to stress. Although these individuals claim to feel little anxiety or anger, they respond to stress with elevated blood pressure and heart rate, which can put them at higher risk for cardiovascular disease. Recent evidence suggests, in fact, that people who use chronic denial to deal with problems are at greater risk for health problems, including heart disease.[4]

A study by Carol Emerson and David Harrison (1990) of the relationships among denial, suppressed emotion, and physiological reactivity looked at forty-five young women between the ages of 19 and 21. On the basis of their scores on the State-Trait Anger Expression Inventory and the Marlowe-Crowne scale, a measure of denial, the women were categorized as being either (1) low in anger and low in denial; (2) high in anger and low in denial; or (3) low in anger and high in denial. Next, all three groups were presented with the same task: they were given color names (red, blue, etc.) printed in colors other than the one named. Subjects were asked to say the actual color of the word (as opposed to the color named) as quickly as possible. While engaged in the task, they were monitored for blood pressure and heart rate.

As expected, both the high anger/low denial and the low anger/high denial groups showed significantly greater physiological reactivity to the task than the low anger/low denial group. More importantly, the group that was low in anger but high in denial was actually more reactive than the high anger/low denial group. The results are particularly significant because, in men, a pattern of competitive drive and excessive anger that is denied (the so-called Type A personality) has been associated with heightened risk of cardiovascular disease, even when other risk factors such as diet and smoking are taken into account.[5]

One example of the level of anger—and denial of it—found among some with Type-A personality comes from a man studied in Friedman and Ulmer's Recurrent Coronary Prevention Project. Using a question-naire measure, investigators asked subjects whether they thought them-selves excessively hostile. One subject actually responded "I do not believe that I have excess hostility; this is due in part to the fact that my intellectual, physical, cultural, and hereditary attributes surpass those of 98 percent of the bastards I have to deal with. Furthermore, those dome-head, fitness freak, goody-goody types that make up the alleged 2 percent are no doubt faggots anyway, whom I could beat out in a second if I weren't so damn busy fighting every minute to keep that 98 percent from trying to walk over me." [6]

The results of Emerson and Harrison's study of women subjects suggest (1) that individuals who claim they are not angry—but who are high in denial—may in fact be angry; and (2) that their suppressed anger may be jeopardizing their health.

Denial, Emotionality, and Cancer   Denial of the symptoms of cancer or their seriousness in some cases prevents people from seeking help that could save their lives. Clinical social worker Margaret Wool and her col-league, Dr. Richard Goldberg (1986), recount the case of a woman who on some level knew all too well the meaning of her symptoms:

> Miss D., a 61-year-old single woman with breast cancer, delayed seeking treat-ment for seven years though she said she had been aware of a lump. She said she knew the lump meant cancer and was not surprised by the diagnosis. She had tried to ignore the growth and eventually applied dressings, which helped her "ignore" it. She finally sought medical attention when she began to hemorrhage. Striking in Miss D's history was that her mother had died of breast cancer and had exhibited the same aspect of denial and delay. Miss D said she felt stupid for not having come in earlier for treatment because she "knew better." (p. 8)

While this is an extreme case of denial and delay, it is by no means unique. Wool and Goldberg cite other examples of patients who waited even longer to go for treatment. One study of women referred to a sur-geon because of breast lumps (Styra et al. 1993) found that denial of cancer symptoms was very common. Although none of the women had yet been diagnosed with breast cancer, they were aware of the lumps and were complying with recommendations for follow-up. Yet, in a structured interview when asked to name three problems in their lives over the last three months, 74 of the 100 women studied failed to identify the breast lump as a problem. The nonidentifiers showed significantly less anxiety than the identifiers, although both groups showed higher anxiety than women in general. In addition, women who did not identify their breast lump as a problem scored significantly higher on measures of problem avoidance and reliance on avoidant coping mechanisms—primarily denial.

In one study of adolescents and young adults up to 25 years old (Tamaroff et al. 1992), denial was associated with failure to comply with treatment once cancer was diagnosed. Using the modified Hackett-Cassem Rating Scale of Denial, investigators compared young subjects who complied with oral medication to those who did not. Compliance with the medication regimen was established by laboratory tests. Non-compliers showed significantly greater use of denial in dealing with issues related to their illness, were more likely to believe that the absence of symptoms implied a cure, and—in spite of mature understanding of both their illness and its treatment—had significantly less insight when it came to issues related to their prognosis or the cause of their illness.

A number of studies have found a link between suppressed emotions and the development of cancer and course of the disease once diagnosed. One of the most famous studies (Thomas et al. 1979) was done at Johns Hopkins Medical School. A large number of students entering the school between 1948 and 1964 completed psychological tests upon entering and were followed up years later to assess their health status. The forty-eight subjects who eventually developed cancer were similar in that they showed little emotion and their relationship with their parents was cold and remote. This personality profile was also characteristic of subjects who eventually committed suicide. Greer (1983) reported finding relationships between the development of cancer and prior depression, feelings of hopelessness, and suppressed anger.

In another study (Weisman and Worden 1975) researchers found that long-term survivors of cancer had stronger personal relationships and better coping skills than short-term survivors, who tended to be passive, to exhibit stoic acceptance of their disease, and to attempt to forget it—an indicator of denial.

We should note here that individuals do not control whether or not they contract a serious illness such as cancer. Not everyone who engages in denial will eventually suffer from cancer, nor do all cancer patients show this pattern of denial. The findings do suggest, however, that there is a relationship between emotional states and physical well-being.

We do not yet clearly understand the mechanism by which suppressing one's emotions might increase the risk of developing cancer. Experiments with animals, as well as humans, provide some clues. Over the years studies have shown that extended stress compromises immune-system functioning by inducing the body to secrete stress hormones, principally one called corticosterone. Corticosterone, however, has a nasty side effect: it decreases the number of white blood cells, which are important for immune-system functioning.[7]

Riley (1981) has shown that either a stressful experience or a direct injection of corticosterone in the absence of stress affects the prognosis of mice implanted with cancerous tumors. The stressed mice and those who received corticosterone had tumor growth four times greater than that of control mice. The connection to cancer may be suggested by the studies of cardiovascular risk discussed earlier: individuals who use denial habitually and suppress negative emotions may be less aware of emotional distress but, at the same time, be more physiologically reactive to stress. In some individuals, this pattern may result in higher heart rate and blood pressure; in others, the physiological price of denial may be higher levels of circulating corticosterone, hence compromised immune functioning and increased vulnerability to viruses and other cancer-causing agents. In effect, the emotions people refuse to deal with may become an ongoing source of stress that ultimately takes a heavy toll on their bodies.

Optimism is not Denial   There is an important difference between being an optimist and using denial. Optimists do not deny that they are facing problems but believe that they will be able to triumph over them. People using denial assert that whatever they are confronting is not a problem.

Scheier and Carver (1985) use the term *dispositional optimism* to describe people who approach the problems of life with the expectation that good will come from confronting them. According to their research, such optimistic people tend to fare better than pessimists. In one study (Scheier et al. 1986), they asked subjects to tell them about the most stressful situation they had encountered during the previous two months. Optimists' accounts indicated that they used coping mechanisms that focused directly on their problems and did not resort to denial (Carver et al. 1989); that is, they did not refuse to acknowledge the existence of a stressful situation. This result is particularly significant, as many studies have found that the use of denial is associated with worse outcomes.

Scheier and his colleagues (1989) also looked at optimism and denial and their effect on patients' recovery from coronary bypass surgery. There was a clear difference in the use of denial between optimists and pessimists: individuals who were high in optimism were less likely to avoid thinking about their recovery; and pessimists were significantly more likely to believe that denial or avoiding thinking about their problems was helpful. But was this denial helpful? Decidedly not. Optimists were less likely than pessimists to have indicators of such physiological problems as irregular EKGs and enzymes related to muscle damage.[8]

Denial, Mental Health, and Coping with Stress

We have seen that while denial, in childhood at least, can protect individuals from the pain and fear engendered by some overwhelming external reality or emotion, it can also impair physical health. It is related to impaired mental health and ineffective coping abilities as well.

Researchers have found that denial is significantly associated with depression, alcohol use, and antisocial behaviors. One group of patients studied for three years (Perry and Cooper 1986) had impaired abilities to function at work and maintain family relationships, as well as a lower overall satisfaction with life during periods when their levels of denial were high. Such high levels of denial have also been related to tendencies to use alcohol or drugs to cope with problems; to disengage from difficulties mentally—for example, by watching television or sleeping a great deal; and to give up trying to solve a problem (Carver, Scheier, and Weintraub 1989). Denial is also related to certain personality traits, such as anxiety, and negatively correlated with such traits as optimism, control, hardiness, and self-esteem.

A recent study of residents living near the damaged nuclear-power plant at Three Mile Island (Collins, Baum, and Singer 1983) documented the toll denial takes on physical and mental health and on the ability to cope with stress. The Three Mile Island accident created a chronically stressful situation for residents because additional radioactive leaks occurred during the year following the initial accident. Many residents believed they were in continual danger from the radioactive gas and water trapped in the reactor building, as well as from the long-term effects of their initial exposure.

People living near Three Mile Island showed signs of chronic stress even two years after the accident, but individuals differed in the extent to which they were affected. The differences appear to be related to coping styles. When asked about the accident, individuals who used denial to cope with the problem tended to respond, "I refuse to believe what is happening." They reported more physical symptoms like nausea, headache, and nervousness, and greater emotional distress, including depression and anxiety, than other subjects. They also performed more poorly on two behavioral tasks requiring concentration: an embedded-figures task and a proofreading task. It is not difficult to imagine that the physical complaints and emotional distress these individuals experienced, not to mention their impairment in concentration, might have had a negative effect in many areas of their lives, including job performance and social interactions.

Denial and the Ability to Think

Leslie Groh (1981) relates denial to the work of Swiss psychologist Jean Piaget and his theory (1951) of how children develop the capacity to think about the world around them. Piaget suggested that a *concept* consists of perceptual, cognitive, and emotional components. For example, a baby's concept about the bottle of milk it drinks from has a perceptual component (the taste, appearance, and feel of the bottle), a cognitive component (what the bottle is used for), and an emotional component (the pleasure of drinking from it). Consequently, when individuals deny the emotional component of an experience—for example, the fear, pain, and anger of childhood punishment—the meaning of the concept *abuse* is lost and the person has great difficulty accepting or understanding information relating to such abuse.

Groh cited in this context the example of a patient whose thinking was impaired:

One of my patients, a twenty-six-year-old housewife suffering from a multiplicity of delusions and cognitive impairment, came to a session somewhat upset after a rather unpleasant meeting with her mother. She described the event in a flat voice and then added that she could almost hate her mother when the latter was so derisive and unreasonable. She then added in a surprised manner: "I feel nothing." After a few second's silence she said: "Everything is strange. Nothing has a meaning any more." She then pointed at the bookcase and asked, "What's that?" The therapist told her then that she could not face her murderous hate of her mother so she denied she felt anything. The patient became rigid, brought her hands up to her face, started to cry violently and said: "My feelings are crazy, they are not real, people don't want to kill their mother." "You do." She answered: "Leave me alone, let me die, I'm rotten." She continued to sob for a while, and when this subsided the therapist asked her whether she had any feelings now. She responded in the affirmative and added that everything looked normal once more. (p. 676)

This case, although extreme, illustrates the most severe consequences of denial: if a person can experience no emotion, then all concepts lose their meaning.[9]

Joe Alford and his colleagues (1988), in a paper discussing the use of denial among Vietnam veterans, link it to *psychic numbing* or constricted emotion. This condition is common among individuals with post-traumatic stress disorder, whether resulting from combat, childhood abuse, natural disaster, or some other very frightening event. Denial of emotions—denial that one has any emotional reactions at all—is one way to avoid being overwhelmed by terrible experiences. It is not uncommon for children to respond to beatings by attempting to control the only thing left under their control—their emotions. They may stifle their tears and pain under orders from adults or because the emotional pain is so great or because they sense that withholding an emotional response preserves their last shred of autonomy.

Despite their denial of emotion, the Vietnam veterans Alford studied often responded behaviorally to stress with extreme anger. They lashed out at partners, walked off their jobs, or otherwise behaved in ways that are self-defeating and that betray tremendous emotions, even while they claimed to feel nothing. The researchers relate this anger to the combat experience in several ways. First, anger and rage are natural reactions to enemy attacks and, perhaps, seeing friends killed. Second, anger—as opposed to sadness, for example—is an emotional response that contributes to a feeling of strength and the belief that one will survive, and even triumph. As such, it is perceived as far preferable to sadness, fear, and vulnerability. Again, the analogy to a child's situation seems straightforward: we would expect children to respond to abuse and physical punishment predominantly with anger, rather than fear or sorrow, both because parents often forbid expressions of sorrow and because anger helps children deny their helplessness and vulnerability and believe they will survive the mistreatment.

Alford and his colleagues argue that the changes in thinking and behavior typical of some veterans are adaptations to combat that become maladaptive when veterans are no longer in a life-and-death situation. Their description of the way veterans adapt their thinking and behavior to combat may remind some readers of what it is like to be a child growing up in a home with alcoholic, violent, or otherwise abusive parents.

Some of the veterans developed a rigid intolerance of mistakes that was reflected both in impossibly high standards for their own performance and anger toward those they perceived to be "screwing up." Their anger was particularly apparent in dealings with bosses and coworkers. In combat, Alford points out, such rigidity and perfectionism was necessary, because one small mistake could cost a life. Later, in a civilian context, it was difficult for the veterans to adjust to the fact that most jobs do not involve life-and-death situations. Adults who have grown up in alcoholic homes, or with a violent parent, often show the same serious, life-and-death attitudes toward problems. If as children they were screamed at or beaten for the slightest failing, they might come to believe that every mistake is potentially fraught with fatal consequences.

Along with rigid adherence to perfectionist standards, some Vietnam veterans engage in what has been called "black-or-white thinking." They see things as either right or wrong, good or bad and perceive other human beings as either totally trustworthy or completely unreliable. The veterans' cognitive rigidity and resistance to changing their thinking may be due, in part, to their intolerance of error. They also seem to be related to fear.

Other researchers (Foa and Kozak 1986) have suggested that cognitive and behavioral responses to fear-provoking situations do not disappear over time—even when the threat is no longer present—unless people learn to modify their perception of threat. If they don't, cognitive rigidity becomes a circular and self-defeating pattern. Traumatized people continue to see dangers and threats all around them, to be hypervigilant to any conceivable threat, and to cling to their defenses.

Denial and Intergenerational Transmission of Pain and Abuse

If—as we would argue—the trauma of physical punishment in childhood has the same effects on thinking, imagine what happens when children who have been beaten or spanked, slapped, shouted at, insulted, ridiculed, or ignored grow up and have children of their own. Mistreated children who develop the sorts of cognitive and behavioral impairments Alford noted among some combat veterans would as parents have rigid standards of performance for their children and be intolerant of the slightest "screw-up." They would hold black-and-white ideas of what is good behavior or bad behavior and would not take into account the natural limitations of young children. They would stubbornly resist changing their thinking or behavior about child rearing. Such parents would also deny the pain they felt as children when they were mistreated and would respond to their own children's slightest misstep with extreme anger—which they might rationalize to their children as the sign of a strong person, a survivor.

The danger of such cognitive and behavioral consequences of trauma is, therefore, that they become long-standing, maladaptive patterns that are handed on to the next generation. That is perhaps the most serious consequence of denial: we recreate for our children the pain we deny from our own childhood experiences, ensuring that they too will grow up angry.

We often hear parents vow that they will never treat their children the way their own parents treated them. Yet they may one day hear themselves saying to their offspring the same abusive things their parents said to them or, in a moment of extreme anger, striking their children as they had resolved never to do. There are at least three reasons, rooted in basic psychological processes, why as adults we tend to repeat with our own children the treatment we received while growing up. First, our working model of the world is based on our childhood interactions with our caretakers. Second, we learn in part by observing the behaviors of others and tend to repeat behaviors that we see are rewarded. Finally, the culture around us supports and even glorifies strength, the use of force, and the belief that parents know best. We address each of these factors in turn.

Children who receive warm, nurturing care from their parents learn to see themselves as valued individuals and so develop strong self-esteem. The same children develop models of their caretakers as warm, nurturing, and available to children when need arises. On the other hand, children who are abused or neglected develop models of the self as undervalued and models of others as unavailable or undependable.[10]

Research has shown a relationship between the way parents talk about the attachment they felt to their own parents and the way their children behave toward them. To assess the strength and type of attachment infants have with their important caretakers, Ainsworth and colleagues (1978) developed a test called the Strange Situation Procedure. Infants between twelve and eighteen months of age were left briefly with a strange adult and then reunited with their parents. The way the parent and child interact following the parent's return was used to classify the attachment between the infant and the parent as either *secure* or *insecure.*

Theories of attachment suggest that when confronted with a strange adult, an infant who has a secure attachment to his or her caretakers will use it as a base from which to explore new environments and go to the parents for reassurance when they return. Other infants are undisturbed when their parents leave the room and may ignore or actively avoid them when they return. This type of relationship is called *avoidant.* Yet other children complain loudly when their parents leave but then alternately demand attention and ignore the parents when they return. This third type of relationship is termed *resistant.*

George and colleagues (1984) developed a parallel procedure for assessing how attached to their parents adult subjects were as children. They used an interview with questions about early relationship experiences of loss, separation, and other instances related to attachment to classify parents as either *autonomous* or *insecure.* Autonomous adults place a high value on relationships, have a considerable capacity for forgiving others, do not maintain idealized images of their parents, and have clear recollections of early childhood experiences. In contrast, detached or insecure adults see their early experiences as irrelevant and exhibit distortions in thinking typical of individuals who use denial. Zeanah and Zeanah (1989) report, for example, that they tend to idealize their parents and childhoods, speaking of them in glowing terms while claiming

Table 2.1
Correspondence between attachment classification of mothers and their infants

Mothers	Infants
Adult Attachment Interview	*Strange Situation Procedure*
Autonomous	Secure
Detached	Avoidant
Preoccupied	Resistant
Unresolved	Disorganized

that they cannot remember particular events. When they do recall specific instances, the latter are usually inconsistent with their descriptions of idyllic childhoods (p. 187).

The classifications of parents resulting from the attachment interview corresponded very closely to independently conducted classifications of their 12- to 18-month-old infants in the Strange Situation Procedure, as Table 2.1 demonstrates. Various researchers have found agreements ranging from 76 to 86 percent in ratings of infants and their mothers.[11]

These findings indicate that differences in the way people learn to relate to each other emerge at an early age. Further, such differences are not simply a matter of chance but correspond closely to the way in which the child's parents learned to form attachments. The results indicate that the positive or negative ways of attaching to others—the working models that individuals carry with them—are transmitted from one generation to the next.

Children not only pick up from their parents general working models of interpersonal interactions. They also see how their parents behave toward themselves, their siblings, and the other parent and observe the consequences of those behaviors. Learning theory, particularly Bandura's social learning theory (Bandura, Ross, and Ross 1963a), would predict that a child subjected to physical, sexual, or emotional abuse will learn those behaviors by observing the abusing parent; that is, the abuser models that behavior for the child.

The classic 1959 study by Bandura and Walters we discussed in chapter 1 found that antisocial boys physically punished by their fathers were less likely to engage in aggressive behavior inside their homes but more likely to be aggressive away from their fathers. One interpretation of this result is that the boys learned from their own experience that violence is an effective way to impose one's will on others who are smaller and weaker. In other studies, Bandura and his colleagues found that children who watched adults beat up a doll learned the violent behavior, although whether or not they acted out the behavior depended on whether the adults they observed were rewarded or punished for it.[12] In everyday life, a physically abusive parent often appears to reap considerable rewards from his or her behavior. Other family members accede to the person's wishes, make efforts to avoid displeasing him or her, avoid bringing up matters that could be a source of conflict, and so forth.

Research on the intergenerational transmission of abuse has largely focused on physical abuse; it demonstrates that abusive parents almost always have a history of abuse from their own childhoods. On the other hand, people who were physically abused do not always physically abuse their own children.

There is, however, clear evidence that children who are physically abused are much more likely to engage in aggressive behavior. Psychologists Kenneth Dodge, John Bates, and Gregory Pettit (1990) interviewed parents of a large sample of four-year-olds and then followed the children over time. They found that children who were abused reacted to provocative situations presented to them on videotape with aggressive suggestions significantly more often than did children for whom there was no evidence of abuse. The abused children were also significantly more likely to approve of aggressive responses when alternatives were presented to them. These findings remained significant, even after controlling for other variables known to predict children's aggressive behavior.

Some people have argued that human aggression is an instinctual, or inborn legacy of our evolutionary development. This argument is seriously flawed on several grounds. Evidence for the instinctual nature of aggression comes primarily from animal studies, and the extent to which we can infer anything about complex human behavior from animal behavior is questionable. Indeed, it is not certain that we can even speak of aggression among animals in any sense that can be meaningfully extended to humans. Some animals kill for food and some establish social hierarchies through the use of highly stylized displays of threat, rather than through inflicting physical harm. Neither of these behaviors is comparable to human aggression. Finally, because a behavior is inborn does not imply that it is either inevitable or unchangeable: both humans and animals show a high degree of flexibility in modifying the expression of even powerful basic behaviors.[13]

While learning theorists focus primarily on the analysis of behavior, clinical and developmental psychologists point out that behavior may be motivated by strong impulses and emotions that are often denied. They explain the intergenerational transmission of abuse not simply as a result of the external rewards attendant on it, but in terms of the strong emotions that result from mistreatment and the way in which denial of such emotions paradoxically ensures that the person will repeat the behavior and engender the same strong negative emotion in his or her own children. Our research, reported in chapter 3, found that there is a high correlation between denial and negative child-rearing attitudes, with individuals scoring high in denial more likely to subscribe to the use of force and the withholding of affection and support from their children.

Alice Miller (1983) describes how abuse in a family is passed down from one generation to the next:

For parents' motives are the same today as they were then: in beating their children, they are struggling to regain the power they once lost to their own parents. For the first time, they see the vulnerability of their own earliest years, which they are unable to recall, reflected in their children. . . . Only now, when someone weaker than they is involved, do they finally fight back, often quite fiercely. There are countless rationalizations, still used today, to justify their behavior. Although parents *always* mistreat their children for psychological reasons, i.e., because of their own needs, there is a basic assumption in our society that this treatment is good for children. (p. 16)

Many may find Miller's assertion that parents always mistreat their children for psychological reasons having to do with the parents' own needs somewhat extreme. Yet the case she builds in defense of it is convincing. What's more, she takes the argument a step further and maintains that social and cultural norms actually support the victimization of children. When we present Miller's argument to students—and the arguments against physical punishment of children in general—they often object to it. Some of their objections point to the unexamined assumptions many people make about children's needs and motives.

In one class, for example, a young woman objected to the idea that one should refrain from using physical force with children. "What about infants?" she asked, "They cry for no reason." When other members of the class expressed shock at the idea of hitting a crying infant, the young woman assured us that, no, of course she didn't think it was right to hit a baby. She was still troubled and puzzled: "What *do* you do, then?" she asked. "Even when they're not wet, or hungry, or sick, babies cry." We suggested gently that you might pick the baby up and hold him or her. The woman became vehement at that point, insisting, "In that case, all they want is attention. If you let them get away with it, before you know it they'll control you completely."

Where would someone get the idea that a newborn infant cries for the deliberate purpose of gaining power over its parents, controlling them, and reducing them to slaves devoted to satisfying its every whim?

This is just one of many comments about child rearing we've heard over the years that seem to be based on an underlying assumption that the parent-child relationship is one involving a contest of wills, of who will control whom, and who will receive consideration and attention for their needs. As we pointed out in chapter 1, Miller argues that culturally accepted child-rearing strategies represent an ideology based on the assumption that children are deliberately willful, even at an early age; and that parents need to break their will and establish themselves as authorities, lest the child's "natural" antisocial tendencies get out of hand. We have already discussed, in the previous chapter, the potential outcomes of such treatment of children—pain, fear, sadness, and rage toward the parents that, if denied, can be displaced onto spouses or children.

According to Miller, it is not simply that adults repeat behaviors they have observed when they were small. The mistreatment of children also serves a double psychological function: it both guards against a reawakening of painful feelings from childhood and allows one to rationalize the behavior of one's own parents. Children taught in childhood that their needs are an imposition on adults and that their very will is an affront to parents will naturally tend as adults to see children as excessively needy and unacceptably willful. If parents react with tremendous anger to any unacceptable behavior, no matter how age-appropriate—whether arguing with a sibling or accidentally dropping a dish—then such "childish" behaviors become anxiety provoking and will be associated with feelings of threat or impending catastrophe. One would certainly attempt to squelch similar behaviors in one's own children as quickly as possible.

Finally, if, in response to mistreatment, children deny their fear and sadness and feelings of vulnerability and rage, as adults they will be incapable of empathizing with their own children's pain. To recognize that pain would require them to recognize their own. As we saw in the case of some Vietnam veterans, acting on anger instead of experiencing grief and fear allows us to feel strong and invulnerable; it lets us believe that we will survive, that we have survived, and that we will never again have to feel helpless, trapped, terrified, or heartbroken. So we shout at our children, slap them, or spank them, or worse, and justify it to ourselves by reasoning that they need to toughen up, that we're only preparing them for the hostile world out there.

According to Miller (p. 97), the true motives behind the practice of poisonous pedagogy are several.

1. The unconscious need to pass on to others the humiliation one has undergone oneself
2. The need to find an outlet for repressed affect
3. The need to possess and have at one's disposal a vital object to manipulate
4. Self-defense: i.e., the need to idealize one's childhood and one's parents by dogmatically applying the parents' pedagogical principles to one's own children
5. Fear of freedom
6. Fear of the reappearance of what one has repressed, which one reencounters in one's child and must try to stamp out, having killed it in oneself earlier
7. Revenge for the pain one has suffered.

By breaking the child's will and squelching the liveliness and energy that got the parents into so much trouble when they were small, parents pass on to their children a set of beliefs and values they heard articulated by their own parents. Here are some of the messages Miller claims parents send (p. 59); our own examples of how they are often conveyed are in brackets.

1. A feeling of duty produces love. ["You'll do it and like it."]
2. Hatred can be done away with by forbidding it. ["You do *not* hate your brother."]
3. Parents deserve respect simply because they are parents. ["I'm your father and as long as you live under this roof . . ."]

4. Children are undeserving of respect simply because they are children. ["Just who do you think you are?"]

5. Obedience makes a child strong. ["If you don't learn to mind now, you'll have a surprise waiting for you out in the *real* world."]

6. A high degree of self-esteem is harmful. ["Watch out that you don't fall off that high horse and hurt yourself, young lady."]

7. A low degree of self-esteem makes a person altruistic. [e.g., "Can't you ever think about anybody but yourself?"]

8. Tenderness (doting) is harmful. ["You're going to spoil that child rotten."]

9. Responding to a child's needs is wrong. ["Before you know it, they'll control you completely."]

10. Severity and coldness are a good preparation for life. ["Don't expect the world out there to come rushing to your side any time you want."]

11. A pretense of gratitude is better than honest ingratitude. ["She's your mother; can't you at least *pretend* . . . ?"] . . .

13. Neither parents nor God would survive being offended. ["Do you want to *kill* your mother?"] . . .

17. Parents are always right. ["Because I said so, that's why."]

All of this, parents tell us (and we tell our children), is "for your own good." In one sense, that is true: they are preparing us to fit into a culture of people just like us, all of whom have been raised to respect authority unquestioningly and to deny feelings. As a result, the culture at large jointly operates on a set of values that glorify strength, fearlessness, discipline, and even ruthlessness, while it condemns what it calls *whining*— a term often applied to the expression of feelings of pain, grief, or confusion.

Imagine a culture in which adults tell children, "You're a big boy now. Boys don't smile. If you have to do that, for heaven's sake, go home and get in the shower and keep your happiness to yourself. There you can smile as much as you need to and get it out of your system." Imagine a culture in which smiling or laughing at work, at a social event, in a grocery store would cast doubt on one's maturity and emotional stability. We take the expression of positive emotions for granted; we even value them and consider them a sign of mental health. But negative emotions—that is, emotions that are seen as evidence of weakness, such as sadness and fear—are censured and subject to shame and ridicule.

The one negative emotion the culture finds acceptable is anger, an emotion we are free to direct against children and members of the society perceived as weaker or blameworthy—welfare mothers, gays, and others.

Conclusion

Denial, a defense mechanism guarding us against unacceptable feelings that may result from childhood experiences, takes a heavy toll on us as individuals and as a society. It puts some people at higher risk for heart disease, cancer, and other physical ills. It impairs our mental health and functioning, our ability to cope with stress, and our ability to think clearly about the world around us. It also ensures that we will pass on to our children the very pain we so strenuously defend ourselves against. Even worse, denial creates a society based on values of toughness in which anger becomes the only negative emotion we can express freely without being subjected to shame and ridicule.

What is the result of physical punishment, abuse, and denial? Miller argues that children react to punishment and abuse with rage. In a family system based on denial, however, they are prohibited from expressing their anger or are trained to deny their feelings, to believe that they have nothing to be legitimately angry about. This unexpressed anger does not go away as we shall see in the remainder of this book.

3

The Politics of Denial

What becomes of all those people who are the successful products of a strict upbringing? It is inconceivable that they were able to express and develop their true feelings as children, for anger and helpless rage, which they were forbidden to display, would have been among these feelings—particularly if these children were beaten, humiliated, lied to, and deceived. What becomes of this forbidden and therefore unexpressed anger? Unfortunately, it does not disappear, but is transformed with time into a more or less conscious hatred directed against either the self or substitute persons, a hatred that will seek to discharge itself in various ways permissible and suitable for an adult. (Miller 1983, p. 61)

In this society, we tend to assume that a person's political attitudes are the result of rational reflection on the issues. In their textbook on public opinion, political scientists Jerry Yeric and John Todd (1989) argue that attitudes represent people's emotional response to particular objects or events and are "derived from the individual's belief system" (p. 29). In other words, the way we feel about, for example, a presidential candidate, is determined by what we believe to be true about him or her and about the qualities we think a candidate should have. This approach overlooks, however, the possibilities that emotions may powerfully shape a person's beliefs and opinions and that such emotional residues of childhood punishment as anger and fear might influence adult political attitudes.

We would expect childhood socialization to be an important foundation for adult personality and the exercise of parental discipline a fundamental aspect of socialization. Because of its potential for abuse, parental discipline may produce negative emotions in some individuals and teach them lessons about the misuse of power. A central element of many political issues, such as capital punishment or the use of military force in international crises, is the theme of punitiveness or retribution. Such issues might serve as an arena for displaced childhood rage, fear, or helplessness and as an excuse for rationalizing the desire for retribution.

Factors such as gender, social class, education, individual experiences, and aspects of the contemporary political environment—taken together—account for some of the variation in people's opinions on particular political questions (Milburn 1991). For example, women and those with a higher level of education are more likely to support legal abortion. The studies we describe in this chapter tested the hypothesis that political attitudes may also be influenced, in part, by childhood punishment.

Previous research has demonstrated that individuals who hold a constellation of conservative and punitive social attitudes, called by Adorno and his colleagues (1950) the *authoritarian personality,* are likely to have been raised by rigid, punitive parents. Individuals scoring high on measures on authoritarianism tend to support punitive and conservative political policies. However, until recently, no researcher has demonstrated clearly that there is a direct link between childhood punishment and adult political attitudes, although such a link has been theorized by political psychologists for many years.

Personality and Political Attitudes

Harold Lasswell, one of the first scholars to consider this connection, theorized in 1930 that political beliefs are influenced by individuals' unresolved personality issues and emotions stemming from relationships with parents and siblings.[1] In the model he proposed to represent this process Lasswell used the concept of *displacement,* hypothesizing that private motives would be displaced onto a public object and rationalized in terms of the public interest. The need for revenge against punitive parents, for example, might take the form of revenge against criminals or a foreign nation. Lasswell argued that an individual might rationalize his or her private motives by coming to believe that it is just and necessary to the security or prestige of the nation to execute criminals or wage war against an enemy.

Through the process of rationalization, people thus construct a subjective reality that permits them to express their negative emotions without guilt: "Primitive psychological structures continue to function within the personality long after the epochs of infancy and childhood have been chronologically left behind. The prominence of hate in politics suggests that we may find that the most important private motive is a repressed and powerful hatred of authority" (p. 76).

Lloyd Etheredge (1975) found evidence for Lasswell's model in his study of U.S. State Department officials. He demonstrated that their judgments about whether to use military force in hypothetical situations were highly correlated with certain personality traits. After comparing their scores on psychological tests with their attitudes and opinions concerning a series of hypothetical international crises, Etheredge concluded that personality was an important factor in their choice of policies: "It became obvious that diplomatic and military opinions are linked intimately with certain private and interpersonal characteristics" (p. 39). Among these State Department officials, distrust of those around them, desire for power, competitiveness, and low self-esteem all predicted greater advocacy for the use of military force in international crises.

Authoritarianism

Earlier, in *The Authoritarian Personality*, Adorno and his colleagues offered a more specific formulation of the relation between personality and political attitudes that nonetheless parallels Lasswell's model. They theorized that children raised by rigid and punitive parents develop a personality type they called *authoritarian*. Parents who cannot tolerate any expression of the child's natural sexual and aggressive impulses and respond to them with exaggerated punitiveness leave the child no alternative but to repress those impulses, that is, to ban them from consciousness. The child, in effect, becomes unaware of any sexual or aggressive feelings.

The problem with repression, however, is that it is rarely completely successful; repressed impulses will threaten to break through into consciousness, producing anxiety. To guard against anxiety, additional defenses must be erected against the impulses, much as one might pile larger and heavier pieces of furniture against a door to keep out an insistent intruder. Adorno and his colleagues theorized that the sexual and aggressive feelings the child must banish are disowned and projected onto—

that is, unconsciously attributed to—someone else—members of despised outgroups, groups whose religion, culture, or race differs from that of the child's family.

The parents' punitiveness produces rage that the child dare not feel—or at least, must not attribute to the parents' behavior. The child denies the parents' abusiveness and idealizes them while displacing the rage onto the despised minority group. The beauty of projection lies in its psychic economy; once one has projected one's own "bad" impulses onto women, Jews, or African Americans, it is only reasonable to take out one's rage against them. After all, they are the ones who are oversexed, aggressive, sneaky, and so on. (It is interesting that many groups from different cultural and religious backgrounds are accused of the same unacceptable traits by authoritarian people.) In addition to venting their anger on minority groups, individuals of this personality type find their own children perfect targets for displacement and treat their children the same way their parents treated them.

Adorno identified a specific constellation of attitudes that are characteristic of the authoritarian personality: for example, rigid adherence to conventional moral standards; a harsh, punitive attitude toward outgroups as well as those perceived as social inferiors; and a glorification of authority figures—for example, the president or religious leaders—within their own group. They also assiduously avoid introspection and are contemptuous of professions or avocations—such as psychology—they associate with introspection. They glorify power and toughness and are cynical about others' intentions and about human nature in general, seeing ulterior motives in even the most saintly behavior. Frequently they are superstitious people who engage in stereotyped behaviors, rigidly practicing the same response to many situations, however maladaptive it may be. They use the defense mechanism of projection a great deal and, owing to the projection of their own sexual impulses, are overly concerned with what they perceive as other people's sexual improprieties.

Adorno's team established the relationship between harsh, punitive child rearing and an authoritarian personality in adulthood by interviewing people who scored high on a measure of authoritarianism called the *F* (for Fascism) *scale*. They found that such people expressed ambivalent feelings about their parents: "It was usually not long after the statements of glorification that a note of complaint or self-pity began to creep into the interview." High scorers often shared a similar background: "Discipline in the families of the more authoritarian men and women was characterized in their accounts by relatively harsh application of rules, in accordance with conventional values, and this discipline was commonly experienced as threatening or traumatic or even overwhelming" (Sanford 1971, pp. 319, 337). The relation between harsh, punitive child rearing, and authoritarian personality was confirmed in another study by Frenkel-Brunswik (1954), who conducted home visits and interviews with parents of children as young as ten years old.

There are many ways in which authoritarianism might affect adult political attitudes, for it represents a complex set of psychological defenses for managing the hostility and insult to self-esteem caused by harsh parenting. Because highly authoritarian people are harsh toward those they see as blameworthy—and tend to see most people outside their own racial, ethnic or religious group as guilty of some offense—we would expect to see a relationship between authoritarianism and attitudes on political issues involving themes of blame, retribution, the use of force, or the imputation of negative motives to others.

The relationship between authoritarianism and political ideology is complex. The original researchers reported that individuals with high scores on the measure of authoritarianism tended to be highly conservative on political and economic issues. Others have since confirmed that the majority of authoritarians fall on the conservative end of the political spectrum; what accounts for the less-than-perfect correlation between authoritarianism and conservatism is variability among conservatives.[2] In other words, virtually all authoritarians are politically conservative, but not all political conservatives are authoritarians. In theory, the connection would be between authoritarianism and the sort of people who in 1992 appropriated the Republican national convention as a forum for their particular constellation of punitive political and social attitudes. These are the individuals we would suspect to be both politically conservative and high on authoritarianism.

Of course, political attitudes do not fall uniformly along a single liberal-conservative spectrum. A political ideology is composed of a number of different issue domains, such as foreign policy attitudes, economic views, and social policy positions. People's views in one domain do not necessarily match or predict their views in another.[3] For example, an individual might be quite liberal on social policies like welfare or abortion but markedly conservative on such economic issues as the need for a balanced budget. Indeed, one of the most interesting developments in contemporary American politics is the increasing tendency of individuals, and even identifiable subgroups within the two major political parties, to espouse liberal attitudes in one domain and conservative attitudes in another. The particular political issues that distinguish authoritarians from nonauthoritarians are those that raise the possibility of punitive action (Christie 1993).

In American politics, high scores on authoritarianism are related to a tendency to vote for conservative political candidates and to support the death penalty. Various researchers have established a relationship between authoritarianism and support for U.S. involvement in the Vietnam war and between authoritarianism and conservative political attitudes. Some recent work on the authoritarian personality concludes that "we know very little about the origins of authoritarian tendencies." There is evidence, however, that the denial of problems originating in early interpersonal experiences is one key to the development of authoritarianism.[4]

Childhood Socialization, Affect, and Ideology

Tomkins offered another way of understanding the relationship between enduring personality traits originating in childhood experience and adult political views. He proposed that people of different personality orientations (what he calls *scripts*) are attracted to different political ideologies. He hypothesized that there are two types of scripts, the left-wing (or *humanistic*) script and the right-wing (or *normative*) script. One's characteristic script, he believed, results from the primary emotional environment experienced during childhood socialization. Parents who engage in childrearing socialization strategies that Tomkins defined as humanistic value the child as a unique and special individual, whereas parents who employ normative strategies emphasize obedience and strict adherence to rules and conventional standards.[5] Tomkins developed his Polarity Scale to assess individuals' normative or humanistic orientation. Subjects who correspond to the normative script tend to describe themselves as being politically conservative.

Tomkins argues (1991) that the manner in which children are socialized about anger influences their adult disposition toward it. *Rewarding socialization* attempts to minimize the experience of anger, and *punitive socialization* increases the child's experience of anger through parents' frequent physical punishment or verbal scolding. Rewarding socialization cultivates adults capable of controlling their anger, while punitive socialization increases the likelihood that the individual will frequently experience anger in adulthood.

As we saw in chapter 2, Alice Miller (1983) also argues that punitive child-rearing practices produce anger toward their parents that children must deny. Anger that is not recognized and dealt with later in adulthood, she suggests, serves as a reservoir of rage that can be displaced onto the political arena. Her poisonous pedagogy consists of child-rearing methods parallel to what Tomkins calls normative child rearing and to what Adorno and his colleagues describe as the antecedents of authoritarianism. Miller further argues that it is not simply harsh punishment or abuse that results in negative emotions that are later displaced in various ways. Rather, it is the denial of the effects or importance of these experiences that results in the adult displacement of the emotions. It is one thing to treat a child harshly in a moment of frustration or anger and then to acknowledge the child's quite justifiable anger. (After all, as adults, we feel our anger is justified when a coworker, spouse, or our children speak to us harshly or treat us with disrespect. Why would not children experience anger under the same circumstances?) According to Miller, the most pernicious effect of poisonous pedagogy is the lie employed by parents when they deny the real nature of their harsh behavior and convince the child that beatings, constant criticism, and severity are signs of their love. Children thus learn to disregard their feelings and to deny the reality of what is being done to them. In adulthood, that denial ensures that individuals will be unaware of the anger they carry within them—and of its true source. They are therefore more likely to engage in the process of displacement that Lasswell described, adopting punitive public policies that can be rationalized and perceived as responses to threats to national interests or security.

We have seen that public opinion research supports Miller's claim that physical punishment is common in American families. Verbal harshness in child rearing is also pervasive. One nationally representative study of 3,346 children (Vissing et al. 1991) found that 63 percent of them were spoken to by parents in an aggressive manner. The researchers defined verbal/symbolic aggression as "a communication intended to cause psychological pain to another person, or a communication perceived as having that intent. The communicative act may be active or passive, and verbal or nonverbal. Examples include name calling or nasty remarks (active, verbal), slamming a door or smashing something (active, nonverbal), and stony silence or sulking (passive, nonverbal)" (p. 224).

Another group of researchers, attempting to ascertain whether experiences of harsh parental discipline during early childhood are associated with later aggression, found a significant correlation. They also argued that maladaptive social information-processing patterns develop in response to harsh discipline. In other words, children who have been treated harshly learn to interpret the behavior and intentions of others in a way that inhibits them from achieving good interpersonal relations. Another study found that aggressive children exhibited a hostile attributional bias—that is, they often attributed malicious or threatening intent to others—and were more likely than a control group to say they would respond to a hypothetical situation with aggressive behavior.[6]

As we have seen, psychologists have theorized that harsh child rearing produces anger that colors adult political attitudes. What remains to be shown is an empirical connection among childhood punishment, a particular personality type or characteristic set of defenses—what Adorno and his colleagues call *authoritarianism* and Tomkins referred to as the *normative orientation*—and adult political attitudes.[7]

Bob Altemeyer (1988) contributed the first step in attempting to test empirically the relationship between childhood punishment and authoritarianism. He studied college students and their parents, asking them both to recall the type of punishment the students received in childhood. Interestingly, there was virtually no agreement between the students' and parents' memories about punishments. In addition, neither the students' account nor the parents' recollection of the amount of punishment meted out correlated highly with students' scores on Altemeyer's measure of authoritarianism, the RWA (Right-wing Authoritarianism) scale. Alte-meyer's failure to examine differences in the way male and female children in our society are taught to handle and experience their anger may explain why he found no clear relationship between authoritarianism and childhood punishment.

The Link Between Childhood Punishment and Adult Political Attitudes

The accumulated theory and research discussed above led us to expect that people who had experienced a great deal of punishment in childhood, particularly physical punishment, would express more punitive political attitudes. We expected this relationship to be particularly strong for individuals uninterested in exploring emotional issues in their childhood.

Punishment, Retribution and Political Attitudes

Revenge and retribution are themes that influence a number of political attitudes. To consider them, we chose to investigate three issues that seemed particularly likely to be affected by displacement of childhood rage: attitudes toward the death penalty, abortion, and the use of military force.

The Death Penalty   Many people support capital punishment in spite of numerous arguments against it. According to Van Gestel (1991), for example,

1. *It costs much more to execute criminals than to imprison them for life.*   According to a Florida study, execution costs $3.2 million, compared to $516,000 to imprison the person for life. Thus, a disproportionate share of legal resources are absorbed by death-penalty cases.

2. *There is little or no evidence supporting a deterrent effect of capital punishment.*   Stack (1987), in a time-series analysis of executions and murder rates, claimed he found evidence of a deterrent effect. Other researchers, however, identified conceptual and methodological problems with Stack's research and, in a reanalysis of the time series, discerned no cumulative effect of capital punishment on murders committed during the execution and in subsequent months (Bailey and Peterson 1989). These findings are echoed by Archer and Gartner's ten-year cross-national study of crime and violence (1984). Gathering data from 110 countries, they

found that capital punishment does not deter murder and that a nation that has just concluded a war experiences an increase in the civilian homicide rate. They concluded that when a nation commits violence against people, either by executing them or engaging in war, it instigates more violence among its citizens than would otherwise occur. Their review of fifty studies on the effect of the death penalty reveals that capital punishment has no deterrent effect on murder rates.

3. *The United States is alone among Western democracies in retaining the death penalty.*   Other countries that continue to employ capital punishment include Iran, Iraq, Libya, Syria, China, Nigeria, and Cuba.

4. *No legal system is perfect.*   Innocent people are convicted and have been executed. When the death penalty was ruled unconstitutional by the U.S. Supreme Court in 1972, 558 men on death row had their sentences commuted to life in prison. Of these, 239 were eventually released (because not all states had mandatory life sentences) and 4 of the 239 men released were later proven innocent (Obligato 1994).

Despite the large body of evidence that it is not effectual, many people support the death penalty for a simple reason: a desire for retribution that is, in part, the result of rage they carry from childhood and of the need to take revenge for their childhood pain. A 1992 study (Grasmick, Davenport, Chamlin, and Bursik) notes that, in the landmark case of *Gregg* v. *Georgia* in 1976, the Supreme Court ruled that public opinion—including the public desire for retribution—can be a legitimate basis for implementation of the death penalty.

In fact, the desire for retribution does appear to be strongly related to public opinion favoring the death penalty. In one survey (Warr and Stafford 1984), 66 percent of Seattle residents, when asked about the goals of punishment, mentioned retribution as one of their first three choices. In another study looking at the psychological bases of attitudes toward the death penalty, 35 percent of death-penalty supporters said they would favor it even if it did not deter crime. Other studies have found even higher percentages.[8] These findings point strongly to the existence of an emotional basis for death-penalty support.

Abortion   Attitudes toward abortion have a similar retributive or punitive component. While many people who oppose abortion base their belief on the sanctity of human life, others argue that sex outside of marriage is immoral and should take place only in the context of procreation.

If a woman gets pregnant through her irresponsible, sinful behavior, they believe she should pay the price. Punishing women in this situation is a way for individuals to reenact the punishment they received as children, at the same time powerfully identifying with a defenseless, innocent "child" who needs protection from its own parents. Since many of the strongest opponents of abortion are men who often felt helpless as children, their opposition is also a way for them to feel powerful, this time at the expense of women.

The work of other researchers supports our hypothesis that emotion from childhood is responsible, at least in part, for adult attitudes on abortion. Allgeier, Allgeier and Rywick (1981) administered measures of sexual knowledge and sexual guilt to undergraduates they classified as pro-choice, antiabortion, or mixed on the basis of responses to ten fictitious accounts of women requesting an abortion. They found that although sexual knowledge did not predict abortion attitudes, the students' scores on the sexual-guilt scale did. The researchers defined *sexual guilt* as "a generalized expectancy for sex-mediated punishment for violating or anticipating the violation of internalized standards of moral behavior" (p. 278). They observed that the antiabortion students appeared to have internalized sexually repressive moral messages and to be punishing the women for not adhering to them.

Use of Military Force   A third political attitude that contains a strong retributive component is support for the use of American military force. It is interesting that governmental officials attempting to justify military intervention (as in the war against Iraq), frequently picture the enemy as a "bully" who has to be stopped before he abuses others. For most people this image evokes childhood experiences of shame, humiliation, or abuse from some older or bigger child. As children we wanted to strike back at our tormentor; now, as adults, we get the chance to do it—this time using smart bombs and B-52s.

Empirical Evidence
In our first study (Milburn, Conrad et al. 1995), we administered a questionnaire to a group of a hundred undergraduates at the University of Massachusetts. We asked them about their political attitudes on a

number of issues, their childhood experiences with punishment, and whether they had ever been in therapy. The political issues we looked at included the death penalty, legalized abortion, defense spending, higher taxes for wealthy individuals, and the use of military force when U.S. interests are at stake. We thought several of these issues—for example, the death penalty—might serve as targets for any punitive feelings individuals might hold. As we saw in the last section, support for the death penalty is strongly related to a desire for retribution and so represents a punitive policy. We also asked students about their political ideology, in other words, whether they identified themselves as liberal or conservative.

To measure childhood punishment, we used a parental punishment scale developed by Bob Altemeyer, a researcher on right-wing authoritarianism. This scale asked such questions as, "If you ruined a nice or expensive toy (e.g., your major Christmas present) by too rough play or abuse, would your parents have spanked you, taken away privileges, scolded you, expressed disappointment, or not punished you?" Since we asked about a range of different situations (e.g., stealing money from mother's purse; hitting a younger brother or sister; using "dirty" or sexual words; talking back to an adult or showing disrespect), we obtained a fairly complete picture of the prevalence of different types of punishment for different offenses.

We expected that denial would play an important role in whether negative emotions from childhood would influence a person's political attitudes. Individuals try to confront emotional issues from their childhood in several ways: through psychotherapy and in community support groups like Alcoholics Anonymous or other twelve-step groups. We hypothesized, therefore, that individuals who had been in therapy or had been involved with such support groups would be more likely to have broken through their denial about childhood and, therefore, less likely to displace anger originating in childhood punishment onto punitive political attitudes.

The initial results were puzzling, in light of earlier research suggesting a relationship between harsh child rearing and punitive political attitudes. We found no relationship between being physically punished as a child and either conservatism or scores on a measure of authoritarianism. There was a moderate relationship between physical punishment and

Tomkins's Polarity Scale, but it was the opposite of what we had expected: people who reported higher punishment scores were more humanistic in their orientation. Some of the correlations were as predicted; for example, conservative political attitudes were highly correlated with scores on authoritarianism, normative scores on the Polarity Scale, and high scores on our measure of denial; and conservative political views were highest among individuals with little or no experience with therapy.

Our results seemed to indicate that childhood punishment was not related to political conservatism, although both gender and therapy were. Like earlier research, our study found that women were significantly more liberal in their political attitudes than men. This led us to wonder whether the effect of physical punishment, and the anger it produces, might be different for women than for men. An examination of the research literature on this issue confirmed that men and women learn different ways to experience and express emotion.

Gender and Emotion

Evidence suggests that males and females are socialized differently with respect to anger. For example, in a study of children aged thirty to thirty-five months, Fivush (1989) monitored conversations between mothers and their children at home and found that, while girls used the words "angry" or "mad" twice as often as boys did in describing their past experiences, mothers of girls never used these words, though mothers of boys frequently did. Fivush concluded that as girls do not hear feelings of anger mirrored or reflected for them, they may come to believe that anger is not an appropriate emotion for them. In effect, then, a young girl who is angry, and says so, never hears her mother say, "Oh, you're angry because Timmy hit you." Instead she may be ignored (and so come to believe that the emotion she has expressed is socially unacceptable) or hear her feelings mislabeled: "You're afraid because Timmy hit you," or "You're sad because Timmy hit you."

There are also gender differences in the socialization of other emotions. Girls, for example, are more empathic than boys. Two literature reviews of gender differences in aggression found evidence that women are less aggressive than men in some situations, apparently because they are more apt to empathize with the victim and experience guilt and anxiety about any harm their aggression inflicts. Both reviews attribute the differences in empathy to gender-role socialization—the way we teach children what girls and boys are supposed to be.[9]

As a result of this differential socialization, women react differently to the internal cues of anger than men do. Hokanson and Edelman (1966) gave electric shocks to both men and women, and both showed increased heart rate and blood pressure, presumably a sign that they were angered by the treatment. Such internal physiological cues may alert us to the fact that we are experiencing emotion. In men, the opportunity to express their anger by retaliating against the attacker produced a drop in heart rate and blood pressure. Women, however, instead of retaliating, tended to be particularly friendly and generous to the attacker, and this placating response produced a drop in their physiological arousal. The implications of this study are that women and men will both attempt to decrease the uncomfortable internal feelings associated with anger, men by directing their anger toward another person and women by being helpful.

In light of these findings on the different ways men and women are socialized, we did further analyses to test the hypothesis that physical punishment in childhood would have different effects on political attitudes for men and women. Men with a background of severe punishment, we expected, would displace their anger outward onto political issues, while women with a background of punishment would be more likely to adopt a generous, empathic attitude toward others and, therefore, might support traditional liberal policies like social welfare programs.

Childhood Punishment and Punitive Attitudes: The Role of Gender

The results we obtained in our new analysis of the data strongly supported our predictions, but the relationship was not a simple one. The effect of having been severely punished in childhood was different for males and females: males who reported high levels of punishment were slightly more conservative than low-punishment males; and females who reported high levels of childhood punishment were more liberal than low-punishment females. These results make sense in the context of the research on differential socialization. Boys are encouraged more to feel angry and in adulthood are more likely to take their anger out on others, while girls' angry feelings are discouraged as they are socialized toward empathy.

Whether individuals had ever been in therapy also interacted with their level of punishment: the effect of punishment differed according to whether people had or had not been in therapy. People who reported high levels of punishment and had never been in therapy held significantly more punitive attitudes than did high-punishment individuals who had some therapy. Therapy made little difference in the political attitudes of individuals reporting low levels of childhood punishment.

Our predictions about the effects of childhood punishment, therapy, and gender were confirmed. Respondents who had not had some sort of therapy to deal with their negative childhood emotions appeared to be displacing them onto their political attitudes. However, the results also raised a number of questions.

Because our sample in this first study was limited to undergraduates, we wondered whether their responses might differ from those of the general population. It is also possible that their responses simply reflected their educational level, or of the education of their parents, as the type of discipline used in child rearing varies by social class (which is related to educational level). We could not test this possibility on a college sample because all the respondents had essentially the same level of education. Finally, we had inferred the effect of negative emotions resulting from parental punishment rather than testing it directly. Although we thought it likely that the reason for the link between childhood punishment and punitive political attitudes was the anger generated by harsh punishment, we could not be sure. Nor could we be sure that harsh childhood punishment *causes* people to adopt punitive political attitudes. Given the way the study was designed, we could conclude only that higher levels of punishment and punitive political attitudes go together.[10]

We therefore designed a second study to test whether we could repeat our earlier findings and resolve some lingering questions: Would a sample of the general adult population respond in the same way that students had? Were the results we obtained simply the effect of education? Does childhood experience actually cause differences in adult political attitudes? Does residual childhood anger mediate or explain why those with a background of high punishment are more likely to espouse punitive political attitudes? We made the same predictions about the effects of gender, therapy, and punishment on political attitudes. In addition, we predicted that if respondents were given an opportunity to vent the anger associated with childhood punishment, their displacement of anger onto their political attitudes would temporarily decrease and their responses would be less punitive.

For this second study we interviewed a probability sample of fifty-three adults living in eastern Massachusetts. We asked the same questions about childhood punishment, therapy, and their attitudes toward the death penalty, abortion, and the use of military force. We also added an experiment embedded within the survey by varying the order of the questions.[11] Half the sample (the control group) answered the political-attitude questions first, while the other half (the experimental or recall/catharsis group) answered the childhood-punishment questions first. Answering questions about their experiences of punishment in childhood, we thought, would remind people of their parents' treatment and arouse any residual anger they still harbored about it. We then asked individuals in this group to respond to a "projective" sentence-completion test, with questions such as "Overseas, they ____"; "My mother ____"; and "My greatest fear ____."

Research suggests that such projective tests can provide an opportunity for emotional catharsis and temporarily reduce a person's level of anger. We expected that arousing childhood anger and then offering a way of releasing it would reduce the amount of anger available for displacement onto a person's political attitudes. If we were right, the political attitudes expressed by individuals in the recall/catharsis group would be less conservative than those of people in the control group, who answered the political attitude questions before having an opportunity to release childhood anger. We could then consider members of the control group as representative of voters who carry around childhood anger and readily displace it onto political issues.

We did not, of course, predict that individuals' political attitudes would be completely transformed by a transient situational manipulation; but even a modest decrease in conservatism would provide evidence that the displacement of emotion from childhood does contribute to individuals' political attitudes.

The overall results of our survey replicated our findings from the first study. Childhood punishment again interacted with psychotherapy and gender to influence respondents' political attitudes. Individuals with high-punishment backgrounds who had not had therapy expressed significantly more punitive political attitudes—supporting the death penalty and the use of military force, and opposing abortion—than high-punishment individuals who had been in therapy. In addition, men who had experienced high levels of punishment in childhood were significantly more punitive in their political attitudes than men who had been punished less. In contrast, high-punishment women were slightly more liberal in their attitudes than low-punishment women. Overall, the biggest differences were found between high-punishment men who had not had therapy and all other groups.

The results of the embedded experiment were consistent with the overall results. Individuals in the control group, those who had answered the political-attitude questions first, matched the pattern of emotional displacement found in the first study and in the overall results of the second study. The responses of the recall/catharsis group, however, were dramatically different. The interactions between punishment and therapy and between punishment and gender *disappeared*. It was as if the emotion the individuals were carrying around with them, which had previously influenced their political attitudes, was gone. Support for the death penalty was significantly higher among individuals in the control condition than for those individuals who had recalled their childhood punishment first. The results from these studies have significant implications for public policy.

A third study (Levine 1996), carried out by a student in our lab, provides additional, physiological, support for the hypothesis that individuals displace childhood anger onto political issues. Levine used measures of political attitudes, childhood punishment, and experience with therapy similar to the ones we employed and made use of the same recall/catharsis manipulation. The political-attitudes scale included items assessing subjects' self-described conservatism; their support for the use of military force, capital punishment, and restrictions on abortion; and their personal feelings about use of the death penalty (e.g., "I feel good when I hear that a convicted murderer has been executed").

To obtain measures of emotion, Levine asked subjects questions about their experiences of anger and depression and measured their physiological responses to the different questions by having them wear heart-rate monitors throughout the face-to-face interviews. Research by Sinha and colleagues (1992) established that, compared to the neutral state, the emotional experience of anger is associated with increases in heart rate.[12]

Levine's results were consistent with our earlier findings. They suggested that punitive political attitudes are partly based on residual childhood emotion. He found that men were significantly more politically conservative than women and that individuals reporting high levels of childhood punishment were significantly more conservative in their attitudes than those reporting low levels of punishment.[13]

Using items from the anger scale developed by Spielberger and his colleagues (1985), Levine asked questions designed to determine the individuals' characteristic level of anger and the way they reacted to different situations. Subjects high on the anger scale responded positively to such items as, "I am quick tempered," "I am a hotheaded person," "When I get mad, I say nasty things," and "When I get frustrated, I feel like hitting someone." These subjects disagreed with statements such as, "I try to be tolerant and understanding," "I calm down faster than most other people," and "I control my angry feelings."

Levine's results clearly revealed the importance of subjects' anger. Subjects who reported receiving higher levels of childhood punishment were significantly more angry than low-punishment subjects. Their anger also predicted the punitiveness of their political attitudes, with subjects expressing higher levels of anger holding more conservative political opinions. Levine's subjects who first recalled their childhood punishment and then expressed their political attitudes had significantly lower heart rates than subjects who answered the political-attitude items first. This indicates that subjects who had not had the opportunity to recall and release their childhood anger were more emotionally aroused by answering political questions—as predicted by our earlier studies.[14]

Public Policy and Childhood Emotions

Several studies indicate that anger resulting from childhood punishment is associated with holding more punitive political attitudes. As we have argued, unresolved anger from childhood provides a poor basis for formulating public policy because it lets citizens disregard evidence of the failure and costs of different policies. "It's beginning to seem," wrote Barbara Ehrenreich in 1992, "as if anger is our national emotion. You can feel it crackling along our highways. . . . It smolders in our cities, where rich and poor, often meaning white and black, face off across a gulf. . . . It shines, all too often, from the faces of our politicians and their handlers. . . . The [Gulf] war was . . . the perfect outlet for a diffuse sense of grievance" (p. 62).

Many of our political attitudes, particularly those we feel strongly about, have their source in childhood. What's wrong with that? Well, the primary problem with acting out or expressing childhood anger, pain, and fear in a contemporary political context is that it frequently results in very bad public policy. The costs of the death penalty are tremendous, and the death and destruction caused by taking military action—instead of making honest attempts to negotiate political solutions—create massive human suffering and the conditions for continuing conflict. Census Bureau demographer Beth Osborne Daponte, calculates that 158,001 Iraqis, including 71,807 women and children, were killed by the U.S. war effort in the Gulf.[15] At home, displaced anger is a divisive force, polarizing public opinion on issues such as abortion and contributing to the murder of doctors and clinic workers.

Yet many Americans continue to advocate the physical punishment of children, sometimes as an article of religious doctrine. In the next chapter, we examine a group of such Americans, Protestant fundamentalists whose child-rearing practices have sometimes included brutal physical discipline. There it is possible to trace some of the political consequences of childhood pain and suffering.

4

Honor Thy Father and Mother

Since the 1970s, one of the most politically conservative segments of American society, a loosely allied coalition of fundamentalist Christians known as the New Religious Right, has gained political sophistication as well as political strength. In this chapter, we investigate the political and social beliefs of religious fundamentalists and the origin of their beliefs in childhood punishment. We also discuss the export of their belief system into the political arena and look at the possible negative consequences of their influence on American politics.

The Christian Coalition

The most influential conservative religious group in America today is the Christian Coalition, which was formed in the wake of Pat Robertson's failure to win the presidency in 1988. The membership of the coalition, a more politically savvy successor to the Moral Majority of the 1970s, was culled largely from the mailing list of his campaign organization. As Robert Sullivan (1993) notes, the Christian Coalition is similar to a political party in that it organizes training seminars, engages in fund-raising, and promotes its views on a range of political issues. The Christian Coalition opposes legislation to protect the civil rights of gays and lesbians, legal abortions, condom distribution in the schools, and inclusion of such New Age "abominations" as the teaching of tolerance in schools.

Sullivan quotes from a 1991 fund-raising letter by Coalition founder Robertson outlining the goals and ambitions of the organization: "We are training people to be effective—to be elected to school boards, to city councils, to state legislatures and to key positions in political parties. . . .

By the end of this decade, if we work and give and organize and train, THE CHRISTIAN COALITION WILL BE THE MOST POWERFUL POLITICAL ORGANIZATION IN AMERICA" (p. 34).

By the fall of 1994 the organization had reportedly grown to include 1.4 million supporters and 1,100 chapters in 50 states, with a mailing list of 30 million. Its tactics are considerably different from those of the Moral Majority; it is much more circumspect about its religious views, choosing to emphasize secular conservative issues such as the fight against crime (Kaufman 1994). In fact, one of its tactics is to run "stealth candidates"—individuals who avoid mentioning their association with the Christian Coalition—in local elections. For example, the Pennsylvania Christian Coalition organizational manual quoted by Sullivan instructs political workers: "You should never mention the name Christian Coalition in Republican circles" (p. 34). According to Kaufman, its members and other conservative Christians now dominate the Republican party in over a dozen states, including Texas, Florida, Minnesota, and South Carolina. It is unlikely that any Republican candidate for president in 1996 will be able to win without the support of conservative Christians, a point that has been made clear by Senator Bob Dole's recent move toward the right on social issues.

The Adkissons, a Christian Coalition family in Oregon profiled by Sullivan, became politically active in the late 1980s because of their opposition to a state executive order protecting gays from discrimination. Sullivan notes the fear of the Adkissons and others in the New Religious Right that their way of life—and they themselves—are being threatened: " 'I finally understood that I was in someone's crosshairs,' Jim says, sitting in his big-backed comfortable chair. 'The things that I believe in and that are important to me, I felt were being targeted. It's like when I was in Vietnam. When someone was targeting you, you knew.' " Jim's wife has similar fears: " 'Obviously,' says Christie, speaking of homosexuals, 'in the last twenty years since they wrote their homosexual agenda, they have had a methodical plan. That's why we've had to wake up' " (Sullivan 1993, p. 42).

What methodical plan, one wonders? To do what? The Adkissons seem genuinely fearful that they are under attack—Christie gives talks on "the infiltration of the gay agenda in the schools"—by a monolithic group of homosexuals who, in all likelihood, have no knowledge of or interest in the Adkissons' existence. The latter's political activity, however, is not merely defensive; it is offensive, and aimed at limiting the civil rights of others. Nor are Jim and Christie Adkisson alone in their view that fundamental institutions and values within American society are in danger.

Fundamentalism in America

Since the 1970s, there has been a resurgence of religious fundamentalism in America. According to Christopher Ellison and Marc Musick (1993), sociologists at the University of Texas, Protestant fundamentalism embraces four central assumptions: (1) "The Bible is inerrant and a sufficient guide for all of life's problems"; (2) "an anthropomorphic, hierarchical, judgmental God . . . participates actively in the lives of individuals"; (3) human sinfulness is ubiquitous; and (4) personal salvation is "the only escape from eternal damnation at the hands of a righteous, punitive God" (p. 381).

While certain religious denominations, such as Southern Baptists, are heavily fundamentalist, fundamentalism is not a religious denomination per se—nor are all Southern Baptists fundamentalists, nor are evangelicals necessarily fundamentalists. Evangelicals share with fundamentalists a belief in the necessity of salvation through faith in Christ and devotion to the Scriptures. Fundamentalists go beyond evangelism in two respects: they are more likely to stress the literal truth of the Bible; and they are committed to a dispensational, premillennialist eschatology—a belief that human history will come to an end in the near future and that the end will be preceded by the Apocalypse, a terrible battle on earth between the forces of good and evil, which only the righteous will survive.

Fundamentalists do not, by and large, fit the stereotype of uneducated, lower-class southerners. As a group, they are quite well educated, tend to be middle-aged, and are similar in social-class profile to the population as a whole. More than half of them are nonsouthern and a significant number belong to churches outside the Southern Baptist convention (Miller and Wattenberg 1984).

It is estimated that 9 percent of Americans consider themselves fundamentalists, while a considerably higher number share the central beliefs of fundamentalism: 44 percent of Americans maintain that salvation through Jesus Christ is the only source of eternal life; 30 percent claim to be "born again"; and 54 percent insist that "the Bible is the actual word of God and is to be taken literally, word for word." In a national survey of 1,000 American adults, *U.S. News and World Report* found that 60 percent of Americans believed literally in the biblical account of the final judgement; 49 percent believed in the biblical account of an antichrist; 44 percent believed in the final battle of Armageddon, and 44 percent in the rapture of the church described in Revelations.[1]

The Roots of Fundamentalism in Childhood Punishment

Rutgers historian Philip Greven (1991) describes the appeal of the warning that to spare the rod is to spoil the child, for centuries the rationale for physical punishment of children among American Protestants, particularly fundamentalists. As Greven points out, the physical punishment of children is, if anything, distinctly un-Christian: neither Jesus, nor even Saint Paul, ever advocated hitting children. When the disciples asked Jesus, "Who is the greatest in the kingdom of Heaven?" Jesus set a child in front of them and told them, "Except ye be converted, and become as little children, ye shall not enter into the kingdom of heaven." He continued, "whoso shall receive one such little child in my name receiveth me. But whoso shall offend one of these little ones . . . it were better for him that a millstone were hanged about his neck, and that he were drowned in the depth of the sea." Jesus also told his disciples, "take heed that ye despise not one of these little ones. . . . It is not the will of your Father which is in heaven, that one of these little ones should perish." Ironically, even the adage "Spare the rod and spoil the child" does not come from the Bible, but from a poem by satirist Samuel Butler written in 1664. The biblical texts that fundamentalists and other Protestants appeal to are, in fact, Old Testament sayings attributed to King Solomon, such as "He that spareth his rod hateth his son: but he that loveth him chasteneth him betimes."[2]

There is thus an enormous contradiction in the attitudes of fundamentalists toward child rearing. Although they insist on following the message of the New Testament as it relates to salvation through Christ, they are fanatical proponents of the Old Testament injunction to use the rod on children. Greven traces the Protestant fundamentalist obsession with the rod through two centuries of influential Protestant leaders who were physically punished as children and, as adults, both practiced and advocated this form of child rearing.

Greven cites several examples of present-day fundamentalists who fit this pattern. "Tammy Bakker remembers seeing her stepfather 'beat' her brother and stepbrother 'with a belt until he drew blood on their backs. . . .' 'To this day,' she noted in her autobiography, 'I can see my mother, tears streaming down her face, wiping the blood off my brothers' backs, and my father hating himself for beating them like he did'" (p. 30). Oral Roberts too was beaten severely: "Papa believed in the stars and stripes. He put on the stripes and Vaden [Oral's brother] and I saw the stars. When he got us home he took down his big razor strap. It was made in two pieces. When he got through with us, we believed it had a thousand pieces" (p. 26). Billy Graham's father "would sometimes withdraw a wide leather belt to apply to him, once when he was discovered with a plug of chewing tobacco bulging in his cheek, another time snatching him up from a church pew where Billy had been fretfully squirming, shoving him on out into the vestibule and there strapping him thoroughly" (p. 25). Oral Roberts, like many other parents, handed the physical punishment on to his own children, whom he and his wife whipped (p. 26).

Physical violence against children is by no means a relic of the fundamentalist past; it continues to be sanctioned today, as Greven makes clear in numerous citations from child-rearing books written by fundamentalist Protestants, including some who are psychologists and psychiatrists. He also describes fundamentalist Christian communities where severe physical punishment, including whippings and beatings, have been administered to children as young as six months in order to break their will and notes that children in these communities have been beaten to death.

Greven cites a fundamentalist endorsement of physical punishment by Beverly La Haye, wife of the Reverend Timothy La Haye, a former leader of the Moral Majority. In her *How to Develop Your Child's Temperament* (1977), "she urges parents who have spanked their child once to repeat their spankings as often as necessary to teach the child who continues to cry after the initial punishment not to voice feelings of 'anger' and 'rage.'

Her advice seems to be designed to train children to suppress their feelings of resentment and resistance, an emotional control brought about by parental blows, violence, coercion, and the purposeful hurting of the child" (p. 79). La Haye's advocacy of physical punishment seems intended not only to command obedience but also to force children to deny their reactions to such abuse. As we saw in chapter 2, abuse plus denial of the resulting emotions is particularly damaging to children.

The Reverend Jack Hyles (1972) is explicit about the necessity for breaking the child's will: "*The spanking should be administered firmly* (his italics). It should be painful and it should last until the child's will is broken. It should last until the child is crying, not tears of anger but tears of a broken will. As long as he is stiff, grits his teeth, holds on to his own will, the spanking should continue" (quoted in Greven, p. 68).

James Dobson, a fundamentalist psychologist whose book *Dare to Discipline* has sold over a million copies, is equally explicit: "The child may be more strong-willed than the parent, and they both know it. If he can outlast a temporary onslaught, he has won a major battle, eliminating punishment as a tool in the parent['s] repertoire. Even though Mom spanks him, he wins the battle by defying her again. The solution to this situation is obvious: outlast him; win, even if it takes a repeated measure" (in Greven, p. 67).

It is important to note, however, that fundamentalists are not alone in their emphasis on teaching the child total obedience. D. Ross Campbell, a nonfundamentalist psychiatrist, for example, writes that "Defiance is one of the few indications for punishment. Defiance is openly resisting and challenging authority—parental authority. It is stubbornly refusing to obey. Of course defiance, as well as any misbehavior, cannot be permitted. At these times, punishment is often indicated, and such times occasionally occur no matter what we do" (in Greven, p. 93).

Advice similar to Campbell's abounds in current child-rearing manuals. Clearly many people still unreflectively assume that obedience to parents and other authorities is the chief virtue to be instilled in children and that any signs of an independent will must be stamped out. The way Campbell uses language to distance himself and the reader from the true import of his advice is very interesting. Throughout the passage quoted, Campbell uses the term *punishment,* which could suggest a range of alternatives, including taking away privileges, being required to perform some exculpatory task, scolding, and so on; even so, it is clear from the context that he is specifically talking about physical punishment. This obfuscation contributes to denial. When he states that "at these times, punishment is often indicated," the very language suggests that the choice is both outside the control of parents and supported by some external authority. In speaking of an illness, we say that a certain type of medication or treatment "is indicated," meaning it is prescribed by medical experts on the basis of scientific evidence of its efficacy. Campbell's language suggests that physical punishment is a "treatment" for misbehavior that has equal status with, for example, antibiotics for the treatment of infection. His assertion that "such times occasionally occur no matter what we do" has the additional effect of suggesting to parents that, as defiance simply happens, it is not the parent's fault or responsibility that "physical punishment is indicated."

While fundamentalists are not alone in their need to force complete obedience, their religious rationale for inflicting physical punishment may reveal something about the true motive for such control. They insist that only total obedience toward God can save the children from eternal hellfire. Their vision of the hell they seek to protect their children from, however, may be a product of their own earthly experience. Greven quotes the Calvinist minister Jonathan Edwards, who describes hell in a way that sounds like nothing so much as a child's memories of being beaten: "Do but consider what it is to suffer . . . in pain, in wailing and lamenting, groaning and shrieking, and gnashing your teeth, with your souls full of dreadful grief and amazement, with your bodies and every member full of racking torture, without any possibility of getting ease; without any possibility of moving God to pity by your cries; without any possibility of hiding yourselves from him; without any possibility of diverting your thoughts from your pain; without any possibility of obtaining any manner of mitigation, or help, or change for the better" (p. 58).

If our interpretation seems exaggerated, consider the experience from the point of view of a child. The emotional response of a child to beatings is hard for us to imagine as adults, both because our emotions are more contained and less extreme and because we have virtually no experience in adulthood of a physical contest this one-sided. A small child weighing

50 or 60 pounds being beaten by a six-foot, two-hundred-pound adult male would be equivalent to that male being assaulted by a creature looming eighteen feet and weighing 800 pounds. Moreover, the child, unlike the adult, has nowhere to turn, no possible help or respite from the attack of an adult upon whom he or she is completely dependent.

Small wonder, then, that adults physically punished in childhood by fundamentalist parents claiming to act as the agents of God learn to see their heavenly father as a wrathful God capable of sentencing them to torture for all eternity; and that they come to believe they must beat their own children mercilessly to protect them from such a fate. Of course, in doing so, they tragically expose their children to the same terrible vision of destructive authority.

Yet, even if fundamentalist Protestants believe that beating children is necessary to save their souls from hell, there seems to be more involved. We can glean from the advice of Jack Hyles and James Dobson that punishing children is part of a battle to subjugate the child's will, to gain total control over another human being. Several of the punishment experiences of Protestant fundamentalists Greven describes also contain elements of humiliation. Ruth Wilkerson Harris, sister of the Reverend David Wilkerson, recalls that their "Dad used prayer both as a soothing balm and to make sure the whipping took. We just weren't allowed to cry and go off then, and pout. No! Our rebellious spirits were humbled even more when we were told to put our arms around Dad's neck and say, if we could in our grief, 'I love you, Daddy. Forgive me for disobeying.' Then Dad would tell us, 'I love you too, but now we must ask God to help you overcome your stubbornness'" (p. 29).

This father's smug self-righteousness is hard to believe, but Greven convinces us with many such examples. It's bad enough that children are physically attacked by an adult; worse, they are humiliated, their self destroyed in the breaking of their wills, and their sense of reality undermined by adults who self-righteously set themselves up as loving and benevolent. The child, held hostage by the threat of more beatings, has no option but to deny what is happening and accept the parent's version of reality—that the parent is loving and benign but the child is so bad that the parent has to protect him from the wrath of his *heavenly* father.

We have seen that nonfundamentalists, too, react with vehemence to any sign of willfulness on the part of the child. In fact, children's natural narcissism—their sense that they are not only right but also the center of the universe—is offensive, even a source of outrage to parents whose own narcissism was thwarted by humiliation and control.

Among fundamentalists the application of the rod seems to serve several purposes: the conscious need to save their children's souls from a terrible fate, as well as unconscious needs to assert themselves, establish their unquestioned authority, and assuage the narcissistic injury they themselves suffered as children subjugated to brutal authority. Fundamentalists differ from nonfundamentalists in rationalizing the use of physical punishment in the name of God, thus ensuring that their children will experience terror—for themselves and others—at the prospect of defying their religious community's particular understanding of God's plan.

Visions of the Apocalypse: St. John the Divine and *Radio Flyer*

The 1992 Tom Hanks film *Radio Flyer* dramatizes the relationship between childhood physical abuse and denial. Hanks plays a father recounting for his two young sons the story of his own childhood and that of his younger brother, the uncle they have never met. In an extended flashback, the movie shows us their brutal upbringing in which their stepfather, a violent alcoholic, targeted the younger brother. The little boy sustains terrible beatings while his older brother attempts to protect him and, failing that, to comfort him when the beatings are over. We witness firsthand the dread with which the boys watch and listen for signs of yet another fit of violence—the sound of a beer can opening, the heavy tread of the stepfather's footsteps, his mounting rage. The one source of joy and consolation in the younger brother's life is his wagon, a Radio Flyer that he is convinced he can convert into a flying machine.

As his stepfather's violence and scapegoating escalates, the little boy conceives a plan to test his flying machine by sailing it off the top of a hill above the neighborhood. At the end of the film, we watch, prepared for the terrible outcome, as he launches his Radio Flyer. He must be killed or severely injured when the wagon plummets off the edge of the hill toward the rooftops below. But that doesn't happen. The older brother, now grown, tells his sons that, while the family never saw the younger brother again, from time to time they received postcards from various exotic places the younger brother visited on his tour of the world.

The most horrifying moment in the film comes not during one of the brutal beatings, nor even during the awful suspense of watching the little boy go sailing toward the edge of a cliff in his wagon, but when we come to the sickening realization that the older boy has denied his brother's death. To replace the probable outcome of the story—that his brother died at the hands of his stepfather or in his attempt to escape by flying away on his wagon—Hanks's character concocted a fantasy. What's worse, Hanks hands on this myth to his own small sons.

At this moment in America, the most common cause of death in children under the age of four is abuse at the hands of parents or other caretakers (*Boston Globe,* December 4, 1995). Abused children might well ask themselves: When will the beatings end? Will there be an end? Will my life be ended?

Denial of childhood abuse leaves grown children with feelings that are mysterious in the context of seemingly benign everyday life: terror, hypervigilance, a feeling of impending doom. Even when they deny what they have suffered in childhood—thus disconnecting these feelings from the events of the past—they must try to make sense of their experience. So they project their feelings into the future and come to believe that they will suffer some terrible fate.[3] For many people, the imagined outcome centers around personal failure, sickness, or loneliness. For many fundamentalists, the catastrophe they dread is nothing less than the end of human history.

Some ten to fifteen million American premillennialist fundamentalists believe we are now living in the "end times," the last days of human history preceding the "great tribulation," when famine, pestilence, and war will be unleashed on the earth and culminate in Armageddon, the final decisive struggle between good and evil. After the battle, according to the biblical prophecy, the triumphant Christ will come down to rule for a thousand years on a peaceful and beautiful earth peopled only by the faithful—the rest of humanity having perished miserably. The faithful will survive because, in the rapture that signals the end of human history and immediately precedes the great tribulation, they will be lifted up out of harm's way.[4]

St. John's visions in the Book of Revelations may well be what humanity has to look forward to, but we would not presume to say whether what Harding (1994) calls the premillennialists' "willfully mad rhetoric" is an accurate forecast of the future (p. 63). What is interesting to us is the way fundamentalists choose to act in the present based on this apocalyptic future, as well as the uncanny parallels between St. John's vision of the suffering of the damned and the way abused children experience their torment.

Greven argues that "the sense of expectation and the urgent wish to see human history end in the immediate future often emerges from the intense suffering generated by painful childhood punishments" (p. 8). We would argue that it is not so much a wish as a fear. Moreover, it is worth noting that the idea of the rapture in which good Christians will be lifted off the earth and kept out of harm's way for the duration of the battle is eerily reminiscent of a defense mechanism abused children often employ. During painful beatings some children dissociate; they mentally remove themselves from their bodies. Although the mechanism involved is still not well understood, it may be similar to self-hypnosis. Adults abused as children sometimes report that they learned to mentally "leave their bodies" during episodes of abuse.[5]

Fundamentalist visions of the future are not entirely a matter of literal interpretation of the Bible. The text of Revelations is ambiguous; postmillennialists, for example, believe that Christ will come again at the end of a thousand years of peaceful human existence that may be brought about by humans with God's help (Kierulff 1992). Moreover, premillennialists themselves engage in a nonliteral reading of the Bible, or at least a selectively literal reading, in that they choose, in the face of the Apocalypse, to try to secure their place among Christ's faithful by obsessively following Old Testament admonitions not to spare the rod while, by and large, ignoring Christ's specific injunction to "love one another, as I have loved you"—a love that made him foreswear condemning an adulteress or tolerate an injury to one of those who came to take him to Pilate.

Such modern-day premillennialists as Hal Lindsey, Tim La Haye, Billy Graham, and Jerry Falwell have added a contemporary twist to the apocalyptic story that is not based on biblical scripture. Hal Lindsey, in his *The Late Great Planet Earth,* which sold eighteen million copies, and Tim La Haye, in *The Battle for the Mind,* moved the battle between good and evil forward into the End Times and politicized it. La Haye interpreted the biblical " 'signs of the times' as the effects of the 'liberal humanist' effort to take over the country, an effort that amounted to a 'pre-Tribulation tribulation' which could 'destroy America' " (Harding 1994, p. 69). Lindsey and La Haye both advised readers that political action was necessary to save the soul of America in the End Times. The political program they have in mind is the imposition of conservative moral and social values on the rest of society.

The Legacy of Rigid, Punitive Child Rearing

Support for corporal punishment among contemporary fundamentalists is not limited to the preachers and writers Greven quotes. In fact, a number of studies have demonstrated that fundamentalists as a group strongly support the physical punishment of children. The original discovery of a link between religious attitudes and attitudes toward corporal punishment came from a little-noted finding reported by Erlanger in 1974. Early analyses of data from the National Commission on the Causes and Prevention of Violence study of the early 1970s failed to find the expected link between childhood physical punishment and social class. (It had long been believed that lower-class parents were more likely to use physical punishment.) Erlanger's analysis found instead that the best predictor of having been spanked as a child was religious affiliation, specifically being raised Baptist.

More recently, other researchers have found that willingness to use physical punishment with one's own children is related to religious affiliation. For example, Harold Grasmick, Robert Bursik, Jr., and M'lou Kimpel (1991), sociologists at the University of Oklahoma, reported a study of a random sample of 394 individuals 18 or older in Oklahoma City. They asked subjects their opinion of corporal punishment in the schools ("Teachers and school administrators should be allowed to spank school children when they are very disobedient") as well as at home ("Parents ought to spank their children when their children are very disobedient"). They also asked about the respondents' religious affiliation and beliefs, including their belief in a literal interpretation of the Bible. They found that, even when they controlled for the effects of gender, race, age, and educational level, fundamentalist Protestants were significantly more likely to support corporal punishment than were liberal Protestants, Catholics, and people with no religious affiliation. Furthermore, this effect was not due only to intensity of personal religiosity (which might be expected to be higher among fundamentalists than among, for example, liberal Protestants). Literalness of biblical interpretation accounted for some, but not all, of the difference between fundamentalists' and liberal Protestants' attitudes toward corporal punishment.

Vernon Wiehe (1990) of the University of Kentucky sampled churchgoers in Ohio, Kentucky, North Carolina, Tennessee, and West Virginia. He divided the subjects into two groups, literalists (Baptist, Church of God, Holiness, Church of the Nazarene, and Pentecostal) and nonliteralists (Roman Catholic, Christian/Disciples of Christ, Presbyterian, Episcopal, Methodist), depending on whether their religious denomination upheld a literal interpretation of the Bible. The two groups of churches were compared on their scores on the Bavolek Parenting Inventory, the measure of child-rearing attitudes we used in the research reported in chapter 3. We found punitive parenting attitudes to be highly correlated with our measure of denial, negatively correlated with therapy, and positively correlated with conservative political views.

The Bavolek Inventory is composed of items that measure four aspects of child-rearing attitudes: 1) developmental expectations (for example, "Children five months of age are seldom capable of sensing what their parents expect"); 2) empathy toward the child's needs ("Parents spoil their children by picking them up and comforting them when they cry"); 3) support for physical punishment ("Children should always be spanked when they misbehave"); and 4) role-reversal between parent and child ("Young children should be expected to comfort their mother when she is feeling blue").

Wiehe found that members of literalist denominations were more likely than members of nonliteralist denominations to support physical punishment of children, to have unrealistic expectations of young children, to show less empathy for the child's needs, and to see reversal of parent-child roles as appropriate (that is, they believed that children should care for and be considerate of their parents rather than the other way around). The findings held even when the effects of gender and education were taken into account.

Wiehe also compared the scores of literalists to scores on the Bavolek scales among a group of abusive parents. Both men and women in the literalist denominations scored as high, or in many cases higher, than abusive parents on support for physical punishment, inappropriate expectations of children, and parent-child role reversal. The one difference between literalists and documented abusers was that literalists showed more empathy for children.

This set of findings raises a crucial question Wiehe does not discuss. Those who would argue for the physical punishment of children are apt to claim that such punishment does no harm, that is, that it produces no long-standing emotional problems with such negative consequences as increased aggression in adulthood. Fundamentalists, they might argue, punish their children physically because the Bible recommends it, not because they harbor anger from being beaten themselves. Nowhere in the Bible, however, does it say that parents and children should reverse roles; the greater role reversal among fundamentalists, therefore, lends support to the notion that they punish their children for powerful nonconscious reasons, not because of the biblical injunction. Having experienced physical punishment and the humiliation and control that often accompany it, fundamentalists are left with rage and with many unmet needs, including those of being cared for, understood, and loved. That they continue to have such needs in adulthood is quite understandable; that they expect their children to meet them is wholly inappropriate.

Fundamentalists' support for physical punishment extends beyond the home and into the schools. Grasmick, Morgan, and Kennedy (1992) point out that corporal punishment in schools is still very much with us, and that it is fundamentalists who most favor its use. In their random survey of citizens in Oklahoma City in 1989, these researchers found that, even after controlling for educational level (which is significantly inversely related to support for corporal punishment), family income, gender, and age, fundamentalists still support corporal punishment to a significantly greater extent than nonfundamentalist Protestants.

In their conclusion, Grasmick and his colleagues relate fundamentalist support for corporal punishment in the schools to other punitive social policies (a matter we take up in the next chapter). "While some voices might be calling for a 'kinder and gentler America,'" they comment, "there also seems to be a growing eagerness to use the death penalty, to prosecute juveniles as adults, to increase the severity of criminal sanctions, and to justify criminal sanctions solely on the grounds of retribution. Our findings raise the possibility that religious beliefs are at the root of a wide range of calls for harshness toward those who would break the rules" (p. 185).

Authoritarianism

In chapter 3 we discussed the theory of Adorno and his colleagues that individuals raised by rigid and punitive parents develop authoritarian personalities. Not surprisingly, several researchers have found a high correlation between authoritarianism and fundamentalism.[6] Adorno and his colleagues theorized that parents' rigid prohibition of the child's natural sexual and aggressive impulses leave him or her with no choice but to repress such impulses—to ban them from consciousness. The repression seldom succeeds, however, in controlling the anxiety the child feels when the repressed impulses threaten to break through into consciousness. As a result, the child projects the unacceptable impulses onto some despised out-group.

We have already seen that authoritarianism is generally associated with conservative political views. In the specific case of fundamentalists, we would predict rigid and punitive child rearing to produce particular consequences: because they believe in adherence to a strict moral code specified by religious doctrine, for example, fundamentalists should advocate the use of the rod in disciplining children; they should idealize fundamentalist preachers, while despising secular authorities and "secular humanism" in general; and they should hold punitive attitudes toward those they see as sinners, particularly when their perceived sins are sexual.

We could also predict that, for fundamentalists, political discourse would always be a moral debate and that action in the public, as well as the private, sphere would often be motivated by anger and discharged only by a projection of one's own sexual, aggressive, rebellious, disrespectful, and subversive impulses onto an out-group. In order to maintain psychological equilibrium, fundamentalist political activists would always need out-groups they can define as distinct from the mainstream. Their opposition to perceived out-groups and the policy issues pursued with respect to them would cluster around the themes of sex, violence, and purity. Abortion, therefore, is a good psychological candidate for fundamentalist activism, although many pro-lifers are logically inconsistent. If they were as committed to the absolute sanctity of human life as they claim, they would also oppose the death penalty. What allows them to pursue their psychological equilibrium within the realm of political discourse—as opposed to violent action—is the compartmentalization of the issues: they can be vociferously antiabortion and pro–death penalty by asserting the innocence of the unborn.

When political activism is thwarted, or political change is slow in coming or despaired of altogether, the depression and grief of childhood may threaten to break through and, for the least-stable activists, the only path left may be to act in anger—bomb clinics, blow up federal buildings, and so on. Douglas H. Spinney (1991), a therapist who has worked with Christian fundamentalists, writes that "depression resulting from the loss of affectional bonds is a dreaded probability that is active in the minds of fundamentalists. Defending against that perceived probability consumes much of their energy" (p. 116). He describes the fundamentalists he has seen as "practic[ing] a narrow piety that is strictly enforced by an intrusive scrutiny and severe discipline" (p. 115) and points out that any deviation from that strict piety carries with it the threat of disapproval—originally, the parents' disapproval—and communal rejection, which they would experience as catastrophic.

Attitudes toward Homosexuals: The Religious Right and Prejudice

One of the earliest and most basic findings of the literature on authoritarianism is that it is likely to lead to prejudice against social out-groups. We might expect, therefore, that fundamentalists would be more prejudiced against such groups and more likely to discriminate against them than nonfundamentalists. In fact, Stephen Maret of Rutgers University found that self-identified fundamentalists were more disapproving of homosexuality than nonfundamentalists (1984). He also documented an interaction between religious affiliation and gender, with female nonfundamentalists having the most tolerant attitudes toward homosexuals and female fundamentalists being the most intolerant toward them.

More recently, McFarland (1989) measured the desire to discriminate against blacks, women, homosexuals, and communists and related it to religious belief. Rather than measuring denomination or the content of religious beliefs, he used a distinction, first proposed by Allport and Ross (1967), between *extrinsic orientation* toward religion—in which religious practice or adherence serves such practical ends as providing security, social status, or comfort—and *intrinsic religious orientation*—in which religion is central to the person's life and motivation. In addition to measuring these attitudes, McFarland added a factor proposed by Batson, *religion as quest* (1971) which captures the extent to which individuals seek religious understanding as part of an open-minded quest for truth.

Previous studies had shown that individuals with an extrinsic orientation toward religion are more likely to be prejudiced against blacks, while a quest orientation predicts a lack of such prejudice. Intrinsic orientation is not related to racial prejudice one way or the other.

McFarland added yet another dimension of religious orientation, fundamentalism, which he assessed with six questions about the inerrancy of the Bible, the importance of adhering to the "true teachings of God's word," and of preparing for heaven and eschewing worldliness. He found a highly significant negative correlation between fundamentalism and quest, meaning that individuals who agreed with the fundamentalism items were less likely to be open-mindedly searching for truth. The quest orientation, on the other hand, predicted a general unwillingness to discriminate against any target. McFarland points out that earlier studies had shown the quest orientation to be positively correlated with both cognitive complexity (Batson and Raynor-Prince 1983) and principled moral reasoning (Sapp and Jones 1986).

On the other hand, fundamentalism, unlike other religious orientations, predicted not simply prejudice, but the active desire to discriminate against people in general, and against each of the specific named groups—women, homosexuals, blacks, and communists. In summing up the results, McFarland commented, "perhaps, as Glock and Stark (1966) and many others have argued, fundamentalism cloaks a general closed-minded, ethnocentric mindset, which is shown here as a general tendency to discriminate" (p. 333).

More recently, Lee Kirkpatrick (1993) attempted to replicate McFarland's study and to distinguish between fundamentalism and Christian orthodoxy—that is, the general acceptance of a set of tenets such as the Virgin birth, central to all Christian denominations. He sampled college students at a state university in the southwest, a small northwest liberal arts college, and a private university in Ontario, Canada. Kirkpatrick assessed respondents' fundamentalism, the orthodoxy of their beliefs, and their discriminatory attitudes toward women, homosexuals, communists, and blacks. The results supported a distinction between orthodox Christian views and fundamentalism: fundamentalism significantly correlated with discrimination against all four groups, while Christian orthodoxy predicted less-discriminatory attitudes or was unrelated to discrimination.

Bob Altemeyer and Bruce Hunsberger (1992) sampled parents of a group of university students by asking them to complete four self-descriptive measures: a prejudice scale; a measure of punitive attitudes toward homosexuals (including the item, "In many ways, the AIDS disease currently killing homosexuals is just what they deserve"); a measure of sentencing attitudes in cases involving a drug pusher, a pornographer, and a person who spat on a government official; and questions asking them "how they would react if the government someday outlawed 'radical' and 'extremist' political movements. Would they publicly endorse such a law, tell police about any radicals they knew, help hunt down and attack members of the outlawed organizations, and support torturing and executing them" (p. 121). Altemeyer and Hunsberger found that both authoritarianism, as measured by Altemeyer's right-wing authoritarianism (RWA) scale, and fundamentalism, as measured by Altemeyer's religious fundamentalism (RF) scale, correlated significantly with prejudice; punitive attitudes toward homosexuals; willingness to track down, torture, and execute "radicals"; and support for severe sentencing of criminals. These findings held even when researchers controlled for subjects' educational level.

Altemeyer and Hunsberger's findings are chilling in the light of a recent string of gay murders in Texas—brutal killings of men whose only apparent distinguishing characteristic was that they were homosexual (Bissinger 1995). What is even more disturbing, if possible, is that these murders have without exception been carried out by teenage boys—not gang members or juvenile delinquents, but teenage boys from "good families"—ordinary kids who, when they weren't "fag-bashing," were going to high school, playing football, applying to college, sitting in church, or writing articles for their high school newspaper. One such article published in a San Angelo, Texas, school newspaper was entitled "Students Declare War on Homosexuality." H. G. Bissinger quotes from the piece at some length in his *Vanity Fair* article.

In the dark of the night after homework is complete, teen-age students scurry to their vehicles to stalk male homosexuals in San Angelo. "I want them to die when we do it," Bob, a student, said. Bashers claim part of the fun is from the adrenaline rush they receive. "A couple of friends and I were driving down the fag drag, when we noticed there was a whole car load of them sitting in the car just kissing, so we got out our baseball bats—most of us carry baseball bats anyway—shattered their windows and dragged them out of the window and just literally beat them," Ray said, a member of the bashing group.
"After we are done, they are on the ground in a bloody heap" (p. 145).

Bissinger makes it clear he believes there is a link between "fag-bashing" and the ascendancy in Texas of an increasingly conservative political and religious agenda that disenfranchises gays and invokes scriptural warrant to do so. At least one Texas politician, a Republican whose campaign was supported by the Christian Coalition, has publicly stated that homosexuals should be executed.[7]

But there seems to be another element present that even Bissinger has not recognized. He describes these Saturday-night "fag-bashers," ordinary teens for whom beatings and murder are a conventionalized recreation, as similar to the Klan: "like the old boys who roamed the quiet, bygone nights, these youngsters relish the obvious terror they create in their victims and are emboldened by the firm conviction that the Bible and their Lord Jesus are on their side" (p. 86). We can, of course, attribute the teenagers' targeting of gays solely to their elders' political and religious agenda. But what about the brutishness of the attacks and the enjoyment of the victims' terror? Although Bissinger ascribes the boys' behavior in part to traditional Texan machismo, he comes closer to a convincing explanation in citing the reaction of Dianne Hardy-Garcia, a gay- and lesbian-rights activist, to one of the witnesses in a trial for murder: "Hardy-Garcia listened to the testimony of a 15-year-old boy who had been part of a group that liked to go fag-bashing in Tyler. What she saw was a child, a 'baby boy' who was scared to death, and she became convinced that what he felt in his heart for homosexuals was the product of an environment in which gays are depicted over and over again as perverts, predators, and pedophiles" (p. 86).

The cruelty of the attackers and the relish they took in their victims' terror adds up to more than Texas machismo. It sounds like the result of environmental factors interacting with fear and rage, perhaps emotions carried over from being terrorized and brutalized in childhood. Were these boys, instead of directing their anger against those actually responsible for their pain, projecting it onto safe and helpless "evil" victims?

What this community has done is not simply disenfranchise gays and disapprove of them; it has established them as acceptable scapegoats by setting them up as monsters who will do terrible things to children—even though the vast majority of pedophiles are heterosexual. This sounds suspiciously like the process Adorno describes: of projecting one's unacceptable feelings—especially sexual feelings—onto a minority group and thereby creating a scapegoat; once the group has been vilified, acting out one's rage against them becomes acceptable and logical.

On January 25, 1995, in response to Bissinger's article in *Vanity Fair*, the television show "Primetime" ran a segment on the murders. They interviewed one of the murderers, Donald Aldrich, on death row. On camera, he seemed anything but the typical unfeeling psychopath. He expressed ruefulness, as well as sadness and distress over the fate of his victim, Nicholas West. Aldrich and two others, according to Bissinger's report, lured West into a truck, drove him to a deserted area, and terrorized him until he defecated in his pants from fear. They then forced him to remove his pants and shoes and "bitch-slapped" him across the face with a .357 Magnum and taunted him to fight back. When he wouldn't, they shot him eight times, in the stomach and finally in the back of the head.

On television Aldrich admitted to the interviewer that he took pleasure in "seeing the fear in someone else." The interviewer, amazingly, let this go by without comment or further question, even though Aldrich had talked quite frankly about his motivation in the *Vanity Fair* article. He had told Bissinger he didn't hate all fags, only "the perverts"—those who preyed on children—and revealed that he had been "forced to perform oral and anal sex on a relative for three or four years from the time he was nine years old" (p. 88).

Bissinger doesn't buy this explanation of why Aldrich, by his own admission, hung out in a public park he knew was frequented by gay men and willingly played the lure in a series of gay robberies, allowing himself to be approached sexually before beating and robbing the victims. Nor does he see it as the reason why the last robbery, of Nicholas West, got so out of hand. Bissinger is skeptical because Aldrich "can offer no independent corroboration" of the sexual abuse he suffered; he is also scornful of Aldrich's claim that he was defenseless against the abuse of a relative seven years older than he was (p. 88). What, then, did Aldrich mean when he said he enjoyed seeing someone else's fear?

The Religious Right and Sexuality
There is reason to believe that for Protestant fundamentalists, sexuality is a complex, contradictory topic. On the one hand, they rigidly oppose premarital sex; on the other hand, a number of prominent fundamentalists and evangelicals, including Jim Bakker and Jimmy Swaggert, have been caught with prostitutes or engaging in extramarital affairs. This is not surprising, given the difficult-to-ignore nature of human sexuality. We might predict that such rigid restrictions would occasionally be overturned by the acting out of sexual impulses in self-destructive ways.

Although there is little research on sexuality among fundamentalists, Longres's 1991 study of seventy-five teenage girls arrested for prostitution in a northwestern city uncovered the curious fact that the majority of the girls' parents identified themselves as Christian fundamentalists. Yet their family backgrounds were full of chaos, owing to what the author calls "impermanent parental sexual relationships" and "strained family functioning" (p. 125). Many of the parents had had multiple sexual partners. The author concludes that a fundamentalist religious background may increase the likelihood of becoming a prostitute. It is also interesting that the majority of parents had at least some college education yet were working at low-level jobs such as janitor or nurse's aid; the mismatch between their occupational level and their educations suggests that emotional difficulties had taken their toll. The vast majority of the parents said they would not feel comfortable turning to their families for support and that, even though they were quite religious, they would not go to a religious leader for help with their problems.

Fundamentalism and Thought

We have seen that one of the likely outcomes of childhood punishment is denial, which can affect the ability to think clearly. Merelman (1969) suggested some time ago that the effect of physical punishment on children is to stunt the cognitive and moral development that is needed to learn to think and act effectively in the political world. He argues that children who are physically punished never have a reason or opportunity to develop internalized moral standards or to think in a complex way about events around them. Instead, they retain the simplistic and concrete thinking of early childhood, in which moral values are absolutes imposed by an external authority.

To examine the thinking style of fundamentalists, Thomas Edgington and Roger Hutchinson (1990) studied ninety-eight students at a fundamentalist Christian seminary in Indiana. They measured a number of variables, including degree of fundamentalism, religiosity, authoritarianism, dogmatism, and cognitive complexity. The latter was measured through short essays and was composed of *differentiation,* the ability to see multiple aspects of a problem or situation, and *integration,* the ability to synthesize different aspects of a problem into a complex whole. Lack of differentiation results in simplistic, black-or-white thinking. They found that fundamentalism was highly correlated with authoritarianism and dogmatism and inversely correlated with cognitive complexity, with the highest levels of fundamentalism associated with the least complex, most simplistic thinking.

In a study of the relationship between cognitive complexity and the content of ethical dilemmas, Hunsberger, Pratt, and Pancer (1994) sampled university students and separated out the high- and low-fundamentalism groups corresponding to the upper and lower quartiles of scores on the religious fundamentalism (RF) scale. They interviewed subjects about dilemmas involving ethical, religious, and environmental issues, some of which were already familiar to students and some which were not. (See table 4.1 for the content of each dilemma and the content

Table 4.1

Dilemma	Content	Familiarity
1. Genetic choice Should parents be able to choose, e.g., the eye color of their children?	Ethical	Low
2. Abortion How should the conflict over legalization be resolved?	Ethical	High
3. North Africa Should water people need be diverted from a river if doing so will also cause damage to plants and animals?	Environmental	Low
4. Jobs versus the environment Should government crack down on a company that pollutes, even if the company could fail and jobs be lost?	Environmental	High
5. Car accident How can parents reconcile their child's death in an accident with belief in a loving God?	Religious	Low
6. Sunday shopping Should stores be open on Sunday?	Religious	High

category.) Subjects gave their views on each dilemma and then answered questions designed to increase the complexity of their thinking on the issues. They were asked, for example, if they could think of other solutions to the dilemma and if they saw the potential for compromise among alternative solutions.

The researchers found higher levels of cognitive complexity—measured by the degree of differentiation and integration in subjects' responses—in response to issues that were familiar to the students and in response to prodding questions about the issues. While fundamentalists' cognitive complexity scores did not differ from those of nonfundamentalists when all six dilemmas were looked at together, they did differ significantly from nonfundamentalists on two dilemmas: those concerned with abortion and the death of a child in a car accident. In their discussion of these two issues fundamentalists showed significantly lower complexity than nonfundamentalists.

Hunsberger and colleagues speculate that these two dilemmas involve what they call existential content or "questions that confront us because we are aware that we and others like us are alive and that we shall die" (p. 341). They also note that the negative correlation between fundamentalism and religion as quest scores in other studies supports the notion that fundamentalists prefer not to deal with issues that involve searching existential questions. Interestingly, in Hunsberger's study, high scores on the RWA measure of authoritarianism were also significantly related to lower levels of cognitive complexity for the same two dilemmas—abortion and car accident.

We hypothesize, however, that there is something other than existential issues involved. We believe the clue lies in the fact that both fundamentalists and authoritarians from nonfundamentalist backgrounds have one thing in common: punitive child rearing that included physical punishment. Similarly, both dilemmas on which fundamentalists and authoritarians show low cognitive complexity involve questions related to the life or death of a child. In the case of abortion, the issue is whether or not a parent has the right to abort a fetus—or, as fundamentalists argue, take the life of an innocent child. Such a question is well suited to re-arousing the fear and the anger experienced in childhood by individuals who were physically attacked by their parents and may well have feared for their lives. The car-accident dilemma shifts the locus of responsibility for the child's death to a heavenly father, but it remains a question of how an allegedly benign authority could will, or at least tolerate, a child's death. We wonder whether it is the thematic content of the dilemmas—injury to a child at the hands of a parent—rather than the existential content that explains why fundamentalists and authoritarians show a drop in cognitive complexity in response to these dilemmas. Denial is a child's only recourse in response to parental abuse, and, as we have seen, such denial is linked to thinking deficits. Dilemmas that arouse residual childhood emotion—which must still be denied in adulthood—are likely to elicit those thinking deficits.

In their study of attitudes toward abortion Stets and Leik (1993) also found differences in the thinking of pro-lifers and pro-choice advocates. Their data show that individuals who hold a pro-life position on abortion have a less complex, more monolithic attitude structure toward abortion than pro-choice advocates, who are more likely to distinguish among various component aspects of the abortion question, such as the morality of abortion versus the legality of abortion. In addition, pro-lifers were more conservative politically and religiously, more given to absolutist moral standards, and more conservative on social issues than pro-choice advocates. Their less-complex thinking on this issue resembled that of the Protestant fundamentalists in Hunsberger's study, whose general social, political, and moral views they shared.

Attitudes toward Abortion

Many observers see the Religious Right's antiabortion stance as more punitive than compassionate, more concerned with power than with morality. As one writer (Simpson 1987) put it, "Moral Majority politics, far from being a symbolic crusade in defense of status, is a struggle for power at the most fundamental level, that is, a struggle that is being waged on and for control of the body (p. 67).

In her *New York Times* essay, Dr. Elizabeth Karlin (1995), a doctor who provides abortions, testifies to the tactics used by pro-life activists: "They've invaded my block carrying grisly pictures of full-term stillbirths with decapitated heads. They've jumped out at me when I walk my dogs at night. Once they invited extremists from around the country to march around my house seven times praying, in the hope that the house would fall down—a Jericho march. They plagued my mother, who was then 86 years old, with hang-up calls every three minutes for two days. . . . They've invaded my office, repeatedly glued my locks shut and vandalized my office building" (p. 32). Karlin argues that "to invite a religious minority to participate in decisions affecting one medical procedure—one that involves only women, and frequently, suffering women—is appalling. It is like inviting Christian Scientists into a discussion of whether to use balloon angioplasty or medication to treat coronary artery disease." And, she points out, "there is only one reason I've ever heard for having an abortion: the desire to be a good mother" (p. 32).

Milburn (1991) illustrates the displacement of anger and pain onto objects in the political environment with the example of Randall Terry, leader of the antiabortion organization Operation Rescue, which has blockaded abortion clinics around the country. Susan Faludi questioned

Terry about his past for her *Mother Jones* article (1989): " 'My wife almost had an abortion a few years ago but I stopped her,' Terry says. They had four kids, and she didn't want another. 'I fought it. I said, "No, no, no." ' In the end he followed her into the examination room, where she was lying in a hospital gown. 'I came in and snatched her and I said, "Let's get out of here. Now!" I'm not going to let her be anywhere where I'm not.' She had the baby, but then she left him. Tears fill his eyes as he says this. He swats at them and explains, 'I'm crying for the unborn babies' " (p. 25).

People often explain their personal pain and anger in political terms, denying the actual source of the emotion they are experiencing. By suggesting that he is crying for unborn babies, Terry can deny the pain caused by his wife's rejection and, more importantly, avoid the pain of considering how he had contributed to the dissolution of his marriage. Antiabortion activism for Terry is also a way to act out his anger at his ex-wife by preventing other women from getting abortions.

It seems clear that far more than abortion is at stake for Randall Terry. As Faye Ginsburg (1993) points out, his larger goal is to reinstitute "traditional Christian values" in America.[8] God, Terry says, "is using us to separate sheep from goats . . . the wheat from the chaff. . . . When the Lord put the vision in my heart, it was not just to rescue babies and mothers but to rescue the country. This is the first domino to fall" (p. 558).

According to Ginsburg, Randall Terry has expressed contempt for the "wimps for life" (p. 563) who constitute the mainstream of the pro-life movement, individuals such as those on the National Right to Life Committee (NRLC), which appeals to individuals from a range of religious backgrounds and limits its attempts to change policy to legal means. Terry's own vision of the antiabortion cause, by contrast, is angry and militaristic: "methodical 'rescues' are embellished with 'covert' and 'intelligence' operations, requiring the stealthy maneuver of 'troops' and a solemn 'chain of command.' He speaks of 'organizing for war' and calls participants 'warriors' " (p. 568). Operation Rescue training camps also offer training in the political skills needed to elect conservative politicians.

During the first of his "rescue missions," at a clinic in Binghamton, New York, Randall Terry was arrested for criminal trespass. After that experience, Ginsburg tells us, he "had a more definite idea of what it was going to take to secure justice again for the children" (p. 566). As Operation Rescue began to suffer legal setbacks, beginning in 1989 when Terry himself was imprisoned for refusing to pay a fine for trespassing, and the courts began to levy heavy fines for blocking access to clinics in defiance of the law, Terry's tone changed. He became both more strident, more severe in his prophetic pronouncements, and more resentful: "We as a nation are doomed to a severe chastening from the hand of God," he claimed, "What kind of justice is it when ten of us are fined $450,000 for trying to stop the murder of innocent babies while the homosexuals who entered St. Patrick's Cathedral and disrupted Mass are fined $100 each?" (p. 569).

His tone began to slide toward paranoia with statements about the "anti-Christian bias of the nation's judicial system . . . the steady diet of anti-Christian bigotry we're seeing . . . police oppression, judicial tyranny and political harassment" against Operation Rescue at the hands of "our enemies" (pp. 579–570). In 1991, participants in a siege of abortion clinics in Kansas referred to themselves as the "Lambs of Christ" or "Victim Souls of the Unborn Christ Child" (p. 571). Rhetoric like this is reminiscent of the way authoritarians interviewed by Adorno and colleagues (1950) described their childhoods; after initially presenting their parents in idealized terms, they quickly shifted to a resentful tone.

In fact, the fight against legalized abortion is psychologically the ideal arena for expressing residual childhood emotions. As Spinney (1991) argues, fundamentalist activists can defend against the anxiety and depression they would experience if their fundamentalist peers rejected them by strictly adhering to an uncompromising pro-life stance. Opposition to abortion becomes a holy mission to protect the innocent unborn child endangered by its own parents. They may themselves have been hurt, or even endangered, by physical abuse in childhood but had no one to rescue them; now the unborn babies will not be harmed. In seeking to protect these innocent victims, activists can assuage their own humiliation and feelings of low self-esteem from childhood by envisioning themselves as heros taking on the courts and the police, while expressing their anger toward women and toward these "corrupted institutions." The institutions serve as substitute parental authorities activists can defy without anxiety—because they will not ratify the local authority of the fundamentalist community. At the same time, fundamentalists may imagine that they can convert and reform these institutions and end the persecution—as they were never able to reform their own parents and end the persecution they suffered in childhood.

The results of a 1989 study revealed a fascinating dichotomy in attitudes among pro-life supporters. While a large number of them believed that abortion was morally wrong because it involved taking the life of an unborn child, very few of them considered the actual well-being of the child in their moral decision. Jacqueline Scott, a psychologist at the University of Essex in England, conducted a telephone survey of a random sample of Americans. She asked respondents whether they believed abortion is morally wrong and why, and also whether individuals should have legal access to abortion. She found that 51 percent of Americans believed abortion is morally wrong but that 27 percent supported legal abortions despite their personal belief that abortion is wrong. Respondents' answers to the question of whether abortion is wrong fell into one of four categories: (1) emphasis on the life of the unborn child; (2) emphasis on the individual woman's right to choose; (3) emphasis on the well-being of the child, including considerations of whether the child, if born, would be unloved or poor; or (4) consideration of the unique circumstances of each pregnancy, whether it resulted from rape, whether the mother's life was endangered, and so on.

Fewer than 1 percent of the pro-life supporters mentioned the well-being of the child when considering whether abortion is right or wrong, compared to 34 percent of the pro-choice individuals. Pro-life individuals were not, however, solely concerned with the life of the unborn child; 21.7 percent of them mentioned the unique circumstances of the pregnancy as grounds for deciding the morality of abortion. Scott also found that pro-life supporters were more likely to adopt a rule-bound stance toward abortion, while pro-choice advocates judged the morality of abortion within the context of responsibilities and relationships.

Although Christian fundamentalists express pro-life attitudes, that does not prevent some of them from having abortions. According to the National Abortion Federation (1990), of the 1.6 million women who had abortions in 1990 (the last year for which statistics were available), one-sixth described themselves as born-again or evangelical Christians.

Attitudes toward the Death Penalty

While fundamentalists are committed to the sanctity of human life in the case of an unborn fetus and equate abortion with murder, they are untroubled by the state execution of citizens convicted of capital crimes. Robert L. Young, sociologist and director of the Criminal Justice Program at the University of Texas at Arlington, conducted a study of support for the death penalty (1992) by using data from the 1988 General Social Survey. He found that males and whites were more apt to support the death penalty than were females or African Americans. He also found that political conservatism, membership in a fundamentalist church, and literal interpretation of the Bible were all significant predictors of support for the death penalty. One fascinating finding is that attending a fundamentalist church was associated with increased support for the death penalty among whites, but not among African Americans. African Americans characterized as evangelicals on the basis of responses to the question "Have you ever tried to encourage someone to believe in Jesus Christ or to accept Jesus Christ as his or her savior?" were the least likely of any group to support the death penalty (p. 81). Young suggests that this finding may reflect the lack of trust African Americans have in the judicial system, combined with the compassion reflected in evangelical beliefs (as opposed to fundamentalist beliefs, which are more rule-oriented and punitive).

In a 1992 study, Grasmick and colleagues investigated the possibility that the desire for retribution against criminals might be related to religious affiliation. They found that fundamentalists scored significantly higher on the desire for retribution than Catholics, nonfundamentalist Protestants, and those with no religious affiliation. The single best predictor of the desire for retribution, it turned out, was the literalness of one's understanding of the Bible. Interestingly enough, individuals who were strongly religious but do not interpret the Bible literally are significantly less devoted to the goal of retribution.

The Ambivalence Inherent in Fundamentalism

As sociologist Frank Lechner (1989) points out, fundamentalism in America is, by definition, an ambivalent stance. On the one hand, fundamentalists reject modern secular society, with its separation of church and state; its efforts to include individuals of different cultures, races, religions, and values; and its support of a pluralistic society in which only the most general values are common to all. Their belief in the absolute authority of the Bible and their quest to impose a particular set of moral standards on all of society are thus rejections of the tenets of modern secular liberal society. Yet their very existence and the ability to make any claims at all are based on those very tenets. As a minority often viewed with derision, they must appeal to the inclusiveness and tolerance of American society to reserve a place for themselves in the cultural debate. Moreover, according to Lechner, fundamentalism bears within itself the inevitable failure of its own project, precisely because of its strong commitment, historically and theologically, to the primacy of every individual's absolute right and responsibility to work out and act on his or her own beliefs.

So, on the one hand, then, fundamentalism attempts to dictate "correct" beliefs and behaviors to its own adherents, as well as to export them to the larger society. On the other hand, it can hardly reject completely the right and responsibility of individuals to base commitments on their own consciences. It becomes necessary, then, to appeal to the broad general values shared by all Americans, which are likely to allow for more tolerance and ambiguity than are consistent with core fundamentalist beliefs.

So fundamentalists are in the position of having to deny either the implications of their own program or the basic values of American society. When Lechner wrote, in 1989, he did not anticipate the current heavy involvement of the Religious Right in politics, nor its reliance on stealth candidates, who win political power precisely by denying and hiding their fundamentalist program.

The Political Impact of the New Religious Right

Given the logical inconsistency built into fundamentalism, one might well wonder whether fundamentalist activism represents a serious threat to American society. In some ways, the Religious Right has not had the impact on American politics it would like. Clyde Wilcox (1994) has argued that, from one point of view, its political program has failed. Pat Robertson failed to win a single primary election in 1992, in spite of spending more money than any other candidate in American history. Although some states have placed restrictions on abortion, *Roe v. Wade* has not been overturned; nor has prayer been reinstituted in the schools. Most local initiatives to restrict the civil rights of homosexuals have been defeated, albeit narrowly in some cases.

Wilcox's insightful analysis of the fate of the Moral Majority of the 1970s suggests that it "failed not because of shifting public sentiments or broad historical trends. Their grassroots efforts failed because of the intolerance and distractions of the Baptist Bible Fellowship preachers" (p. 249). Apparently, the ministers of the Baptist fellowship entrusted with the task of organizing grassroots support for the Moral Majority spent more time splitting the world into increasingly specific out-groups than they did building a broad base of support for the movement. According to Wilcox, "Baptist Bible Fellowship pastors are an intolerant lot. At one sermon before an organizational meeting of the Ohio Moral Majority, the preacher railed against Catholics, Methodists, pentecostals, evangelicals, and even other Baptist denominations" (p. 248).

So, what reason is there to believe that the New Religious Right will have a greater political influence than the Moral Majority? We believe conservative Christians are likely to affect American politics in the near future by several important means.

Helping elect Republican candidates. The Christian Coalition was the only solid voting block that supported George Bush in the 1992 Presidential election (Kaufman 1994). It was also a major influence in bringing about Republican majorities in the House and Senate in 1994.

Pushing mainstream Republicans to the right. The stronger the Christian conservative movement grows, and the more it infiltrates party politics at the state and local level, the more indebted to it moderate Republicans become. As theologian John Swomley put it (1995), "The mere existence of an extreme right-wing party, even if it does not ultimately control the government, has its value to those in power in the political and economic system. They tend to want to make concessions to conservative and authoritarian religious forces in order to gain the fundamentalist vote, whether those concessions weaken or destroy certain constitutional values such as separation of church and state or equal protection of the law. In so doing, they take the country further down the authoritarian religious road that sacrifices long-held democratic values" (p. 6).

Defining the terms of the presidential contest. In 1988 the campaign focused on "flags and furloughs" rather than more crucial concerns. Again, for much of the 1992 campaign, the Republican party attempted to define the campaign as about "family values," a vacuous concept that simply encourages groups to vilify each others' life-styles. We actually heard the Republican vice president scold a fictional character on a television sitcom for having a child out of wedlock. In an even stranger development, Candice Bergen and the producers of "Murphy Brown" got their revenge by incorporating Dan Quayle's lunacy into the story line of the show.

Contributing to a mood of intolerance in the society. Sociologist John H. Simpson (1994) has documented a disturbing trend in recent national elections. Comparing data from the General Social Survey (GSS) conducted by the University of Chicago's National Opinion Research Center in 1980 and 1988, he examined answers to five questions on homosexuality, abortion, and pornography—issues traditionally of great concern to conservative Christians. The items he chose allowed him to contrast individuals' moral positions on the issues with their readiness to grant civil rights protection to individuals who might hold opposing views. For example, one question asked whether sexual relations between two adults of the same sex are wrong—a moral judgment—while another asked whether a male homosexual should be allowed to teach in a college or university, an item that inquires about the rights of individuals conservatives often deem to be morally wrong.

Simpson found that Americans fall into three camps on these social issues. What he terms "consistent liberals" refrain from moral judgments against homosexuals and other groups and support their civil rights, whereas "consistent conservatives" both condemn homosexuality, abortion, and pornography on moral grounds and seek to limit the legal freedom of homosexuals and the legal access to abortion and pornography. The group Simpson labeled "ambivalent" were conservative in their moral judgments but were unwilling to abrogate others' civil rights. While they might condemn the behavior of a man who was homosexual, they were unwilling to see him banned from university teaching.

What is disturbing is that while the number of liberals showed a negligible increase from 1980 to 1988, the number of individuals who were morally conservative but upheld civil rights decreased substantially, a decline that was matched by a corresponding increase in the number of people in the consistently conservative camp. The results seem to suggest not so much an increase in conservatism on the issues as a decrease in tolerance for others who hold different moral views.

There is also evidence that such a shift in moral climate indeed affected voting in the 1992 presidential election. Hammond, Shibley, and Solow (1994) used the GSS data from 1980, 1984, 1988, and 1992 to make this point. First, they distinguished between what they call the Christian Right contribution to voting patterns—adherence to conservative theological beliefs—and a family-values component that combines traditional conservative views on abortion, premarital sex, homosexuality, and women's roles in society. They also examined three other aspects of conservatism: anticommunism, antigovernment attitudes, and a "law-and-order" stance, which included support for the death penalty, opposition to laws requiring a permit to carry a gun, and belief that the courts are too lenient on criminals. In sum, Hammond and his colleagues measured five indicators of conservatism: (1) Christian right theological beliefs, (2) family values, (3) anticommunism, (4) antigovernment attitudes, and (5) law-and-order orientation.

Compared to the findings for 1980–1988, the picture that emerged from the 1992 data is quite different. In 1980, 1984, and 1988, the researchers found, individuals' choices for president were overwhelmingly related to the political party they identified with—Democrats voted for the Democratic candidate and Republicans for the Republican candidate. There was, however, a significant, if small, contribution of conservatism (measured by the combined five components above) to voting behavior over and above party identification. So, conservative opinions did contribute to voting patterns in these years, although party identification was a much more powerful predictor of voters' choices.

In these elections, Hammond concluded, Christian right theological beliefs had no independent impact on voting beyond party identification and conservative opinions in general—that is, the five components combined. (Fundamentalism, however, did predict voting for Republican candidates for House and Senate races in 1980, even after Miller and Wattenberg [1984] controlled for party identification and liberal/conservative political ideology.) In 1984, the family-values component had a very slight independent effect on voting beyond party identification and conservatism in general.

In the 1992 election, however, the situation changed. Although party identification was still the most important predictor of voting preferences, the contribution of conservative ideology (the combined five indicators of Christian right beliefs, family values, anticommunism, antigovernment attitudes, and law-and-order orientation) increased from 13 percent of the impact of party identification in the 1980 to 1988 elections to 22 percent of the impact of party identification in the 1992 election. It appears, then, that conservatism in general—as opposed to identification with the Republican party—is increasingly driving the vote. In addition, for the first time, the influence of the Christian right and family-values components each exceeded the impact of the combined index of conservatism. What's more, the family-values component had a much more powerful impact on the vote than did the Christian right component. It may be that what we are seeing is a general increase in intolerant attitudes toward the way other people live their lives.

James David Fairbanks (1982) has argued that the influence of the New Religious Right has been more a matter of strengthening conventionality—what he terms the civil religion—than of inculcating any specific religious beliefs. As he puts it, "The demands of the civil religion actually are quite conventional; no one is called upon to sell all they have and give to the poor or renounce the world and all its vain things. Symbolic gestures toward conventional norms are sufficient. . . . The priority issues of the social agenda are those concerning the respect and recognition given to the nation's religious heritage, to traditional sexual mores, and to traditional patterns of family life" (p. 334).

Encouraging a climate of extremism.   We have argued that individuals who bear the pain and grief of childhood punishment will, in the final analysis, attempt to stave off depression by acting on their anger. When that anger is displaced from childhood onto political issues and is given legitimacy as a means of policy debate, a few individuals may adopt violent means of making their beliefs known. Faye Ginsburg (1993) notes that, in nearly every case, individuals apprehended for violence against abortion clinics between 1983 and 1985 were not mainstream pro-life activists prior to the assault. That also seems to be true of John Salvi, the man alleged to have murdered two women at two clinics in Boston in 1994.

In this chapter, we have seen that the political views and actions of Christian fundamentalists seem to be directly related to the tradition of punitive child rearing advocated by generations of Protestant fundamentalists. Fundamentalists, however, are not the only Americans subjected to physical punishment in childhood. The majority of us have suffered from child-rearing beliefs that are the same in principle, if less extreme in practice. It should not surprise us to learn, then, that America is a very angry and punitive society, as we see in the next chapter.

5

The Punitive Society

The United States is a society remarkable for the degree of punitiveness that pervades its families, its schools, and its criminal justice system. Supported by an ideology that values personal toughness, this punitiveness not only has a range of negative consequences for individuals, it also distorts public policy. In this chapter, we document the way punitiveness spills over into our schools and prisons to produce even greater damage to individuals and society. We also continue our analysis of the negative political consequences of punishment, a discussion we began in chapter 3, by looking at national survey data.

As we pointed out in chapter 1, support for the use of physical punishment in child rearing has always been high in the United States and continues at high levels today. The punitive spirit that characterizes many American families serves as the foundation for policies in the larger institutions of society.

The Schools

In September of 1981 an ABC/*Washington Post* national survey of 1,500 people found that 54 percent of respondents approved of allowing teachers to use corporal punishment. A more recent Harris Poll, taken in 1988, asked respondents, "Do you think that it is all right for teachers to hit, spank, or otherwise physically discipline students in the school?" A total of 43 percent of the sample agreed that teachers should be free to use physical discipline either "sometimes" or "whenever the teacher decides." While these results suggest a considerable decrease in support for corporal punishment in the last decade and a half, an April 1988 Gallup poll asking respondents whether they approved of schools physically punishing "children who do not respond well to other forms of discipline" produced a 50 percent support for corporal punishment.

Physical abuse in schools remains legal in many states. As of January 1994, twenty-three states still allowed teachers to discipline students physically, a practice that sets the United States apart from Japan, Canada, England, Ireland, most of western Europe, Israel, and the countries of the former Soviet Union. States in the South and Southwest—for example, Florida, Texas, Alabama, and Arkansas—are leaders in the use of such punishment.

According to Rust and Kinnaird (1983), teachers and administrators who use corporal punishment tend to be more authoritarian and dogmatic, inexperienced, and neurotic than their colleagues. This is not surprising, as punitiveness is one of the primary characteristics of authoritarianism.

Irwin Hyman, director of the National Center for the Study of Corporal Punishment and Alternatives at Temple University, has written extensively on the use and effects of punishment in schools and in the family. He estimates that 750,000 incidents of corporal punishment occur annually in the United States, a large number of them in fundamentalist Christian schools and academies. As we documented extensively in chapter 4, people who identify themselves as fundamentalists, literalists, Baptists and evangelicals are more likely to hit their children than are individuals of other denominations. In the schools, Hyman notes, children who are poor or black are four to five times more likely to receive physical punishment than middle- or upper-class white children.

The National Center has documented numerous instances of abuse of schoolchildren that, Hyman claims, represent only a fraction of the actual cases. Paddles, leather straps, electrical cords, a broomstick, and metal and steel pipes, among many other objects, have been used as instruments of punishment. Students have also been closed up in storerooms, closets, and school vaults for up to seven hours, subjected to strip searches, choked, and tied to chairs. A range of physical injuries have resulted, including sciatic nerve damage from paddling, skin and muscle injuries, a rupture of one student's testicles, and possible permanent damage to the legs and buttocks.[1] As in the case of families, the use of punishment in schools primarily serves to allow expression to the teacher's rage and does not deal constructively with behavior problems. To believe that this kind of treatment enhances the mission of an educational institution is to maintain a high level of denial, as discussion of the consequences of school punishment makes clear.

Consequences of School Punishment

An increasing number of professional organizations have called for the abolition of physical punishment in schools. In 1992 the Society for Adolescent Medicine issued a statement concluding that "CP [corporal punishment] in schools is an ineffective, dangerous, and unacceptable method of discipline. The use of CP in the school reinforces the notion that physical aggression is an acceptable and effective means of eliminating unwanted behavior in our society. It is recommended that CP be banned and that nonviolent methods of classroom control be utilized in the school system."[2]

Although some have proposed paddling as a punishment for graffiti writing or other vandalism, evidence indicates that corporal punishment is an important cause of vandalism in schools, rather than an effective response to it. A national study called the Safe Schools Study found that when there is a substantial amount of misbehavior in a school, corporal punishment makes the problem worse. Intense or repeated instances of corporal punishment can even result in post-traumatic stress disorder (PTSD). In fact, most serious incidents of physical abuse of children begin as physical punishment and then escalate in intensity.[3]

The Criminal Justice System

Following the controversial caning of teenager Michael Fay in Singapore, legislators in various states began proposing the reintroduction of physical punishment in the criminal justice system. The *Boston Globe* reported on November 11, 1995, that a Republican legislator in New Hampshire had recently proposed the public paddling of convicted vandals 12 years old and up. In the fall of 1994, the Mississippi House of Representatives passed a bill to allow judges to order paddlings instead of prison sentences (Reuters 1995); other such bills have been proposed in state legislatures all around the country. Being beaten with a large piece of smooth wood is very painful and can cause severe physical damage. It has come, however, to be regarded as innocuous and harmless, another example of denial that physical punishment inflicts *real* pain.

According to some public opinion polls, public support for the use of beatings is high. An April 1994 *Newsweek* poll found that 38 percent of the public supported the caning of Fay; when a Yankelovich poll taken in the same month asked the question in more detail, stating that Fay was "to be hit six times with a bamboo cane, which may leave permanent marks," 46 percent of the public approved.[4]

There are also increasing calls, particularly by conservative politicians running for office, to increase the punitiveness of the prison system. In Massachusetts Governor William Weld's gubernatorial campaign in 1990, he promised to reintroduce prisoners to the "joys of busting rocks." In the 1996 Republican presidential primaries, Senator Phil Gramm of Texas stated he would "Stop building prisons like Holiday Inns, take out the air conditioning, the color televisions and the weight rooms" (Nyhan 1995). Confusing prisons with Holiday Inns is a particularly distorted way of thinking. As Abbe Smith, deputy director of the Criminal Justice Institute at Harvard Law School wrote in 1995, "Make no mistake about what goes on in prisons. Though penal institutions came about as part of a social reform movement as an alternative to harsh labor camps and public torture, there is no question that we mean to break the spirits of those we imprison. The intense deprivation that imprisonment imposes puts prisons on a continuum with other forms of torture" (p. 82).

Consequences of Punitiveness in the Criminal Justice System

Mandatory sentencing and the "three strikes and you're out" rule are the latest innovations in the criminal justice system pushed by conservative politicians and backed by frustrated citizens increasingly fearful of crime. These sentencing practices have dramatically increased the prison population of the United States, which now has the highest incarceration rate of any country in the world.

Yet our prisons are failing. From national recidivism rates of about 35 percent, it is clear that our criminal justice system does not prevent crime or adequately rehabilitate those who serve time in our prisons. Moreover, the costs of incarceration are substantial; the annual costs for prison construction and maintaining inmates is currently around $21 billion (Smo-lowe 1994). Building more prisons and locking up more criminals is not the answer. A 1991 study by Israeli researchers Cohen, Eden, and Lazar compared the likelihood of recidivism of two groups of individuals convicted of serious felonies. One group was sentenced to terms of up to seven years, the second was granted probation. Police records show that for a five-year period following release from prison, there was no difference in the number of crimes the two groups committed.

Conservative politicians, with the support of the punitive public climate of the 1990s, are working to eviscerate the few prison programs that do work. Illiteracy and a lack of education have long been linked to crime; a recent study (Smith 1995) of serious offenders found lack of education to be the strongest predictor of committing another crime. Nonetheless, funding for GED programs in prisons is threatened and Pell grants to prisoners to enable them to pursue higher education have been eliminated, even though such programs have been found to reduce recidivism. Our prisons are failing; yet, because of the current climate of punitiveness and budget cutting, the government is eliminating the very programs shown to help prisoners escape the cycle of crime and imprisonment.

It is well-known that prison is often a training ground for new criminal skills. According to Michael Sheahan, the sheriff of Cook County, Illinois, "They start as drug offenders, they eventually become property-crime offenders, and then they commit crimes against people. They learn this trade as they go through the prison system." Moreover, because vast numbers of nonviolent offenders arrested on drug-related charges fill up prison space, violent offenders are serving less time (Smolowe 1994).

In addition, the brutal treatment nonviolent offenders receive in prison and the rage it creates may actually serve to increase crime. Consider this prisoner in an Ohio penitentiary who wrote to Professor Philip Zimbardo of Stanford University in the early 1970s:

I was recently released from solitary confinement, after being held therein for 37 months. The silent system was imposed upon me, and even a whisper to the man in the next cell resulted in being beaten by guards, sprayed with chemical mace, blackjacked, stomped, and thrown into a strip cell naked to sleep on a concrete floor, without bedding, covering, wash basin, or even a toilet. Because of my refusal to let the things die down and forget all that happened during my 37 months in solitary, I am the most hated prisoner in this penitentiary, and called a hard-core incorrigible. Prof. Zimbardo, maybe I am an incorrigible, but if true, it is because I would rather die than to accept being treated less than a human being. I have never complained of my prison sentence as being unjustified, except through legal means of appeals. I have never put a knife on a guard's throat and demanded my release. I know that these must be punished, and I don't justify stealing even though I am a thief myself. But now I don't think I will be a thief when I am released. No, I am not rehabilitated either. It is just that I no longer think of becoming wealthy or stealing. *I now only think of killing. Killing those who have beaten me and treated me as if I were a dog.*[5]

Brutal conditions in prison are not a problem of the past. In February 7, 1994, *Time* magazine quoted the assertion of University of Miami criminologist Paul Cromwell that "Prison systems are 'criminogenic': they create criminals. . . . The chronic beatings, stabbings, rapes and isolation ignite fury. As one prisoner reported, 'They are so blind with rage that they can't think about the consequences.' "

Besides the potential of physical attacks by guards and other inmates, male prisoners also face the horrific probability of rape by other prisoners. A 1993 *New York Times* story by Stephen Donaldson documents this serious situation: "For too long, we have turned away from the rape crisis in these institutions, which now hold 1.3 million men and boys. In most of them, rape is an entrenched tradition, considered by prisoners a legitimate way to 'prove their manhood' and satisfy sexual needs and the brutal desire for power." Donaldson estimates that approximately 290,000 males are raped each year in prison, compared to a Bureau of Justice Statistics estimate that 135,000 women are raped each year. Since the risk of AIDS transmission is very high in this type of sexual assault, such rapes may amount to a death sentence.

Donaldson notes that while officials have known about the problem for many years, they have done very little. Generally they are loath to admit that such brutalization of individuals in their custody occurs. In the words of Vermont Commissioner of Corrections John F. Gorczyk, "Society reacts with a combination of fear, disgust, and denial." Moreover, nonviolent offenders are the most likely victims of such attacks; and some of them may become rapists themselves when they are released, repeating the violence that was done to them.[6]

As Supreme Court Justice Blackman wrote in the June 6, 1994, decision in *Farmer* v. *Brennan,* in which a prison inmate sued prison officials for not protecting him against being raped: "Such brutality is the equivalent of torture, and is offensive to any modern standard of human dignity. The horrors experienced by many young inmates, particularly those who . . . are convicted of nonviolent offenses, border on the unimaginable. Prison rape not only threatens the lives of those who fall prey to their aggressors [through AIDS], but is potentially devastating to the human spirit. Shame, depression, and a shattering loss of self-esteem accompany the perpetual terror the victim thereafter must endure."

So, what are politicians doing about this problem? The Republican-controlled Congress is trying to make it worse. A proposed law entitled STOP passed by the House (H. R. 667), submitted to the Senate (S. 400), and supported by Senator Phil Gramm would deny courts the power to remedy constitutional violations in prison conditions—whether in juvenile centers, jails, or prisons. This legislation would have the effect of substantially limiting prisoners' right to seek redress for such crimes as rape.

The bill is opposed by a host of professional legal associations and mental health associations, including the American Bar Association, the American Psychiatric Association, the American Psychological Association, the National Association of Social Workers, the National Mental Health Association, National Rainbow Coalition, National Women's Law Center, the Southern Poverty Law Center, and the Youth Law Center, among others. Former U.S. Bureau of Prisons director J. Michael Quinlan calls the bill "extremely misguided." Even the American Correctional Association opposes Senate passage of the bill without prior hearings. There were no hearings on the House bill.

Given the destructive and brutalizing effects of prison rape on previously nonviolent offenders, the policies of the punitive political culture embodied in current conservative political philosophy can only contribute to an ever-increasing cycle of retribution and increased violence and criminality.

The Social Consequences

Public Support of Spanking
Why do so many people support using physical punishment in raising children? A 1988 Harris survey asked a national sample of respondents about the physical punishment they received as children. ("How often did

your parents or guardian hit, spank, or physically discipline you when you misbehaved?") It also asked whether it was all right to physically punish children and the extent to which parents in the sample had punished their own children.

Consistent with earlier research, the survey found that males were spanked significantly more often than females, and those with higher education were spanked significantly less often. Having been spanked or hit as a child predicted both approval of the use of spanking and respondents' actual use of spanking. Respondents were given only three or four possible responses (e.g., "Never all right; Sometimes all right; All right whenever the parent decides"). This type of measurement reduces the variability of the punishment measures and consequently, reduces the apparent size of the correlations between or among variables—for example, between being spanked as a child and spanking one's own children. Had support for punishment or actual punishment been measured more accurately, we believe the effects discussed below would have been stronger.

Support for the use of punishment in families and in schools would seem to reflect the same punitive and retributive emotions resulting from childhood punishment that lead to support for capital punishment and the use of military force. Some critics might argue, however, that the correlation between having been spanked and current approval of spanking is spurious; that is, that the relationship is explained by some third variable, such as education. This alternative argument would hold that people with less education are spanked more, and people with less education approve of spanking more, but having been spanked doesn't cause approval of spanking.

To address this question, we conducted a multivariate analysis to predict the individual effect of six variables—having been spanked, education, income, type of job, age, and race—on respondents' support for spanking. This analysis allowed us to test the effect of a person's having been spanked on their support for spanking in general by controlling for—or holding constant—their level of education. The results did show that education had a significant effect on support for spanking one's children, as we expected. Yet the analysis also showed that, *within* groups of respondents with comparable levels of education, being spanked as a child made one significantly more likely to support spanking now. None of the other variables we tested were significant predictors of support for physical punishment.[7]

The Climate of Punitiveness

As support for the physical punishment of children has been high for many years, we must ask why this punitiveness is now finding expression in policy debates. The political climate, which in 1994 allowed the GOP to capture both houses of Congress for the first time in forty years, appears to be much angrier and more punitive in spirit in the 1990s than it was in previous decades. Numerous public opinion polls have revealed the pervasiveness of support for mean-spirited public policies.[8]

A Harris Poll taken in July of 1990, for example, asked whether the rights of convicted murderers should be restricted so they can be executed more quickly. Sixty-four percent of the sample approved of such restrictions, even though our imperfect legal system has in the past sentenced hundreds of innocent people to death. The same poll found nearly half of Americans (44 percent) in favor of taking welfare benefits from teenage mothers—presumably to punish girls for being poor, having sex, and conceiving a child without being married. Respondents must have known that this action would hurt the children more than it would their teenage mothers. A quarter of those favoring the policy also approved of Newt Gingrich's proposal to put the children of unmarried teen mothers into orphanages.

In a telephone survey of one thousand adults in April of 1994, respondents were asked whether they preferred a candidate who would deal with the root causes of crime—lack of education, poverty, broken families, and illegitimacy—or one who favors tougher sentencing, reducing the appeals process, and building more prisons. Fifty percent of the sample favored the tougher candidate, while only 36 percent wanted to address the root causes of crime.

Public opinion of illegal immigration is another indicator of social fear and punitiveness. Studies have shown that neither legal nor illegal immigration pose an economic threat to this country. An article by Richard Rayner in the New York Times Magazine (January 7, 1996), "What Immigration Crisis?", reports that a nonpartisan research organization, the Urban Institute, found that the cost of educating all immigrants, legal and illegal, is only 5 percent of total U.S. expenditures on education. Immigrants pay almost twice as much in taxes as they receive in services; illegal immigrants alone pay over $7 billion in taxes.

In spite of this evidence to the contrary, a recent *Times-Mirror* national poll showed that fully 61 percent of the public believed that stopping illegal immigration should be a "top-priority" foreign policy effort; an additional 32 percent thought it should be "a priority." A remarkable 35 percent of the public favored building a wall along the border with Mexico; 50 percent favored denying illegal immigrants the use of schools and hospitals; and 62 percent favored issuing national identification cards to differentiate citizens and legal residents from illegal immigrants.

Authoritarianism and Economic or Social Threats

How can we explain the current climate of punitiveness? Writing a number of years ago, Seymour Lipset (1959) argued that the higher authoritarianism of working-class individuals was a response to economic threat. In a test of this hypothesis (1960), psychologist Milton Rokeach found the dogmatism and punitiveness of statements by the Catholic Church Council to be highly correlated with the council's perception of threats to the Church.

Some years later, psychologist Stephen Sales (1972, 1973) used time-series analysis to compare various indices of authoritarianism with the rates of increase in church membership of authoritarian and nonauthoritarian churches. Using descriptive information on U.S. denominations by Mead (1965) and Williams (1969), Sales classified the Presbyterian Church, the Congregational Christian Church, churches of the Northern Baptist Convention, and the Protestant Episcopal Church as nonauthoritarian. He classified the churches of the Southern Baptist Convention, the Church of Jesus Christ of Latter-day Saints, the Seventh-day Adventists, and the Roman Catholic Church as authoritarian institutions. Sales found that during transitions from prosperity to economic stress or social conflict (e.g., 1920–1939 and 1964–1970), there were increases in conversions to three of the four authoritarian churches and decreases in membership in the four nonauthoritarian churches.

Sales also compared various social indicators of authoritarianism for the same periods. For example, to assess authoritarians' glorification of "power and toughness," he looked at the number of championship prize fights and the popularity of attack dogs; to assess "authoritarian aggression," he looked at support for the death penalty; and for "authoritarian submission," he counted the number of loyalty oaths required. There were increases in all the indices for at least one of the two time periods examined, which supports the hypothesis that authoritarianism is more common in times of economic or social stress. More recent research has sustained this proposition.[9]

Many people feel threatened by the economic conditions of the 1990s. Retail sales figures for the 1995 Christmas season were among the worst in recent years, which some analysts attribute to low levels of consumer confidence; more bankruptcies and store closings are predicted (Reidy, 1996). This could account for our current results. However, if this general proposition is correct, we would expect the negative consequences of childhood punishment on political attitudes we reported in chapter 3 to be evident at other times of social stress as well.

The year 1968 was particularly turbulent, both politically and socially; fortunately, that same year a Harris national survey asked questions that are directly relevant to the relationship between childhood punishment and adult attitudes of authoritarian punitiveness. The data from the survey paint a picture remarkably similar to the results of our own experimental and small-scale studies, which demonstrated a significant relationship between adult political attitudes and physical punishment in childhood.

The Harris survey of 1,175 adults asked respondents about their family history of childhood punishment and use of spanking as parents as well as a series of political-attitude questions measuring punitiveness and militarism. Only 5 percent of the sample reported that they were never spanked as children; 32 percent said they were spanked frequently; and 60 percent stated they were spanked sometimes. Thus the questions provide an opportunity to assess the effect of punishment in a national sample.[10]

Harris asked about a number of political issues parallel to the questions we asked about in our research. The frequency with which individuals reported being spanked in childhood was significantly correlated with political attitudes: that is, the more spanking a person reported receiving in childhood, the more punitive were his or her political attitudes. The following are some of the categories and specific social and political attitudes we found to be significantly correlated with childhood punishment. We report specific correlations in the Appendix.

Strict child rearing
(1) What young people need most of all is strong discipline by their parents;

Rigidity of thinking
(1) Everything changes so quickly these days that I often have trouble deciding which are the right rules to follow;
(2) People were better off in the old days when everyone knew just how he was expected to act;
(3) Sex criminals deserve more than prison, they should be publicly whipped or worse. [This is a question Adorno used on the original F-scale designed to measure the authoritarian personality.]

Support for violence
(1) When a boy is growing up, it is important for him to have a few fist fights;
(2) Groups have the right to train their members in marksmanship and underground warfare tactics in order to help put down any conspiracies that might occur in the country;
(3) In dealing with other countries in the world, we are frequently justified in using military force;
(4) Any man who insults a policeman has no complaint if he gets roughed-up in return.

Tolerance of violence in politics
(1) Some politicians who have had their lives threatened probably deserve it;
(2) Human nature being what it is, there must always be war and conflict;
(3) If people go into politics, they more or less have to accept the fact that they might get killed;
(4) Politicians who try to change things too fast have to expect that their lives may be threatened;
(5) A lot more people in government and politics will probably be assassinated in the next few years.

A particularly chilling question, given the 1995 bombing of the federal office building in Oklahoma City and the rhetoric of militia groups in this country, was also correlated with childhood punishment: "The government in Washington is the enemy, not the friend, of people like me."

Individual responses to these questions tended to be highly correlated with one another; for example, people who strongly agreed that young children need discipline also tended to agree that the government is the enemy of people like them. In our analysis of the Harris data, consequently, we created a composite variable of responses to all the items we saw as indicative of punitive attitudes. Individuals who reported a high frequency of spanking in their childhoods held significantly more punitive political attitudes.[11]

The 1968 Harris survey also asked respondents if they would approve of sentencing a person to death for certain crimes: for example, "The person has threatened to kill the President of the United States"; "The person has been found guilty of first degree murder"; "The person was proven to be a traitor". People who reported a high level of spanking expressed significantly more support for the death penalty in these situations.

As we indicated in our analysis of the results of the 1988 Harris Poll on spanking presented earlier in the chapter, some critics might offer a different explanation for the results. They might argue that something in an individual's background—for example, education or social class—is responsible for his or her political attitudes, not childhood experience with punishment. This argument would suggest that individuals who are less well educated tend to be more politically conservative and to use spanking more in child rearing, so that the correlation between having been spanked and holding punitive political attitudes would indicate no real causal effect. The Harris data are, in fact, consistent with this argument; individuals with less education tended to express significantly more punitive attitudes and to report having been spanked more. People with lower incomes also said they were spanked more frequently.[12]

To rule out this alternative explanation, we conducted another multivariate analysis, which enabled us to test the relationship between childhood punishment and punitive attitudes while controlling for the background variables of education and income. We performed an analysis of covariance to test the effect of different levels of childhood punishment (never, sometimes, frequently) and gender (male or female) on the two composite variables we had created—punitive attitudes and support for the death penalty. In this analysis we controlled for the influence of education and economic level. The results (contained in the Appendix) indicate that even after controlling for education and economic level, significant effects of childhood punishment on support for the death penalty and on more punitive political attitudes remain. These findings mean that even after removing the effects of education and income on political attitudes, the more an individual reported having been spanked, the more punitive were his or her political attitudes.

Conclusion

While support for punitive policies in the United States is traditionally high, research shows that authoritarian attitudes emerge even more strongly at times of economic and social stress. There are many sources of stress in the 1990s. Economically, Americans are very insecure: corporate downsizing, stagnating or declining real wages, young couples facing the prospect of doing worse economically than their parents—it all presents a pretty dismal picture. Add the threat of AIDS and the emergence of antibiotic-resistant bacteria when many people are worried about health care costs and only a pink slip away from being uninsured. New standards of racial and gender relations have left many white men insecure, and angry, about their status. All these sources of economic and social stress could contribute to higher levels of punitive authoritarianism.

The national survey data from 1968 demonstrate, like the smaller sample results of our own studies described in chapter 3, that a background of frequent harsh childhood punishment is significantly related to developing punitive attitudes, including support for the use of violence in disciplining children and for the death penalty. The vengeful tone of today's political climate appears to have its source, in part, in childhood experiences of physical punishment—a poor basis for public policy. Evidence of the failure of punitive public policies in families, in the schools, and in prisons is already very clear.

A number of conservative politicians, eager for votes and burdened with childhood issues of their own, have worked to exploit and amplify the mean-spirited potential of the U.S. electorate. In the next chapter, we examine several of these political figures, their backgrounds, and the connection between the public policies they advocate and the anger- and fear-based election campaigns they run. We also describe research that demonstrates clearly the negative effects of exposure to such emotion-laden mass media presentations.

6

The Seduction of the Electorate

It was two weeks before the 1990 gubernatorial election in Massachusetts, and it was looking good for John Silber, the tough-talking, controversial president of Boston University. A *Boston Globe*/WBZ-TV poll just released showed Silber with a six-point lead over his Republican opponent, William Weld (Mooney 1990). This was very good news, as a poll taken four-and-a-half weeks earlier, just after the September 18 primary, had shown a slight lead for Weld (Lehigh and Phillips 1990).

Silber had come a long way in this campaign. In the spring, he had almost been excluded from the Democratic primary. To gain a spot on the primary ballot, he needed 15 percent of the votes of party regulars at the Democratic convention held in Springfield. Only when some delegates committed to liberal candidate Evelyn Murphy were instructed to vote for Silber—perhaps in the hope that Silber would siphon votes away from Murphy's more conservative opponent, Frank Bellotti—did Silber receive enough votes. Murphy eventually dropped out of the race, and Silber, after trailing in the polls, staged a come-from-behind victory in the Democratic primary.

Two weeks before the election, *People* magazine had run a three-page spread on Silber and he was fielding questions about a run for the presidency in 1992. As Silber had long harbored national political ambitions (in 1986 he had commissioned a poll to test the waters for a presidential run in 1988), being elected governor was an important step. A story in the *Boston Herald* headlined, "Silber's the toast of national press" noted that "The *New York Times* this week anchored a corner of its front page with a story trumpeting the Democrat Silber as 'the prophet of the politics of rage'" (November 4, 1990, p. 6).

The Politics of Anger

Silber was angry, and he was hitting a responsive public chord. He was maintaining a lead over Weld, despite controversies over various "Silber shockers." These included his comment that "Cambodians were attracted to the state by its welfare magnet" and his refusal to make an appearance in Boston's high-crime Area B because he didn't see the value of "talking to a bunch of drug addicts." He called the English Department at Boston University a "damned matriarchy" and referred to one woman faculty member as "Henry VIII with tits." [1]

Despite other hot-tempered comments in the final weeks of the campaign—including calling opponent Weld "a backstabbing son of a bitch" and an "orange-headed WASP"—Silber appeared to be doing well. Most political observers believed he had won the final gubernatorial debate on October 30, a week before the election.

Then, on the Monday before the election, a *Boston Globe*/WBZ-TV poll taken over the previous four days showed Weld and Silber in a statistical dead heat, with Silber leading 44 to 41 percent with a margin of error of 3 percent. More disturbing for Silber was the fact that Weld was ahead 43 to 42 percent among voters polled in the preceding forty-eight hours. The trend was real. Weld became the first Republican to be elected governor in Massachusetts in eighteen years, beating Silber 51 to 49 percent.

The loss was likely to hamper severely Silber's plans for national office; he was 64 years old and had never won an election or held public office. In contrast, when Ronald Reagan was elected President at age 67, he had been governor of California for eight years. So, what happened to Silber? Why did he do so well, only to fail in the end?

What turned the tide in Weld's favor was an apparently innocuous interview of Silber by local anchorwoman Natalie Jacobson. Jacobson, a fixture on the Boston news scene for many years, co-anchors the Channel 5 news at 6:00 with her husband, Chet Curtis. She is one of the most beloved local news figures in Boston.

Jacobson interviewed both candidates at home with their families. After asking various questions about his background, she asked Silber what his strengths and weaknesses were. Weld had answered this question by admitting to "a slight lazy streak," but Silber snapped at her, "You find a weakness. I don't have to go around telling you what's wrong with me." Glaring at Jacobson, he alleged that the media had already "manufactured about 16,000 nonexisting" flaws for him.

John Moffit, a political aide for Weld, called the contrast in the interviews between Weld and Silber "chilling." During the final week of the election the Weld campaign even used a clip from Jacobson's interview with Silber in their campaign ads. Moffit's assessment of Silber's self-presentation was shared by the public. It's fine for an angry candidate to appeal to many in the electorate by expressing anger against Cambodians or drug addicts, but when he directs his anger toward a popular public figure, he crosses the line. The day after the election, Margery Egan wrote in the *Boston Herald:*

Anger is OK for the voters, but not for the candidates. "I just can't stomach Silber anymore," I heard over and over this week, even from women leaning toward Silber because they are concerned about education and affordable childcare.

Said Judy Barry, a mother, state worker and Weld voter from Burlington yesterday: "When I saw him talk to Natalie, I actually got shivers. It shocked me. When she asked him about weaknesses, wow. He was so terrible to her." (November 6, 1990, p. 6)

The anger that typifies John Silber's style was displayed again a few days before the election in an interview with another woman reporter, Leslie Stahl. He accused her—despite the negative press he had received for expressing his anger toward Natalie Jacobson—of distorting his record. It was as if he couldn't control his rage. The issue of temperament that had floated in the background of the election campaign now emerged to take center stage.

Anger often plays a role in politics, generally being used by politicians to show their toughness. For instance, a major step in Ronald Reagan's successful 1980 run for the presidency came just before the New Hampshire Republican primary in a candidate debate. Candidate George Bush had attempted to reduce the primary to a contest between himself and Reagan by preventing the other candidates from participating in the debate. When Reagan welcomed the others onto the stage, Bush tried to get the microphones turned off. A national audience saw Reagan angrily protest, "I paid for that microphone!" Reagan went on to win the New

Hampshire primary and the White House with the image of a Clint Eastwood "make-my-day" tough guy.

As long as Silber railed against Cambodian refugees in Lowell and drug addicts in Roxbury he was successful. The anger of the electorate, fueled by years of corruption and patronage in Massachusetts and a state tax burden increased by the skillful shifting of federal responsibilities to the states by the Reagan administration, could be targeted to these groups with "straight-shooting" comments by Silber. He was saying what a lot of people thought, even though he later claimed his comments were taken out of context. His anger showed the toughness the governor was supposed to need to straighten out Massachusetts' fiscal mess while providing a symbol of angry protest that many voters could identify with. But Silber went too far when his anger spilled out onto a popular local newswoman. Many voters shifted in that last week, and many previously undecided voters came out against him. His primary campaign strategist observed, "He missed an easy one."

Silber is a man with a Ph.D. in philosophy, a man some have described as brilliant, a man successful enough in the academic world to ascend to the presidency of Boston University and survive many controversies. All he needed to say to Natalie Jacobson was "Well, I have a temper sometimes" and he might well have been governor. How could he have blown such an easy question? Although there are undoubtedly many facets to the anger of a complex personality like John Silber, the strict and unforgiving unbringing he received both at home and at school must be among the most significant.[2]

John Silber was born in Texas in August of 1926; his father was a German-born architect and his mother a schoolteacher. His upbringing was apparently quite authoritarian. He was instructed by his parents to believe in God without question and to obey authority. His father "was a product of Kaiser Wilhelm's Germany: he laid down the rules till Silber left home at twenty to marry." He also saw to it that the family engaged in "ruthless debates" around the dinner table.

Silber was born with a withered arm at a time when attitudes towards the disabled were not positive, to say the least. His disability made him a focus of other children's ridicule; the *New York Times* (September 20, 1990) reported that "Schoolmates nicknamed him 'one-armed Pete' and he became a target in fights."

Schools are a major breeding ground for shame in childhood, as anyone knows who has been picked on by other children or ridiculed by a teacher. A powerful example from Silber's life shows how his disability and the shame he endured as a part of education were interrelated. During an interview with Renee Loth of the *Boston Globe* (1986) Silber described what must have been an important childhood experience. When he was 12 years old he and his classmates were assigned to write an essay about the occupation they wanted to pursue when they were adults. At that time Silber wanted to become a veterinarian. He worked very hard on his essay, interviewing veterinarians and drawing pictures of them working on cows and pigs. Loth writes that Silber

was very proud of his essay, but as the teacher was reading it to herself in the classroom, she began roaring with laughter.

"All of the kids looked up," Silber recalls. "The teacher said, 'You know what I am doing? I am reading the occupation theme of one John Silber. You know what he's going to be when he grows up?' And everybody said, 'No, what?' 'He's going to be a veterinarian. Let me correct myself. He *thinks* he's going to be a veterinarian. John Silber, I want to tell you something. You aren't going to be a veterinarian.' And then she throws her head back and roars with laughter."

Silber insists he did not find this experience humiliating. The teacher explained to him that he was physically very slight and that farm animals are very big. Veterinarians were simply much bigger and much stronger than Silber would ever be. "She probably had in mind, 'You've also got one arm, kid, and you might put that into the hopper.' She didn't say that, but she could have, and it would have been perfectly reasonable. If teachers don't tell you the truth, they don't do you any good, because one of the most important aspects of education is self-discovery" (p. 38).

It is virtually impossible to imagine how this kind of ridicule could have been anything but unbearably humiliating and shaming to a 12-year-old. Yet Silber denies any such effects. He even says it would have been reasonable for the teacher to ridicule him further by pointing out that he had only one arm. Silber framed this event as an important instance of self-discovery and strongly insisted that adversity develops talent and virtue.

Coming from an educator and a college president—and a man who has been in control of public schools in a Massachusetts community for 10 years—Silber's interpretation of this event is deeply troubling. His interpretation of this event also shows how thought processes can be negatively affected by denial. Silber is correct when he argues that a primary goal of education should be self-discovery. But, because it was necessary for the boy Silber to idealize his teacher to protect himself from the pain of her ridicule, as an adult he appears unable to distinguish between constructive ways of promoting self-discovery and humiliating and destructive ways to provide it. Silber's example of self-discovery is really stripping a child of his dreams. Education should be empowering, not destructive, and provide a safe context for children to make their own discoveries. His version of self-discovery is like discovering a board by being smacked over the head with it. It is not surprising that some of Silber's opponents at Boston University assert that his favored model of education is instruction by intimidation and humiliation. Because of his background, Silber cannot see how high standards can be maintained without punitive harshness.

It seems likely that shame, and the denial of that shame, has been a primary factor operating in Silber's life. It is also probable that the source of the incredible anger he carries with him is the internalized shame of years of humiliation by teachers and peers. Being humiliated produces anger toward the attacker but also toward the self, as well as shame, grief, and the pain caused by injury to the sense of self-worth. When a child has no one to validate the pain of repeated experiences of humiliation, he or she must deny that pain to protect the self. For an adult who has not done the necessary grieving over such experiences, the result may be self-destructive behavior. It may, alternatively, be abuse of others through projecting the shameful self onto others and displacing the resulting anger onto them. It is revealing to examine Silber's political beliefs and personal ideology in this light.

In Silber's *Straight Shooting,* he argues that important values children used to learn in school—before they were condescended to—are missing from today's education. He cites as examples of important moral lessons two aphorisms from old reading primers. His choices are revealing: "The idle fool is whipped in school," and "Job felt the rod yet blessed his God." For Silber to cite these aphorisms as examples of good moral education is astonishing, yet consistent with his earlier experiences of shame and abuse.

Silber's foreign-policy beliefs are also decidedly conservative. He is virulently anticommunist and favors U.S. military intervention around the world. He was a supporter of the contras in their fight against the Sandinista government in Nicaragua, the *mujahedin* rebels fighting the Soviets in Afghanistan, and the UNITA rebels fighting the socialist government of Angola. However, he opposed the use of sanctions against the apartheid government in South Africa.

Morning in America

To maintain denial a person needs alternative positive images to replace the hard reality. We saw in chapter 1 how the child who feared his father transformed him in fantasy into a tame lion (A. Freud 1946). Wangh (1989) too notes that "denial in order to be sustainable is often buttressed by means of positive, substitutive images, by 'dreams of glory,' self-invented or gleaned from the mythologies of the people, by dreams of the might of, and identification with, fairy-tale figures, and more often than not, by solid appearing rationalizations, or by religious consolations of afterlife. One might call all these 'positive hallucinations'" (p. 12).

Ronald Reagan was a master at the invocation of positive images, from his "shining city on the hill" speech in which he argued that the U.S. is a model for the rest of the world, to his Morning in America presidential campaign in 1984. In a 1984 campaign memo Reagan White House operative Richard Darman described Reagan's identification with a "mythic America" or, as *Newsweek* put it, "America as it imagined itself to be— the bearer of the traditional Main Street values of family and neighborhood, of thrift, industry and charity instead of government intervention where self-reliance failed" (Quoted in Cannon 1991, p. 494).

Lou Cannon, a journalist who covered Reagan in his days as governor of California and then followed him to Washington after the 1980 election, reveals that Reagan's father was an alcoholic.[3] Cannon describes Reagan as an outstanding example of the "successful children of alcoholics" who are characterized by an achievement orientation, a positive self-image, and a belief in the importance of self-help.

Reagan did not escape, however, one consistent and pervasive aspect of life in alcoholic families—the use of denial. He was very adept at using denial as a way to relate to the world. His resistance to changing his mind, even when there was clear proof that he was wrong, amazed even his advisers. A dramatic example of Reagan's capacity for denial is demonstrated in the speech he made to the nation after release of the Tower Report on the Iran-Contra affair: "A few months ago I told the American people I did not trade arms for hostages. My heart and my best intentions still tell me that is true, but the facts and the evidence tell me it is not" (*Boston Globe,* March 5, 1987).

Conservatives and Denial

Many other conservatives have authoritarian childhood stories that parallel that of Democrat John Silber. After the death of his father in 1957, the mother of Texas Senator Phil Gramm decided he needed more discipline and sent him to the Georgia Military Academy.

Patrick Buchanan, a conservative Republican presidential candidate in both 1992 and 1996, advocates the end of affirmative-action programs and has criticized primary opponents Bob Dole and Phil Gramm for voting for the 1991 Civil Rights Bill. He has also called for the repeal of the 1964 Voting Rights Act. His message of economic patriotism—which would punish U.S. corporations that move plants abroad—and his opposition to the U.S. economic bailout of Mexico and military intervention in Bosnia have their roots in the sort of isolationism that opposed U.S. entry into World War II.[4] Buchanan has also suggested that Supreme Court decisions be made subject to voter approval (*Boston Globe,* January 10, 1996) and asserted in a 1996 Republican primary debate in Iowa—without presenting any evidence—that the violence of present-day U.S. society results from the killing of unborn children, that is, from abortion.

If one considers the emotions that Buchanan utilizes and appeals to, and the source of that emotion, the basis of his support becomes much clearer. Fear, insecurity, and anger are at the heart of his message. Although, some analysts suggest, his economic message is liberal in nature, it depends for its appeal on scapegoating and fear. He often blames affirmative action, foreign competitors such as Japan, and illegal immigrants for America's economic problems, rather than recognizing structural changes in the economy. Anger—like fear of outsiders, blacks, and gays—is an essential part of his message.

Given the emotional themes of the campaign Buchanan waged in the 1996 Republican primaries, it is not surprising that the core of his support is among those concerned about social or moral issues such as abortion, rather than economic issues. A February 1996 Gallup national poll found that 59 percent of Buchanan supporters believed moral problems were the most important issues, while 38 percent saw economic problems as most important (Gallup 1996). Buchanan supporters were very different from both Dole supporters (57 percent economic problems versus 39 percent moral problems) and Alexander supporters (54 percent economic problems versus 41 percent moral problems).

The childhood roots of Buchanan's punitive, authoritarian political views are clear. He grew up in Washington, D.C. with a father who valued toughness and violence. "Pop" Buchanan, a man proud of his Mississippi Confederate heritage, was the son of an alcoholic, abusive father. He too was given to angry outbursts and did not hesitate to use his belt when Pat and his brothers were disobedient. In his memoirs, *Right from the Beginning* (1988), Buchanan discloses that denial was an important aspect of his childhood: "To show emotion and feeling was considered an unmanly thing to do; we were to be stoic about pain. Take your punishment. Don't let anyone see you cry. Whenever I read in today's press about some individual, especially some man, 'revealing himself' (e.g., bleeding and bleating in print about his 'feelings' and 'hurt') I always feel a profound sense of embarrassment" (p. 75). Buchanan had a lot to be stoic about. Mary Otto reports in the *Charlotte (N.C.) Observer* (March 3, 1996) that Buchanan's Roman Catholic father used to hold his children's hands over lighted matches "to impress them with the pain of eternal damnation." (p. 1C)

Pop Buchanan wanted his boys to know how to use their fists. When Buchanan and his brothers missed their daily practice on the punching bag, their father beat them. A *Los Angeles Times* story (December 17, 1995, p. A1) quotes from Buchanan's memoirs: "Whenever we were arrested for fighting or came home bloodied, we were not punished by my parents, so long as we had fought fairly. Pop was usually more interested in how well we had done." Charles Lane, writing in the *New Republic,* states that Buchanan's father encouraged his sons to respond to slights against them or their friends with violence. In fact, Buchanan lost his scholarship and was kicked out of Georgetown University after he assaulted two police officers who had pulled him over for speeding; he kicked one, he brags, where he "thought it might do some good."

Buchanan is not the only conservative whose angry outbursts and violence have attracted attention. Bob Dornan is a U.S. congressman from Orange County, California who may be best known nationally for suggesting during the 1992 presidential campaign that there was something sinister in Bill Clinton's trip to Moscow when he was a college student. Dornan is also known for aggressive confrontations in the House of Representatives. Once in 1985 he grabbed the shirt and tie of fellow Congressman Tom Downey (D-N.Y.) and called him a "draft-dodging wimp." In 1992 he held a shouting match on the House floor with Democrat W. G. (Bill) Hefner of North Carolina.

Allegations of violence have surrounded Dornan for years. His wife, Sallie, filed four separate divorce actions against him between 1960 to 1976, alleging that he had subjected her to extreme mental cruelty and had beaten her. In 1961 she signed a statement saying that Dornan had, "dragged her about the home . . . by her hair and . . . exhibited a revolver." In the course of events, a judge found Dornan guilty of a "violent attack" on his wife and sentenced him to jail, although he apparently never served any time. Sallie Dornan has subsequently claimed that her husband was not a violent man and that the statements she made were false allegations induced by her addiction to prescription drugs and her experience with an abusive mother. She reported that the gun was a toy and that her husband "didn't have any guns then." [5]

Newt Gingrich (R-Ga.), the current speaker of the House, is another politician whose childhood experiences apparently shaped his political ideology and resulted in patterns of distorted thinking and denial. One example of his confused thinking is his reaction to the gruesome murder in Chicago of a mother and her two children. He claimed it was a result of a "welfare state" that had produced a "drug-addicted underclass with no sense of humanity, no sense of civilization and no sense of the rules of life" (*Boston Globe,* December 1, 1995, p. 3). According to historian Linda Gordon (1988), murders more gruesome than these have occurred for centuries. Her examination of the records of child welfare agencies has documented the pervasiveness of family violence—including physical abuse, neglect, incest, and wife-beating—that long predates the modern welfare system. These kinds of emotional reactions and broad generalizations that lack empirical foundation are typical of Speaker Gingrich. Where might they originate?

The picture that emerges most strikingly from Gail Sheehy's portrait of Newt Gingrich (1995)—for which she interviewed seventy of his friends and relatives—is a child whose life was dominated by a harsh and punitive father and an adult filled with anger. Gingrich's life, not unlike Silber's, appears to illustrate our model of displacement of anger from an abusive childhood onto an adult belief system that embraces a range of aggressive and punitive public policies.

When Gingrich was three years old, his father, "Big Newt" McPherson, surrendered his parental rights and allowed his ex-wife's second husband, Bob Gingrich, to adopt "Little Newt" in exchange for four months of child-support payments. Gingrich still feels anger over this abandonment. While talking about the adoption, Sheehy reports anger flashed across his face as he related how furious he was when, at the age of 16, he discovered what his father had done. This event also reflects the intergenerational transmission of pain, anger, and family disfunction we discussed in chapter 1; for Gingrich's father was himself abandoned by his father. Moreover, Sheehy reports, Newt Gingrich's stepfather, Bob Gingrich, was also abandoned; he was a foster child who was not adopted until he was sixteen. Describing his two fathers, Gingrich observed that, "They're both angry. They both served in the military. They're both physically strong. They both believe in a very male kind of toughness. They're both totalitarian." Gingrich's sister confirms that everyone in the family was terrified of Bob Gingrich.

Bob Gingrich himself recalls that some people thought he was too tough on young Gingrich, although support for physical punishment of children was higher then than it is today. He also admits he never hugged the boy. Sheehy relates Gingrich's recollection of a John Wayne movie in which Wayne throws a six-year-old boy into a lake to force him to learn to swim. In the context of his own childhood, Gingrich observed, "that made sense." He recalls that he and his stepfather were constantly in conflict from the time of his adoption until he was 19 years old.

On one level, Gingrich is aware of the influence his painful childhood has had on his adult political life. As he said to Sheehy, "I found a way to immerse my insecurities in a cause large enough to justify whatever I wanted it to." Yet his political attitudes continue to reflect underlying anger. When Sheehy asked him whether he is compassionate, he replied he was not sure what the word meant. He described feeling rage on hearing about a child who had gone through school without being taught to read and concluded, "Now, is that compassion, or is it just rage?" Gingrich seems unable to experience empathy and can feel only anger.

Like Reagan, Gingrich's primary sources of reference are movies, such as those starring John Wayne or Jimmy Stewart, that helped create his ideals of heroism. Sheehy observes that Speaker Gingrich embodies a new cultural myth, "the Angry White Man Strikes Back," a perfect description of the displacement of rage onto public policies characterized by punitiveness and retribution. It is interesting that the "angry white man" is angry at women, at minorities, and at recipients of government aid. Men mistreated in childhood and expected to be stoic might well feel enraged and cheated—and not merely economically—when they see themselves as the only group in the culture whose needs are not being addressed. The culture has changed in the last fifty years to acknowledge—at least partially—the pain experienced by women and minorities who have been discriminated against and oppressed. It has become acceptable for them to talk about their experiences and to receive support and a sympathetic hearing. It is still, largely, not acceptable for men to talk about their pain and fear and to receive some acknowledgement of it; doing so only invites ridicule.

One outcome of Gingrich's unresolved anger occurred in the middle of November in 1995 during stalled budget negotiations between the Republican congressional leadership and the White House. Gingrich and Senator Robert Dole had accompanied President Clinton on the president's plane to the funeral of Israeli president Yitzhak Rabin. Gingrich requested a meeting with Clinton on the flight back to talk about the budget, but Clinton declined. Gingrich subsequently offered the president a much tougher budget proposal than he had previously planned, reportedly because he was irritated at Clinton's refusal to meet with him and angered by not being allowed to leave the plane by the front door, where the reporters were waiting.

Gingrich, of course, anticipated that Clinton would veto the tough budget proposal, thereby shutting down the federal government and furloughing hundreds of thousands of federal workers. "It's petty . . . but I think it's human," he said at a Wednesday breakfast meeting with reporters after his return from Israel, acknowledging that the tough budget proposal was a reaction to his feelings of anger over his perceived mistreatment. Gingrich's childhood issues of abandonment, rejection, harsh punishment and family conflict make this episode a convincing illustration on a microlevel of the relationship between childhood pain and adult politics. One individual's unresolved anger *can* have an effect on the direction of public policy, a fact that students of politics often deny.

Not being allowed to talk with the president (the primary figure of power in the country), being made to sit at the back of the plane, and then being forced to exit from the back of the plane and miss out on the desired publicity—all these events together may have evoked painful emotions from his childhood. Now, however, Gingrich had the power to strike back in anger—and to bring the government to a standstill. Historian Doris Kearns Goodwin (1995) observes of Gingrich that "There seems to be some pattern of anger underneath for people who don't give him the right kind of approval or prestige. When somebody in power acts that way, it's a very unsettling thing to see; there are always encounters with people who have more power or less power than you, and you have to know your ground and be proud of who you are" (p. 98).

Clinical psychologist Robert Godwin's analysis of Gingrich in the *Journal of Psychohistory* (1996) draws on the Sheehy interview:

Gingrich has come to represent what psychoanalyst Harry Guntrip felt was the most dangerous sort of political leader, combining the traits of extreme introversion (tense, grandiose and compensatory fantasy life), narcissism ("I want to shift the entire planet. And I'm doing it. . . . I'll get credit for it"), self-sufficiency ("Newt reads books . . . He doesn't do friendship"), sense of superiority ("People like me are what stand between us and Auschwitz"), and emotional deadness ("He completely ignores [his wife]"). The deeply withdrawn core self exists in an intellectual citadel, free from impingement or dependency upon others, forming an emotionally closed system, without the capacity for true empathy ("Compassionate? I'm not sure what the word means"). (p. 256)

Gingrich's anger is directly reflected in the emotionally loaded phrases and images he uses in his election campaigns and in his instructions to fellow Republicans. As general chairman of GOPAC, the political action committee created in 1979 to help elect Republicans to state and local offices, Gingrich instructed candidates—through conference calls and audio tapes—in the techniques of incendiary campaigning (Kranish 1994). According to a *Time* magazine profile by Gibbs and Tumulty

(1995), "Democrats were to be described as traitors and with such adjectives as sick, corrupt and bizarre" (p. 80). In addition, his training tapes recommended that, as Republicans would probably be criticized for lacking compassion, campaigns should create a "shield issue" to counter the charge, perhaps an image-driven photo opportunity of the candidate "holding up a baby in a neonatal center."

Many observers have decried the low level of political discourse to which this country has fallen in recent years. In the final section of this chapter, we look at the dramatic techniques used by television news and the effect they have on viewers'—their ability to recall what they see and to look at the issues from more than one, negative, perspective. The kind of emotionally loaded campaign rhetoric Gingrich advocates seems to produce a similar, negative effect on discussions of important political issues. His own first successful campaign for the House is an apt illustration of the method.

In 1978, while running against state senator Virginia Shapard, Gingrich, criticizing her plan to commute to Washington while her children and husband stayed in Georgia, implicitly attacked her commitment to her family. Gingrich's slogan was, "When elected, Newt will keep his family together." It was an issue irrelevant to the public-policy issues he would confront in Washington; it was also soon to be irrelevant to his personal situation. Within a year and a half of going to Washington, Gingrich arrived at the hospital where his wife Jackie was recovering from surgery for uterine cancer to discuss the terms of their separation. Godwin suggests that by this abandonment of his wife, and his comment that she was not pretty enough to be a president's wife, Gingrich was projecting onto her the negative qualities he perceived in himself in an attempt to separate himself from them.

Liberals and Denial

Denial can operate in moderate and liberal politicians, too, although its outcomes are usually different from conservative denial. President Clinton, like Newt Gingrich, grew up in a home with a violent stepfather. He has advanced some liberal causes, such as supporting the rights of gays in the military, but remains an adamant supporter of the death penalty; he even flew back to Arkansas during the 1992 election campaign to approve an execution. Clinton would most appropriately be termed a moderate Democrat who holds both liberal and conservative attitudes.

The existence of an "authoritarianism of the Left" is a controversial subject in the psychological literature. Critics of the theory of the authoritarian personality discussed in chapter 3 argue that early measurements of authoritarianism were biased in a conservative direction.[6] Psychologist Milton Rokeach, for example, argues that a personality dimension he calls *dogmatism* is independent of left-wing/right-wing political beliefs. Similarly, psychologist Hans Eysenck argues that—in addition to the left/right political dimension—political beliefs are affected by an independent personality dimension he labels *tough-mindedness/tender-mindedness*. However, empirical evidence indicates that Rokeach's dogmatism scale is itself highly correlated with standard measures of authoritarianism. Moreover, Milburn (1991) concludes from a review of the literature on left-wing authoritarianism that although some individuals with rigid, authoritarian personalities do espouse left-wing political views, the preponderance of research evidence indicates that authoritarianism is overwhelmingly a right-wing phenomenon; three-quarters of authoritarians fall on the political right.

Television, Emotion, and Thinking

Many conservative candidates who experienced the sort of childhood punishment and pain known to contribute to punitive attitudes in adulthood rely on political campaigns filled with angry rhetoric. What is the effect of such campaign messages on the political discourse of the United States? Research on the relationship of emotional images in television indicate that the effects are profoundly negative.

In an episode of Bill Moyers's "Image and Reality" series on PBS, he interviewed Paula Drillman, a woman who develops product advertising campaigns. In the program she begins a focus group by asking the assembled women "to tell me the first thought that comes to your mind when I say to you, 'how do you feel about your baking?'" The women's responses are revealing; they all revolve around basic emotions about their children and families and their self-images as good mothers. For these parents, the smiles on their children's faces when they return from school and realize that something good is in the oven are powerful rewards.

For many people, being parents provides the opportunity to reexperience their own childhoods and to do it differently. Thus, the mothers in the focus group tell Drillman, without being aware of it, of their own needs for love and nurturance. The advertisers use this information to associate their product with these emotional needs, so that buying a cake mix becomes a symbol of loving one's children and, indirectly, a means of experiencing feelings of being loved. As Drillman tells Moyers, the challenge for the advertising agency is to blend together the product information and the emotion-arousing images so seamlessly that consumers are unaware that the commercials contain two messages.

Political advertisers make use of the same techniques, but the stakes are ultimately much higher. Elections determine the policy directions taken by the various levels of our government; therefore, activating negative emotions from childhood and using them to influence electoral outcomes runs a serious risk of distorting public policy.

We have seen how themes from childhood are repeated and transferred to the political arena by adult politicians whose stands on political issues seem to be influenced by these themes. We have also looked at the way these politicians use highly charged emotional themes in their campaigns. Silber, for example, did quite well with Massachusetts voters when he aroused anger over unemployment and, in dramatic soundbites, targeted Cambodians, drug addicts, and female intellectuals. We might ask, what, then, is wrong with politicians' reliance on such emotional appeals to get their message across? To consider this question, we need to examine research that measures the effect of dramatic, emotionally arousing television news stories on people's processing of the information in them.

Drama in the News
In his 1996 book, *News: The Politics of Illusion,* University of Washington political scientist W. Lance Bennett analyzes the characteristics of television news, particularly the way it is dramatized, fragmented, and personalized. He notes, for example, how, during the Gulf War, dramatic techniques were especially apparent in the "highly stylized images, music, delivery, and news plots" (p. 44) used to generate viewer interest. Patriot

missiles intercepting Scuds; smart bombs knocking on the doors of their targets; and war-game boards used to chart military maneuvers—all captured viewers' interest.

Central to drama, and particularly to melodrama, are the figures of good and evil, the hero and the villain. "Our troops" at the front played the heroes and Saddam Hussein, of course, was the villain. But the White House and others interested in a military response were not content to let his actions speak for themselves; Saddam had to become the next Hitler.

The government of Kuwait paid Hill and Knowlton, a public relations firm, $11.5 million to increase U.S. public support for military action to liberate their country. Hill and Knowlton ran focus groups and discovered that the image of Adolph Hitler was what frightened people the most. White House officials and members of the press corps, therefore, made extensive use of the comparison between Saddam and Hitler to drum up support for intervention. A content analysis of news accounts in the months prior to the Gulf invasion reveal hundreds of references to Saddam as the equivalent of Hitler, the personification of evil in the modern world.[7]

Vivid, dramatic images of evil were also carefully orchestrated to produce outrage against the Iraqi government. A Kuwaiti girl named Nayirah, who claimed to have witnessed such events, testified before a congressional committee that Iraqi troops stormed into a Kuwaiti hospital, removed babies from incubators, and threw them on the floor to die. There were reports of up to 312 "documented" cases of such deaths. Only later did reporters learn that the woman giving the reports was the daughter of the Kuwaiti ambassador to the United States. After the war, the press was unable to verify these events, and Nayirah changed her testimony; she said she had only seen one baby removed from an incubator. By then, however, the vivid melodramatic image of Iraqis as baby killers had been widely publicized and almost certainly played a role in garnering support for military intervention in the Gulf (Rowse 1992).

Research evidence suggests that the dramatic content of television news broadcasts results in a simplification of issues in the minds of viewers. In a study conducted in the 1980s, Michael Milburn and his colleagues (1991) interviewed adults in Massachusetts; they found that the more television subjects reported watching, the less complex were their explanations of terrorism. The simplest explanations attributed terrorism to the personal characteristics of terrorists (e.g., "They're all crazy"); more complex causal attributions acknowledged both the personal characteristics of individual terrorists and the historical and political context of their actions. Even after researchers controlled for viewers' educational level and style of thinking, the effect of television was significant. Other researchers have obtained similar results. Sociologist David Altheide (1987) compared American and British coverage of an IRA bombing in London and concluded that the way terrorism is generally covered "retard[s] understanding of the complexities of international affairs in the mass audience" (p. 174).

Part of the problem with the medium's coverage of terrorism and other acts of violence is that television news provides no historical background or context within which to understand these events. Moreover, our own research indicates that the dramatic presentation of violence in the news provides powerful situational cues that evoke emotional responses that can inhibit rational, complex thinking about political issues.

One aspect of *drama* is its characteristic evocation of emotional response. In his comparison of dramatic and epic theater (1957), playwright Bertolt Brecht lists the ways drama appeals to an audience: it provides spectators with sensations; it involves the spectator in an experience; and it emphasizes feeling rather than reason. American television news actually goes beyond drama into *melodrama,* in which the emotions evoked are simplistic and false. The characters in melodrama are one-dimensional representations of clearly defined moral valences—the hero all good and the villain all bad. In melodrama, only one resolution is possible—the victory of the forces of pure good over sheer evil—and the audience has only one option—to applaud the hero and boo the villain (Wagner-Pacifici 1986). Hero and villain are never one and the same. Melodrama, by obscuring the complexity of human motives and emotions and the ambiguity of many human actions, operates as a kind of thought suppressor. When reality threatens to intervene, as in the case of O. J. Simpson—a hero charged with the murder of his ex-wife and her friend—television news is reduced to abject silliness in its attempts to maintain the familiar framework. Every commercial network in America carried live coverage of Simpson's journey to nowhere in his white Bronco, while fellow sports figures and newscasters made bathetic appeals to turn himself in and gawkers along the route cheered him on.

Another defining characteristic of drama and melodrama is their dependence on some underlying myth. In television news myth is perpetuated by the careful selection of stories that fit within a culturally defined worldview. To capture and hold a large and diverse audience, news producers must appeal to a myth many people can relate to and understand. In his *Philosophy of Symbolic Forms,* Ernst Cassirer (1955) argues that the mythical world is woven into a whole, and "all reality is smelted down into concrete, unifying images" (p. 62). The unifying or "smelting" of images makes it inevitable that some of the complexity of the world the image represents will be lost.

Milburn and his colleagues have demonstrated a number of the negative effects on political thinking resulting from dramatized, emotion-arousing news. Milburn and Anne McGrail (1992) developed a scale to measure the dramatic content of broadcast news images and selected five news stories that scored high on dramatic content. They then created alternative versions of these stories by editing out all the dramatic images (e.g., South Koreans burning a giant pack of cigarettes with stars and stripes on it to protest U.S. trade policies). They showed the two sets of news stories to two different groups of subjects, then measured (1) the individuals' recall of the issues raised in the stories, and (2) the cognitive complexity with which subjects thought about the issues.

More complex thinking was defined as the ability to see multiple aspects of an issue and to integrate them in devising a solution. Controlling for various background variables that also affect the complexity of people's thinking (such as education, political ideology, and gender), Milburn and McGrail found that individuals who had seen the original, dramatic version of the news remembered significantly less information and showed more simplistic thinking about the issues involved than did individuals who saw the nondramatic version.

In a second study, Milburn, Luster, and Fine (1994) attempted to repeat the results of Milburn and McGrail and to test the hypothesis that it is the emotional arousal created by dramatic news images that interferes with both recall and cognitive complexity. They created a new television stimulus videotape, using two stories from Milburn and McGrail—on

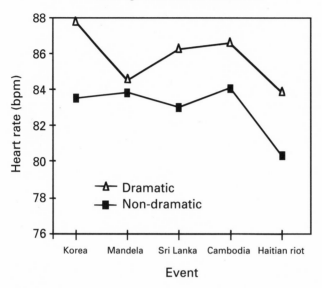

Figure 6.1.
Average maximum heart rate (Milburn, Luster, and Fine 1994).

United States–South Korea trade relations and a terrorist bombing in Sri Lanka—and added three new stories—on the return of the Khmer Rouge in Cambodia, Haitians violently protesting in Miami, and the Nelson Mandela tour. These stories were also edited to create alternative versions in which the dramatic images were absent. When possible, the tapes were edited so that the voice-over remained, thus leaving verbal content unchanged while the video image was replaced with nondramatic images. For example, while the voice-over talked about the possible return of the Khmer Rouge, a scene showing a Khmer Rouge soldier wielding a gun and threatening a woman clutching her baby and cowering in fear was replaced with footage of Secretary of State James Baker speaking.

Wearing heart monitors, subjects viewed either the dramatic or the nondramatic versions of the tape, then wrote down what they could remember of the news stories and answered open-ended questions about United States–Korea trade relations or the situation in Cambodia. Figure 6.1 shows the average maximum heart rate recorded for the two groups while watching each of the five stories. Analysis of the results shows that exposure to the dramatic news stories has both direct and indirect effects on cognitive complexity. Exposure to dramatic news, in and of itself, produced a significant decrease in the cognitive complexity of subjects' thinking, independent of measured emotion. In addition, the emotional arousal evoked by the dramatic news tape—as measured by heart rate—was correlated with a significant decrease in cognitive complexity. Thus, there appeared to be both a direct effect of the dramatic images—reduction of complex thinking—and a significant mediated effect on cognitive processing from the emotional arousal produced by the dramatic images. There was also a significant effect of increased heart rate on recall of verbal material; individuals who were exposed to dramatic news and reacted with increased heart rates remembered less about the stories they had seen than those who saw the nondramatic versions. The researchers concluded that exposure to dramatic news images, including violent scenes, has a negative effect on information processing, inhibiting both recall for the content of the news and complex thinking about the issues raised. They found some evidence that dramatic news produces these effects by arousing emotions that inhibit rational thinking.

What's more, Milburn and McGrail found that the effects of dramatized news are particularly significant in individuals who rate themselves as politically conservative. Conservative individuals exposed to dramatic news scored significantly lower on recall and cognitive complexity than did more liberal subjects exposed to the same dramatic news. How are we to understand this difference? We saw in chapter 3 that severe childhood punishment predicts conservative views on a number of political issues, including the death penalty, abortion, and the use of military force. We suggested that individuals subjected to harsh punishment in childhood carry residual feelings of anger, fear, and helplessness from the punishment and that, in adulthood, they displace those negative emotions onto the political arena and advocate policies that allow them to express their anger—toward women seeking abortions, defendants accused of capital crimes, and other targets. If, as the research suggests, one of the effects of drama is arousal of emotional responses, and if conservatives carry residual negative emotions from childhood punishment, then graphic images of war, crime, and so on may awaken that residual anger and fear, which then interferes with information processing.

News and Childhood Experiences

A recent study from our lab in fact confirms the hypothesis that violent images on television can activate residual emotion from childhood and influence individuals' perceptions of the world (Conrad, Casimira, and Milburn 1995). We showed one group of subjects a set of television news stories with violent, dramatic images, and another group a set of nonviolent news items. The extent of subjects' childhood abuse, both physical and sexual, was measured. We also measured subjects' fear of intimacy, perceptions of an ambiguously described person, and the extent to which they dissociated in response to violent news images.

Psychologists define *dissociation,* a self-protective mechanism in response to trauma, as a "psychophysiological process whereby information—incoming, stored, or outgoing—is actively deflected from integration with its usual or expected associations" (West 1967, p. 890). In other words, when individuals are faced with a traumatic experience or traumatic sights and sounds, they process information differently. The traumatic experience or information is compartmentalized, or split off, from the rest of the contents of consciousness. This type of information processing has several consequences. Individuals may have no conscious memory of the trauma or less recall for traumatic, violent news stories; at the same time, the compartmentalized traumatic material may influence their behavior and perceptions in ways they are not aware of. The simplest example of this mechanism is a person who has been beaten or sexually abused in childhood by an alcoholic parent and later, in adulthood, is drawn to people who drink.

In our study, adults with a history of childhood abuse, either sexual or physical, dissociated in response to violent news. In addition, previously traumatized individuals exposed to violent news showed a decrease in motivation or capacity for intimacy. Another interesting finding of this study was that men and women who were exposed to violent news stories but reported no history of childhood physical abuse differed in their perceptions of "Joe," a hypothetical person we described to them. Men in the violent news condition perceived him positively, as adventurous, in charge, and committed in his relationships; women exposed to the violent news, however, saw Joe as a risk taker and as dangerous and possessive.

Because the perpetrators of the violence reported in broadcast news are overwhelmingly male, men who observe other men engaging in violence may come to see such behavior as acceptable—even admirable—a positive evaluation that may carry over to the ambiguously described Joe. It would appear, then, that men exposed to violent news come to admire—perhaps even identify with—tough, risk-taking, potentially violent men.

What is especially disturbing is that women with a history of abuse also seemed to interpret Joe, the ambiguous male target, in a positive way after they were exposed to violent news. It may be that women abused in childhood, due to distorted perceptions resulting from the abuse, failed to pick up on the potentially dangerous cues that nonabused women saw; perhaps they were attracted to the male violence in the news because of their exposure to abuse in childhood. These results suggest one way in which charismatic leaders such as Reagan, Gingrich, and Buchanan are able to exert political influence.

The early research on hypnosis may provide another clue to this effect. The research literature has long shown a connection between hypnotizability and the use of dissociation as a defense against trauma. Adults with a history of physical punishment are hypnotized more easily than other people, according to psychologist Josephine Hilgard (1970); the more severe the punishment, the greater the susceptibility to hypnosis. Moreover, any amount of punishment affects hypnotizability, even if it is not the dominant form of discipline (Atlas 1990). Some theorists see dissociation as a form of self-induced hypnosis that allows traumatized individuals to escape the pain of, for example, childhood beatings. Hilgard found that physically punished children deal with abuse by using fantasy, imagination, and dissociation. These responses also tend to be typical of individuals who utilize denial as a coping mechanism in adulthood.

Our study confirms that individuals with a childhood background of abuse respond with dissociation to dramatic, violent television images. The pervasiveness of such abuse in this country we documented in earlier chapters suggests how effective such images may be. Gingrich's instructions to the GOP candidates who helped capture the House of Representatives in 1994 emphasized the use of dramatic, vitriolic characterizations of opponents—the kind of campaign our research suggests would influence individuals with a background of punishment and abuse.

Conclusion

Most people would agree that political campaigns should be about the issues that affect voters. In recent elections, however, American political discourse has been dominated by emotional, incendiary language that research on television news suggests can reduce voters' comprehension of the issues involved, lower the complexity with which they think about the issues, and produce dissociation. Because public-policy issues are generally complex and not amenable to simple solutions, campaigns that utilize such approaches run the risk of electing candidates ill-suited to governance. We have seen many examples of politicians whose personal issues—particularly those of anger and punitiveness—intrude into the political arena, exerting a damaging effect on policymaking. As part of his Contract With America, Gingrich, for example, promised to "make the death penalty real" (Linebaugh 1995).

A common theme of politicians with significant backgrounds of physical punishment and denial is the denigration of specific groups as inferior or undeserving. The next chapter explores the use of denial in denigrating one such group, African Americans, and in dealing with the contemporary legacies of slavery and racism.

7

Denial, Slavery, and Racism in America

Many white Americans were shocked and dismayed when they heard the jury's verdict in the O. J. Simpson trial. In contrast, most black Americans found it an occasion for celebration. Why was there so great a disparity between black and white opinion on the question of O. J.'s guilt? The reason, simply put, is racism and the denial of racism. For most black people in the United States encountering racism is a daily occurrence. Together, the history of slavery and racism in the United States and white America's pervasive denial of its contemporary reality go a long way toward explaining the rejoicing of black America.

Slavery in America

It is well known that slavery in this country was an institutionalized socioeconomic system that engendered physical abuse and rape. The physical and psychological effects of such a system on the slaves have been widely documented. What is not always acknowledged, however, is that the effects of that system have reverberated across generations since the freeing of the slaves and—in combination with still-widespread racial prejudice and discrimination—continue to exact a fearsome toll on people of color. Scholars have also documented the psychological effects of slavery on the white slaveowners and their families.

Physical Abuse and Slavery
A few historians have argued that the cruelty of slavery has been exaggerated. According to writers like Robert Fogel and Stanley Engerman

(1974), slave owners strived for the optimum use of force—just enough to obtain compliance without crossing the line into cruelty and perhaps causing slaves to run away (pp. 242–43). This analysis minimizes the extensive evidence that slaves were physically punished and that they suffered the psychological abuse that is inherent in the ever-present threat of violence.

According to most historians (e.g., Genovese 1974), the typical slaveowner made frequent use of his whip. There are many published accounts of slaves dying from being whipped too severely; running away was the offense most likely to bring on this punishment. Because slaves who were badly scarred had a lower market value, some slaveholders developed alternative punishment techniques, such as the use of a cowhide paddle that inflicted considerable pain but left no scars.

The psychological effects of such beatings were profound. One former slave recalled a beating received from a new master: "I's just 'bout half died. I lays in de bunk two days, gittin' over dat whippin', gittin' over it in de body but not de heart. No, suh, I has dat in de heart till dis day" (Genovese, p. 66). In the Civil War, the behavior of black regiments made up of former slaves reflected the psychological effects of the abuse they had suffered. Thomas Wentworth Higginson observed that black troops "appeared insensitive to the pain they could inflict and would unfeelingly raze a town if ordered to" (p. 66). People who experience the trauma of physical abuse frequently deal with it by denying the feelings it evokes; those who deny their own pain cannot empathize with the pain of others.

Whipping was not the only physical punishment used. Castration for a variety of crimes, although more common in the eighteenth than in the nineteenth century, never completely ceased. It was particularly likely to be used on a slave who was competing with his master for the attentions of a desirable black woman. Cutting off a slave's ear, branding, and other mutilations also decreased during the nineteenth century but continued to be used occasionally. The use of force is an inescapable tool for regulating and controlling the enslaved.

In the early days of American slavery, it was not illegal for a master to murder a slave. By the 1800s, however, the law differentiated among killing a slave with premeditation, killing in the heat of passion, and causing death by "undue correction." Nevertheless, penalties for harsh physical punishment of slaves were not severe; in 1840, a woman convicted of killing her slave by undue correction was fined only $214.28.

The psychological consequences of living under what Eugene Genovese called the "most evil of social systems" were destruction of the soul, hardening of feelings, and rage, which sometimes resulted in open rebellion.

Sexual Abuse and Slavery

Some scholars (Fogel and Engerman 1974) have suggested that the sexual exploitation of slave women by white owners was not widespread and that slaveowners in fact preferred white prostitutes (pp. 134–35). Nonetheless, the sexual abuse of slaves has been widely documented. One indication of the extent of sexual abuse is the number of children with white ancestry borne to black women. In 1850, 37 percent of the free black population in the United States was partly white, as was at least 10 percent of the slave population. As all sexual relations do not result in offspring, these figures must greatly underestimate the extent of sexual relations between whites and slaves.[1] Historian Genovese offers these generalizations about sexual relations between whites and slaves:

1. Enough violations of black women occurred on the plantations to constitute a scandal and make life hell for a discernible minority of black women and their men.
2. Much of the plantation miscegenation occurred with single girls under circumstances that varied from seduction to rape and typically fell between the two. (p. 415)

Because of power differences, it is impossible for a child to give willing consent to sexual relations with an adult (Herman 1981). A child who is dependent upon his or her parent for love and care is unable to refuse such a request, particularly because cooperation can be forced by the greater physical strength of the parent. A similar analysis can be offered for sexual relations between slaves and their masters. A master holds the power to feed or deny food to his slaves and to punish them physically as much as he wants. He may even be free to kill them with impunity. How then could a slave refuse sex with the master? Given this inequality of power, it is remarkable that many slaves, particularly married ones, did resist effectively enough to hold the number of such attacks to a low level.

The statement that sexual relations between single slave women and their masters generally fell between seduction and rape bears examination as well. It implies that the slaves were not completely willing partners who cooperated with their seducers, but also that they were not all beaten into submission and taken completely against their wills. However ambiguous such relationships may have been, sexual relations that are not fully consensual have serious negative consequences.

Even though white overseers were discouraged from sexually exploiting black women because of the discontent it produced in the slave community, many overseers did so anyway, often with the knowledge of the masters, as documented in plantation and slave records. As Angela Davis has noted (1981), "Virtually all the slave narratives of the nineteenth century contain accounts of slave women's sexual victimization at the hands of masters and overseers" (p. 25).

Slavery also allowed slaveholders to exploit the reproductive capacity of black women to increase their net worth. The more children a female slave had, the more slaves an owner had to do field work or to sell. Thus, the fertility of black women was an important aspect of their value, particularly after the abolition of the slave trade in 1808. That economic value brought new opportunities for sexual abuse. Historian Herbert Gutman (1976) relates the story of Rose Williams, whose master forced her to take as her husband a slave called Rufus. According to Rose, the master told her: "Woman, I's pay big money for you and I's done dat for de cause I wants yous to raise me chillens. I's put yous to live with Rufus for dat purpose. Now, if you doesn't want whippin' at the stake, yous do what I wants" (pp. 75–76).

Whether one would call this coerced rape or forced prostitution is uncertain; there is a definite parallel to a male pimp forcing a woman into prostitution for his own economic gain. It is clear, however, that the power over a woman's reproduction was a powerful form of sexual abuse that had significant consequences for both the woman and the children of such a "marriage"—consequences only hinted at in Rose's case by the fact that she left Rufus as soon as she could, after bearing two children, and that she subsequently wanted to have nothing to do with men.

The Effects of Slavery on the Black Family
Slaves were at risk of physical abuse not just from their white masters but also within the slave family. Slave parents punished their children harshly,

in part to try to protect them from the very real threat of white abuse. They whipped and beat them to teach them to obey—because the risk to their lives if they did not was so grave. Genovese explains that "Slave parents knowingly carried a heavy responsibility. They had to teach their children how to survive in an extraordinarily dangerous world. They had little margin for error and could not permit their children to learn from their own mistakes. A slave who grew to manhood without the special kind of self-control required in a system of strict racial and class subordination would get himself killed" (p. 510).

Anger was a forbidden emotion. Both parents and owners demanded that slave children suppress their anger when being beaten. We described in chapter 2 the heavy psychological costs of enduring this kind of abuse and emotional denial. The fact that the denial of feelings was needed to survive in a world where expressions of outrage at injustice could be met with death did not make the pain of being treated this way by parents any less.

It is clear that abusive behaviors have been transmitted intergenerationally in black families, just as they have been in white families. Theodore Rosengarten's oral history of Nate Shaw, *All God's Dangers* (1974) recounts the life of Ned Cobb (later known as Nate Shaw), an Alabama sharecropper whose father, Hayes, was a slave for fifteen years. Cobb's father beat his wife and children as he had been beaten while a slave, and Cobb carried lifelong psychological scars from being beaten and watching his mother being beaten. Black families in this century have clearly carried the legacy of this perceived need for physical punishment. African American author Ralph Ellison (1964) wrote:

One of the Southern Negro family's methods of protecting the child is the severe beating—a homeopathic dose of the violence generated by black and white relationships. Such beatings . . . were administered *for the child's own good* [italics ours]; a good which the child resisted, thus giving family relationships an undercurrent of fear and hostility, which differs qualitatively from that found in patriarchal middle-class families, because here the severe beating is administered by the mother, leaving the child no parental sanctuary. He must ever embrace violence along with maternal tenderness, or else reject, in his helpless way, the mother. . . .

Even parental love is given a qualitative balance akin to "sadism." And the extent of beatings and psychological maimings meted out by Southern Negro parents rivals those described by the nineteenth century Russian writers as characteristic of peasant life under the Czars. The horrible thing is that cruelty is also an expression of concern, of love. (p. 96, 101)

Recent compelling documentation of the intergenerational effects of abuse and violence come from Fox Butterfield's *All God's Children: The Bosket Family and the American Tradition of Violence* (1995). This chronicle of the life of Willie Bosket, considered the most dangerous man in the New York prison system, traces his violent roots back to his father, grandfather, and great-grandfather. Willie Bosket, now in prison for life, killed his first man at the age of 15. Willie's father Butch was in jail for murder when Willie was born, and his grandfather, James, and great-grandfather, Pud, also led lives of violence.

Some scholars (e.g., Coccaro 1993) have explained the presence of violence within families generation after generation as a heritable predilection. While there is some evidence that certain personality traits have a genetic basis, the environment a child experiences has a dramatic impact on the inherited tendencies. Harvard psychologist Jerome Kagan (1994) suggests that as many as 25 percent of people may be born with an "uninhibited" temperament. These individuals do not react with fear when challenged for breaking the law; if they are raised in a high-crime neighborhood, they are at a much greater risk of delinquency.

Inadequate, inconsistent discipline also puts these uninhibited individuals at risk. The evidence we examined in chapter 5 suggests that brutal discipline might also predispose such individuals to violence. Butterfield reports that harsh physical punishment was an ever-present fact of life for Willie when he was young: "Sometimes, she (his mother) slapped him around with her hand until the veins popped out, or she would give him a whipping with a belt" (p. 143). Butterfield sees in Willie the anger that such abuse creates and suggests how it was displaced: "The seeds of Willie's problems were planted early. When he was older, he looked back and felt there had always been an anger in him. It started with his childhood hatred of his mother. Then, as the years past, he identified it as a hatred of the American system. It might all have been the same rage" (p. 144). It was most probably also rage at the violence of whites toward blacks in this country, which was transmitted in early childhood by his own mother.

When Willie was nine his mother was unable to cope with him and petitioned the family court to commit him to a juvenile institution. He was sent to Wiltwyck, a place then considered a model for juvenile rehabilitation. Ironically, his father had been sent to the same place at the same age. Given the prevalence of prison rapes (discussed in chapter 5), it is not surprising that one of Willie's first experiences at Wiltwyck was an attempted rape by an older boy—"taking buns," the boys called it.

The Bosket family can be traced back to South Carolina in a region of continual violence known as Bloody Edgefield. Butterfield sees the roots of the Bosket family's constant resort to force as a continuation of the tradition of violent defense of a man's "honor" that was pervasive in Edgefield from the time of the Revolutionary War, through the antebellum period, and into the decades after the Civil War. He believes the violence of present-day street gangs, whose members may kill someone for "disrespecting" them, is a legacy of this cultural code of honor.

Another interpretation of Willie's family would stress the psychological effects of physical punishment and abuse that develop in abused individuals a need to respond to even minor slights with deadly force. Physical punishment and abuse by one's parents strike powerfully at self-esteem and create fear, helplessness, and rage. As Miller (1983) suggests, these emotions created in childhood do not disappear but are expressed in some way, either as anger toward the self or toward others. The code of honor that Butterfield traces from Edgefield to the inner city gangs says, in effect, "I feel so badly about myself, that the smallest insult against me threatens to overwhelm me, so I must lash out to defend what small part of me is left."

The larger context of this rage is important. African Americans live with the rage left by generations of cruelty, racism, and discrimination. At best, they have been treated as if they were invisible; at worst, they have been the focus of contempt, blame, and violence. And, far from being a thing of the past, this opprobrium continues today. How many black people in America are routinely followed in stores by clerks and store detectives? Stopped in the street or pulled over on the highway because they happen to be in the "wrong" neighborhood? Shunned by whites who won't sit next to them in the streetcar?

Slavery did not by itself create parental cruelty to children in black families. This treatment was also a characteristic of West African families (Gutman 1976). What the system of slavery did was to create a need in black parents to use physical abuse to break their children's spirits as a protection from even greater harm. Historian Nell Painter (1995) uses Miller's term *soul murder* to describe this effect of slavery, the range of psychological effects—including depression, rage, self-hatred, and low self-esteem—of the plantation system. Thus, black children growing up in slavery were forced to endure both the physical abuse of whites and the abuse white racism compelled their parents to administer to them.

Today's black parents who physically punish their children are unwittingly, and tragically, reenacting the harm done to them by parents and grandparents who lived under tremendous stress. This is surely one of the cruelest consequences of slavery—transforming black parents into the punishers of their own children—a pattern that contemporary racism induces some parents to continue.

The Effects of Slavery on the White Family

Slavery also had powerful psychological and emotional effects on white slaveowners. Owning slaves emphasized the authoritarian as opposed to the democratic values in American culture. Painter (1995) observes that, "Patriarchal families, slavery, and evangelical religion further reinforced one another's emphasis on submission and obedience in civil society" (p. 142). Slavery helped sustain the values of hierarchy and obedience, which were frequently enforced by violence within white families. Wife-beating was often used by women as grounds for petitioning for divorce, yet "legislators and church leaders routinely urged women to remain in abusive unions and to bear abuse in a spirit of submission" (p. 144).

As the male children of slaveowners grew to adulthood, an important aspect of learning to be a man was to suppress and deny any feelings of compassion for slaves in order to administer harsh punishment, as one slaveowner put it, "without remorse." Identifying with the aggressor was thus a prime requisite of manhood (Painter, p. 143).

Slavery and Denial

The history of denial concerning the negative effects of slavery is rich, and sometimes confusing. In the 1930s a popular history of the United States (Woodward 1936) described slavery in the following outrageous terms: "The slave system . . . did incalculable harm to the white people of the South, and benefitted nobody but the negro, in that it served as a vast training school for African savages. Though the regime of the slave plantation was strict, it was, on the whole, a kindly one by comparison with what the imported slave had experienced in his own land. It taught him discipline, cleanliness and a conception of moral standards" (p. 412).

The enormous capacity for denial of reality among white southerners during the pre–Civil War period is revealed in an influential historical work, Louis Hartz's *Liberal Tradition in America* (1955). Hartz reviews extensively the writings of prominent southern intellectuals who attempted to justify slavery through political theory. He sees southerners as "geniuses in the art of evading reality" whose thought was "thrown into fantastic contradictions," and among whom "meaningful thought was practically impossible." [2]

The core of Hartz's analysis is his belief that the United States was from its inception a liberal nation, in the Lockian sense, born of an escape from European oppression, avoiding the European development of feudalism, rooted in majority rule, and embodying the belief, in Tocqueville's words, that citizens are "born equal." The southern intellectuals' attempt to justify slavery within that context failed miserably. Hartz points to the contradictions that emerged in attempting to make the case, such as John C. Calhoun's denunciation of the North's enslavement of the South, while maintaining that God had ordained the enslavement of the Negro. As Hartz notes, "if Calhoun's God ordained the one, how could he have failed to ordain the other?" (pp. 159–60).

The writings of some slaveholding southern apologists were filled with fantastic assertions. Writing in the 1850s, Virginian George Fitzhugh, author of *Sociology for the South* and *Cannibals, All! Or, Slaves Without Masters,* argued that slaves in the South were better cared for than workers in the North, since "only a 'property' right in another man can make one truly care for him." Supposedly, "the 'affection' between slave and master was one of the finest things about Southern life." Fitzhugh proposed the theory that societies around the world would experience an increasing concentration of capital and the consequential "wage slavery" of workers, which would result in a revolution on behalf of slavery (Hartz, pp. 186–87). The level of denial that belief in such statements requires is daunting, given the brutality of the slavery system.

Fundamental to a justification of the system of slavery was a belief in the inferiority of blacks compared to whites. Sadly, these beliefs persist today, as a discussion of the work of some contemporary theorists reveals.

The Denial of Racism

Race and Intelligence

We have seen that various writers have attempted to whitewash the practice of slavery, to argue that it wasn't so bad, and, specifically, that many slaves had better living conditions than free blacks. There are also periodic efforts to lay the blame for the effects of slavery and institutionalized racism on the victims themselves. The most recent such effort is *The Bell Curve* (1994), by the late Harvard psychologist Richard J. Herrnstein and Charles Murray, who is affiliated with the conservative American Enterprise Institute. They argue that the average fifteen-point difference between the IQ scores of blacks and whites is largely genetic in origin. They state further that the existence of a black underclass is due to these IQ differences—not to environmental conditions related to racism—and that attempts at remediation have failed. In the past few years, the denial associated with Herrnstein and Murray's position has helped create an ideology that perpetuates racism.

Bad Science   These intellectual efforts to blame the victims fail when evaluated as science, as various reviewers, such as Harvard biologist Stephen Jay Gould (1994), point out. Since publication of *The Bell Curve,* two volumes of critical analyses have documented the conceptual and methodological inadequacies of the work. In addition, Gould, in his *New Yorker* review, identifies several important problems with the assumptions and the statistical analyses of Herrnstein and Murray.

The standard method of IQ testing Herrnstein and Murray rely on evolved from the IQ tests devised in the 1920s and 1930s. It tends to focus on a narrow range of mathematical and linguistic skills. Psychologist Howard Gardner (1983) has advanced an alternative theory: that individuals have a range of different of types of intelligences that are relatively unrelated to each other. He lists such intellectual aptitudes as linguistic, musical, logical-mathematical, and spatial intelligence, as well as body-kinesthetic and personal intelligence. In his *The Mismeasure of Man* (1981), Gould deals extensively with the logical and mathematical difficulties that arise from uncritically accepting the one-factor theory of intelligence, as Herrnstein and Murray do. Arthur Jensen, an earlier advocate of racial differences in IQ, made the same error. Gould points out that Herrnstein and Murray's argument for average differences in IQ between groups (pp. 234–320) assumes a single factor of intelligence, "Spearman's *g*," which represents only "one mathematical solution among many equivalent alternatives" (Gould 1994, p. 320). Given the evidence for multiple aspects of intelligence, the Herrnstein and Murray argument collapses. It is inappropriate to base significant, and racially biased, public-policy recommendations on the assumption that there is only one type of intelligence and that IQ tests measure it without any social bias.

Herrnstein and Murray also make important statistical errors. They rely on the use of the statistical procedure called multiple regression to test how differences in IQ among individuals predict various social problems, such as school dropouts, crime, and so forth. A serious statistical problem, however, and one important for the interpretation of multiple-regression results, is the issue of *multicollinearity,* or high degree of correlation among predictor variables. If two predictors are highly correlated with one another, say for example, IQ and social class, then the statistical coefficients that estimate these variables' association with the dependent variable, for example, poverty, can be biased. Herrnstein and Murray do note this problem (p. 124) in their explanation of why they use socioeconomic status (SES) and not education as a predictor variable. The problem, however, is that the SES variable they use is also highly correlated with IQ, thus rendering their results impossible to interpret. The regression equations in their Appendix 4 all appear to make this mistake; and nowhere is there a discussion of the intercorrelations among the predictor variables they use—an essential piece of information for understanding their results. The results they report explain only a small proportion of the variation in the problems they point to; and the results themselves are uninterpretable.[3]

But there is more. Although the scholarship of M. D. Storfer (1990) is not widely known, he has done extensive analyses of the relationship of environment and heredity to IQ. If African Americans and whites were, on average, equal in terms of family background and class, it might be possible to make a simple statistical comparison to test the effect of race on IQ. As there are substantial differences in the lives of blacks and whites, however, a researcher needs to control statistically for an entire range of additional variables known to have an effect on the development of intelligence. Some of these variables relate to the disadvantages of black people in a racist society, such as poverty; other variables are family size, birth order, age of parents at the time of birth, and birth weight. Storfer conducted statistical analyses controlling for all these factors and found that the racial differences in IQ that writers like J. P. Rushton, Arthur Jensen, and Herrnstein and Murray attribute to genetic factors simply disappear.

An important related question is the extent to which social remedies for the disadvantaged position of African Americans are doomed to failure because of the purported genetic contribution to lower average intelligence. Herrnstein and Murray argue against remediation. Their argument, however, overlooks substantial evidence that environmental influences upon intelligence are substantial. James R. Flynn's 1987 article in the *Psychological Bulletin* presents data from fourteen countries showing increases in average IQ from five to twenty-five points in a single generation. Animal studies also show that increases in brain mass occur when rats are raised in an enriched environment with toys, play wheels, and so on. The fact that the authors of *The Bell Curve* could so easily overlook important scientific evidence in their single-minded attempt to influence the policy debate on issues relevant to race suggests, at a minimum, the kind of intellectual rigidity characteristic of individuals high in denial.

A central element of Herrnstein and Murray's argument is that environment, as opposed to genetic intelligence, plays only a small role in students' cognitive development and academic achievement. To support their opposition to attempts to equalize opportunities for poor and minority students, they cite the 1966 Coleman Report findings that per-student expenditures on equipment and facilities explained very little of the variance in students' cognitive functioning. They ignore the substantial and numerous problems with the quality of the data and statistical analyses in the Coleman Report; various scholars have identified these problems and, in effect, invalidated its conclusion. Interestingly, the problem is the same one that Herrnstein and Murray themselves make in their own regression analyses. Their repetition of this invalid result supports the conclusion that their ideological position and desire to prove the genetic inferiority of black students have blinded them to legitimate evidence about environmental effects on intelligence and academic achievement.

The core assumption of Herrnstein and Murray's argument is that American society is one of equal opportunity to which African Americans as a group have the same access as whites. As some black people have failed, Herrnstein and Murray reason, the cause must be genetic difference. This classic example of "blaming the victim" overlooks both the emotional burden carried intergenerationally from the legacy of slavery and the decades of racism that have contributed to the development of a racial underclass.

Perhaps the most insidious effect of the persistent argument that blacks are genetically inferior to whites is that a stereotype of inferiority can become a self-fulfilling prophecy. Research published in 1995 by social psychologists Claude Steele and Joshua Aronson found that when taking a standardized test, black students told that it is diagnostic of their ability performed significantly less well than white students. If they were not told that the test is diagnostic, they performed just as well as white students did. The research also demonstrates that the same effect occurs in women and in white males comparing themselves to Asian-Americans.

An anecdotal footnote to the Herrnstein and Murray debate comes from the family of Willie Bosket discussed above. Willie's father was very bright, being the first prisoner in history to be elected to Phi Beta Kappa and to be admitted to graduate school to study for a Ph.D. in sociology. Willie was also very intelligent, having an IQ well above average. Their intelligence, however, did not enable them to succeed; early experiences of abandonment and abuse had too great an impact. Willie's father was abandoned as an infant, and he was in prison for murder when Willie was born. Both were incarcerated off and on from the age of nine. Childhood experiences do matter.

The End of Racism?   The most current contribution of conservative denial to the discussion of racism is Dinesh D'Souza's recent book, *The End* *of Racism* (1995). Its author makes some astonishing claims that are generally unsupported by his arguments or the evidence. One such claim is that "American slavery, like slavery around the world, bore no necessary link to racism" (p. 79) because slavery existed elsewhere in the world, African nations practiced slavery, and "several thousand free blacks and American Indians owned slaves" (p. 75). D'Souza's argument reflects the pervasive denial about American racism we have documented, and he seems unaware of the great body of evidence that confounds his argument.

First, D'Souza fails to understand the way in which brutality and violence are learned and transmitted. He observed that many free blacks who owned slaves had been slaves themselves and that some were very brutal masters. Given the substantial amount of evidence presented in this and earlier chapters about the way violence is repeated across generations, we should not be surprised that former slaves who were brutalized would mistreat others in the same way. This fact in no way discounts the racism of slavery. D'Souza also notes that some free blacks "bought their wives to ensure their good behavior" (p. 77). The sexist exploitation of women by black men does not, however, disprove the racism underlying slavery. Moreover, if U.S. slavery were not in fact racist, whites could have become slaves; but, of course, as D'Souza himself admits, "there was no legal right to enslave whites" (p. 76). Perhaps without recognizing their contradictory effect, his own words substantiate the racist underpinnings of slavery: "The American institution of slavery became driven and maintained by the assumptions of racial superiority" (p. 86).

A central part of D'Souza's argument is that black culture is pathological. In fact, the criminal justice system has played a major role in creating a destructive culture for inner-city youth, a culture that has significant negative consequences for our society. Going to prison has become so common that, for many youths, it is just part of growing up. Anthropologist Felipe Bourgois, author of *In Search of Respect: Selling Crack in El Barrio* (1995), observes that "prison has become one of the central organizing institutions of growing up poor in the inner city, and instead of going to high school, instead of going to college, you go to prison and you learn to survive prison and you learn to become a better criminal in prison" (Hinojosa 1995, National Public Radio).

The conservative denial of racism, the belief that the poor (including African Americans) are poor because of their personal qualities (e.g., low intelligence, laziness, or moral weakness) and not because of centuries of racism, has been successfully communicated to the American public. Public-opinion polls indicate that whites disregard racism as a cause of poverty and believe African Americans are better off than whites, despite clear evidence demonstrating exactly the opposite.

A telephone survey sponsored by the *Washington Post*, Harvard University, and the Kaiser Family Foundation (Morin 1995) found that only 38 percent of whites believed racism to be a significant problem in the United States today, in contrast to 68 percent of blacks. Similarly, only 36 percent of whites believed that "Past and present discrimination is the major reason for the economic and social ills blacks face," while 71 percent of blacks believed this to be the case. The same survey found that 44 percent of whites believed that the average African American is "'just as well off' as the average white person in terms of income." No blacks indicated a belief in this statement. Similarly, a majority (51 percent) of whites believed that the average African American is just as well off as the average white person in terms of jobs"; only 13 percent of blacks agreed with this statement.

These public beliefs are in stark contrast to a study of the Economic Policy Institute written by Jared Burnstein and reported in the *Washington Post* (November 2, 1995). It shows that the gap between the hourly wages of blacks and whites has increased over the past twenty years and that the difference is greater between blacks and whites with a college or graduate degrees than it is for those without such degrees. Consistent with this finding, government statistics indicate that whites, on the average, earn 60 percent more than blacks (Morin 1995). The decline in blacks' wages relative to whites' has occurred even though the average SAT scores of African Americans, relative to whites, have risen over the same period.

What accounts for this denial of racism? In part, our educational system is at fault. James Loewen's well-researched *Lies My Teacher Told Me* (1995) documents the "invisibility of racism in American history textbooks" with a review of twelve popular history textbooks. Although the black experience of slavery is no longer "sugarcoated," Loewen observes that explanations of slavery typically minimize white complicity in establishing and maintaining it and obscure the causes of the Civil War. The textbook *The American Way* writes that southerners fought "for the preservation of their rights and freedom to decide for themselves," not to preserve slavery (p. 186).

Loewen also found that most textbooks repeated the Confederate myth of Reconstruction, that "carpetbaggers" from the North and greedy, incompetent former slaves dominated southern governments until ten years after the war, when federal troops withdrew and white southerners regained power. The reality, he writes, was that "African Americans never took over the Southern states. All governors were white and almost all legislatures had white majorities throughout Reconstruction. African Americans did not 'mess up'; indeed, Mississippi enjoyed less corrupt government during Reconstruction than in the decades immediately afterward" (p. 149).

In addition, while "Republican governments for the most part attempted to govern fairly," they "had to face the continual violence of racist ex-Confederates" (p. 149). Violence of whites against blacks was a central problem for Reconstruction governments. Attacks on the newly freed slaves continued after Reconstruction, especially from 1880 to 1910, the period one historian calls the "nadir of American race relations" (Logan 1970). In the South, legal restrictions against blacks increased everywhere during this period, and lynchings reached an all-time high. Communities in the North as well as those in the South were segregated. Blacks who had played major league baseball in the 1800s were forced out by 1889; black jockeys were banned from the Kentucky Derby after they won fifteen of the first twenty-eight derbies. The racism directed against blacks far exceeded that experienced by other ethnic groups, a reality many textbooks gloss over. Loewen concludes:

When textbooks make racism invisible in American history, they obstruct our already poor ability to see it in the present. The closest they come to analysis is to present a vague feeling of optimism: in race relations, as in everything, our society is constantly getting better. We used to have slavery; now we don't. We used to have lynchings; now we don't. Baseball used to be all white; now it isn't. The notion of progress suffuses textbook treatments of black-white relations, implying that race relations have somehow steadily improved on their own. This cheery optimism only compounds the problem, because whites can infer that racism is over. (p. 163)

The truth is that racism is far from over in the United States.

Racism Today

The reactions to the O. J. Simpson verdict reflect a substantial gap between whites and African Americans on the issue of racism. As we noted above, almost 70 percent of black Americans believe that racism is a problem, as opposed to less than 40 percent of white Americans. For the jurors the issue of domestic violence was clearly subordinate to the issue of police misconduct and racism. There is, unfortunately, substantial evidence of racism in police forces across the United States.

Police Racism   From the post–Civil War period to the present, police have often joined white citizens in attacking and killing blacks. In cities such as Detroit and Atlanta police killings of African Americans only declined when, in recent years, black mayors were elected and greatly increased the percentage of black police officers (Hawkins and Thomas 1991).

Apologists have tried to say that the beating of Rodney King by Los Angeles police officers that was captured on videotape and the overt racism of Mark Furman are isolated examples that are not representative of police forces across the country. However, there is a growing body of evidence for police and law-enforcement abuses. John DeSantis's *The New Untouchables* reports dozens of cases of questionable use of violence and deadly force by law-enforcement officials who suffered little or no consequences as a result. From the beatings of black motorists to the tragic raid on the Branch Davidian compound in Waco, Texas, law-enforcement officials are generally immune from prosecution.

The pervasive nature of police misconduct toward minorities is documented in another recent book, *Beyond the Rodney King Story* (1995), by Charles Ogletree. It is the result of an investigation by the Criminal Justice Institute at the Harvard Law School and the National Association for the Advancement of Colored People. After holding hearings in seven cities around the country, researchers found evidence that black

Americans are more likely to be arrested than whites, often for being insufficiently deferential to the officer. The study found that (1) excessive force has become a standard part of police arrest procedures; (2) physical abuse by police officers is neither unintentional nor unusual; and that (3) verbal harassment and abuse are the most common forms of police misconduct and are standard procedure in many minority communities. The study concludes that racism among a core of police officers is pervasive in this country. Another, earlier study found that many police officers believe that being a minority actually indicates a general propensity to commit a crime (Johnson 1983).

Incarceration of Blacks   There is a widely cited figure that on any given day nearly a third of black men aged 20–29 are either incarcerated, on parole, or on bail awaiting trial. The rate of incarceration of young black men has disproportionately increased in recent years, compared to whites. Why is this? University of Minnesota criminologist Michael Tonry says that the so-called war on drugs is a major cause. Between 1980 and 1990, the proportion of drug offenders in U.S. prisons rose from 22 percent to 40 percent. During the same period, the percentage of blacks among the prison population rose from 39 percent to 53 percent. African Americans are more likely to be apprehended and jailed on drug charges (the percent of blacks arrested on drug charges rose from 24 percent to 40 percent) because much of the dealing in urban black communities is done on the street where arrests are fairly easy to make. All these arrests, however, have not affected the rate of narcotics use, which had been decreasing for the five years before the war on drugs began. Arrests of small-time drug dealers do not, of course, have much impact on the extent of drug use in the country; it is the heads of the drug cartels who make most of the money, and they are much more difficult to apprehend.

The war on drugs has its roots in the punitiveness of American political culture. Americans are ready to punish those who use drugs (although not alcohol or prescription tranquilizers) and those who sell them, regardless of the amount. In August of 1986 a CBS News/*New York Times* poll found that 68 percent of the public would pay more in taxes to build new prisons so that first-time offenders who sold crack or cocaine could be sent to jail. Many Americans see individuals who use drugs as "bad" people who, consequently, must be punished. Yet many studies conclude that drug use and addiction are often a result of abuse experienced in childhood, a life circumstance the drug user did not choose. Drug use is a self-destructive behavior, and addicts need help, as well as no small amount of personal courage, to quit. Small-time users often sell drugs to support their own habit, while some are attracted by the lure of huge profits and try to expand their operations. The frequently heard argument that large drug traffickers are evil because they sell substances that destroy people's lives could just as easily be made of people who sell cigarettes or tobacco products or unsafe cars.

Racism and the Death Penalty   Historical analyses show that black Americans have been subject to the death penalty considerably more often than whites (Wolfgang and Riedel 1973). Between 1930 and 1967, whites committed the majority of murders, but blacks were more likely to be executed for murder. For rape, the disparity was even greater; 89.5 percent of the people executed for rape were people of color (Flowers 1988).

This discrepancy in executions for rape is also associated with the race of the victim. In the same period, a black man who raped a white woman was far more likely to be put to death than one who raped a black woman. In Florida, no white men were executed for raping black women between 1960 and 1964, while 54 percent of black men who raped white women were executed. It is hard to explain this substantial difference as due to anything but racism.

In *Furman* v. *Georgia* (1972) the U.S. Supreme Court ruled capital punishment unconstitutional and found evidence of "arbitrary and discriminatory" sentencing. Following the reinstatement of the death penalty in 1976, the disparity was reduced. From 1977 to 1985, of the fifty people executed, 34 percent were black and 66 percent were white (Flowers 1988). Nevertheless, current statistics show that the race of the victim still greatly influences the application of capital punishment. If the victim is white, the death penalty is imposed significantly more often than it is if the victim is black.

Affirmative Action

Affirmative action, a policy to promote hiring and educational opportunities for people of color and women, was devised in part to remedy past discrimination and in part to discourage future discrimination. In his review of the effect of affirmative-action programs, economist Jonathan Leonard of the Haas School of Business at the University of California, Berkeley, who is also a research associate of the National Bureau of Economic Research, found that "affirmative action has been successful in promoting the integration of blacks into the American workplace." In a direct test of the effect of affirmative action on productivity he found no evidence of adverse effects.[4]

Nonetheless, affirmative action programs have come under attack in recent years. George Bush laid the groundwork for his 1992 presidential campaign with an assault on "quotas" and a refusal to compromise even with moderate senators of his own party on civil rights legislation. In a September 1991 article in *Rolling Stone,* William Greider observed that Bush's behavior amounted to "The Politics of Diversion" and accused him of implicitly encouraging voters to blame their economic troubles on blacks who were purportedly stealing their jobs.

Conclusion

Conservatives have latched onto the arguments in *The Bell Curve* as justification for jettisoning a host of liberal programs such as the School Lunch Program and Head Start. Herrnstein and Murray argue that attempts at improving school performance through such programs are doomed to failure because the programs do not increase IQ; the implicit assumption is that IQ is the only factor that influences success in school. In fact, a recent study of 14,837 eighth graders by University of Michigan researchers Valerie Lee and Susanna Loeb (1995) indicates that an important reason for the "fade out" of Head Start cognitive gains in later years is that children who attend Head Start programs generally end up attending schools of substantially lower quality than children of comparable family and demographic backgrounds. (They defined quality in terms of "social composition, academic rigor, safety, and social relations.") Lee and Loeb concluded that "No matter how beneficial Head

Start was initially for its young participants, such benefits are structurally undermined if students are subsequently exposed to schooling of systematically lower quality" (p. 62). Herrnstein and Murray's argument, which rests on the assumption that the United States is a society of equal opportunity, is therefore demonstrably false.

Moreover, it appears that interventions such as Head Start should occur even earlier. Psychologist Burton White (1994), in "Head Start: Too Little and Too Late," advocates support for programs such as Missouri's New Parents as Teachers, which aids children from birth to three years of age, a period of crucial development.

The attack on such remedial programs is another example of the way denial contributes to a distortion of public policy. Stephen Jay Gould (1981) states eloquently the consequences of using bad science to support a racist ideology: "Few tragedies can be more extensive than the stunting of life, few injustices deeper than the denial of an opportunity to strive or even to hope, by a limit imposed from without, but falsely identified as lying within" (p. 29).

By following the proposals put forth by writers who deny that racism exists in the United States today, those who call for the end of support for teenage mothers and programs like Head Start, for less money for education and more money for prisons, will doom another generation of poor and minority children to poverty and violence. Following these proposals will also contribute to more racism, violence, and social rage. Both black and white families and the arms of government that represent them must take steps to change the way children are raised and deny no longer the negative consequences of physical punishment and emotional abuse.

8

Governmental Violence and Denial

We have seen that white Americans deny the injuries and injustices suffered by African Americans and other people of color, and that certain intellectuals still perpetuate and rationalize racism by arguing that black people are biologically less intelligent than whites. The argument is frighteningly reminiscent of the race theories the Nazis used to justify the extermination of six million Jews and some five million other "undesirables"—gypsies, Poles, handicapped people, and homosexuals.

In this chapter, we first explore some of the ways governments successfully appeal to residual childhood emotions of rage, fear, and shame to gain public support for war and genocide. We then examine how these emotions make it possible for individuals to collaborate with and even participate in atrocities sanctioned by governments. Finally, we look at the way societies deny the long-term consequences of war for both victors and victims and the way that denial can contribute to a cycle of continuing violence.

The Institutionalization of Violence

Powerful psychological forces in the form of anger, shame, helplessness, and fear, together with political, economic, and social factors, contribute to war and genocide. Social scientists commonly dismiss the idea that emotions are important factors in the outbreak of wars, preferring to emphasize what they see as objective economic, historical, and geopolitical factors. This preference is itself a way of denying the role of emotion in history and public policy. As individuals and nations, we want to believe that our behavior is based on rational considerations and not on what we consider the embarrassing, petty hurts of childhood. Although emotions are only a contributing cause—along with many other factors—in the outbreak of wars, their role is a significant one we should not discount. One of the principal ways emotions affect the decision to wage war is through creation of public support for governmental violence.

The Creation of Shared Denial

How do governments seduce the population into military adventures? We argue in earlier chapters that physical punishment in childhood often produces denial of the violence perpetrated by parents and other authority figures and a propensity to project the associated feelings of weakness and shame onto despised outgroups. To the extent that individuals idealize the government and national leaders, as they do the parents who punished them, they will follow leaders' cues to displace their anger onto those defined as enemies of the nation. They can thus maintain their idealization of the parents and denial of the parental misuse of force. As we report in chapter 3, a high level of childhood punishment is associated with support for the use of military force. Other researchers have also found that authoritarians tend to approve of past wars, including the Vietnam War, more often than nonauthoritarians.

In a classic article on the subject, political scientist Murray Edelman (1971) argues that governments attempt to generate a series of public perceptions in support of their actions. These perceptions do not necessarily have anything to do with reality; in fact, they often represent a simplified version of events, if not a deliberate falsification. They include perceptions that

(1) popular views and participation influence political decisions;
(2) governmental leaders are able to cope with issues too complex for the public to understand;
(3) particular groups in the world are evil;
(4) other groups in the world are friendly; and
(5) certain kinds of actions are evil.

The first of these perceptions is quite often false, precisely because governments create public opinion to support their actions as often as their actions reflect it.

One important way government officials create the perception that certain groups are evil—and that others are friendly—is through language. Ronald Reagan, for example, labeled the Soviet Union "the evil empire." Government officials use melodramatic language, which is echoed and often heightened by the media, to present opposing nations as villainous and its own people as virtuous and heroic. Moreover, government and military officials disguise their use of force with antiseptic metaphors, leading the public to perceive both their own and other nations in simplistic ways that encourage the use of force. If the enemy is evil and this moral failing is the source of its actions, then negotiation, after all, is pointless; we have no choice but to fight.

An examination of recent U.S. military actions illustrates how governments' appeals to residual childhood emotions help create public support for the use of force.

Light at the End of the Tunnel

For eight years, from 1964 to 1972, the United States fought a war it never declared. The U.S. government and three of its presidents lied to the American people about the true nature, extent, and purpose of the war. Denial pervaded all aspects of the war effort in Vietnam: from the beginning, when U.S. policymakers painted a heroic image of our fighting men defending the free world against the spread of communism, to the neglect and minimization of the suffering of the veterans who returned from Vietnam alive. The government lied about its actions and motives in Vietnam for the sake of public opinion; later, it entered into a massive denial of the failure of its policy that led to escalation of the war.

There were a number of reasons, including economic and strategic considerations, for U.S. involvement in Vietnam. More private motives apparently also played a role. According to David Halberstam (Schmookler 1988), Kennedy's decision to escalate American involvement in Vietnam from an advisory status to combat was a direct consequence of his disastrous meeting with Khrushchev in Vienna in 1961. Gary Wills alleges that "Khrushchev led him by the nose all during the week and Kennedy was simply on the ropes at the end" (Schmookler, p. 128). Halberstam believes that Kennedy wanted to show Khrushchev he was not the weak, inexperienced young man the Soviet leader thought him. If Halberstam is right, Kennedy's action is a frightening example of the power of personal motives to initiate policies that later take on a life of their own.

Vietnam quickly became a quagmire from which the United States could not extricate itself. Enormous expenditures—two billion dollars a month in 1966, for example—massive bombing, fresh infusions of troops, and a one-sided battle—in which eight times as many North Vietnamese and Vietcong as Americans were reportedly killed—had seemingly little effect on the enemy's motivation and effectiveness. The commitment the United States had already made to the war effort required all of those involved to deny the failure and futility of the effort. As journalist Frances FitzGerald (1972) put it,

In 1968 the job of the American ambassador, the military command, the heads of the aid programs, the CIA operations groups, and their counterparts in Washington, was not to discover if the American effort was morally wrong or doomed to failure, but to make that war effort a success. . . . To admit that the war was excessively destructive or that it was not being won was to admit to personal as well as institutional failure. . . . The circle of self-interest created a complete circle of self-deception that began and ended in the office of the President of the United States. (p. 487)

The U.S. military command, three American presidents, scores of intelligence and diplomatic officers, as well as soldiers in the field in Vietnam had to cope with the conflict inherent in the knowledge that, despite the use of more and more destructive attacks, the war was not being won; nor was there a sign that it ever would be. Further, they had to come to terms with, and justify, the human lives already lost in an ill-conceived war. The enormous investment of troops and resources in Vietnam, induced many to believe that the commitment was justified, that the war was looking better every day, and that it would eventually be won. Government officials rationalized the war to the public in terms of values sacred to Americans: freedom, democracy, self-determination, and the defense against communism.

For its part, the military command gamely produced "kill ratios" day after day and offered them up to journalists in the daily briefings the press dubbed the "Five O'Clock Follies." Because territory won yesterday was often lost again within days or weeks, the body count was the only visible evidence officials could point to to foster the illusion that they were making progress. Yet they were also in the awkward position of having to chart the war's progress in dead bodies without actually acknowledging that people—especially Americans—were being killed.[1] Hence, according to Herr (1977), "the cheer-crazed language of the MACV Information Office, things like 'discreet burst' (one of those tore an old grandfather and two children to bits as they ran along a paddy wall one day, at least according to the report made later by the gunship pilot), 'friendly casualties' . . . 'meeting engagement' (ambush), concluding usually with 17 or 117 or 317 enemy dead and American losses 'described as light'" (p. 240). The very language used by the military denied the reality of death and destruction.

Soldiers faced with the horrors of combat could not fall back on euphemisms and policy abstractions. Although cruder, their strategy was essentially the same as that of the military command: deny the humanity of the dead on both sides. "The living, the wounded and the dead flew together in crowded Chinooks, and it was nothing for guys to walk on top of the half-covered corpses packed in the aisles to get to a seat, or to make jokes among themselves about how funny they all looked, the dumb dead fuckers" (Herr, p. 25).

Many young soldiers who went to Vietnam had doubts about the war from the beginning. Some went because it was the alternative to prison or exile; some felt it was their patriotic duty; and yet others, it seems, went to avoid their parents' disapproval. One of the latter was Tim O'Brien:

I have done bad things for love, bad things to stay loved. Kate is one case. Vietnam is another. More than anything, it was this desperate love craving that propelled me into a war I considered mistaken, probably evil. In college, I stood in peace vigils. I rang doorbells for Gene McCarthy, composed earnest editorials for the school newspaper. But when the draft notice arrived after graduation, the old demons went to work almost instantly. I thought about Canada. I thought about jail. But in the end I could not bear the prospect of rejection: by my family, my country, my friends, my hometown. I would risk conscience and rectitude before risking the loss of love. (O'Brien 1994, p. 52)

Regardless of their reasons for going, when soldiers got there they had to find a way to deal with the fear and grief caused by the things they did and the things they saw done to their friends and comrades. Most simply denied their emotions: "Don't mean nothin," they would say. (As we have seen, complete denial of affect renders all experience meaningless.) Some men came to inhabit a realm in which information was beside the point. Journalist Michael Herr recounts a story told to him by a man who was on his third tour in Vietnam: "'Patrol went up the mountain. One man came back. He died before he could tell us what happened'" (p. 5). There were horrors that no language was adequate to describe. Indeed, the indiscriminate slaughter of both sides in a firefight left soldiers with nothing to say; the conflict that pitted them against each other became meaningless and moot.

People in the federal government came to believe their own rhetoric. What may have started as an attempt to maintain a foothold in Indochina, both for the sake of access to its resources and for its strategic value, seems to have become an ideological matter, a matter of conquering hearts and minds. When it became clear that that goal was impossible to attain, that the South Vietnamese, as well as the North Vietnamese, could not be molded to American cultural images, the government and the military resorted to carpet bombing.

Bush and Panama

For years the Panama Canal has been an important issue for conservatives. They fought fiercely against the Panama Canal Treaty, which turned the operation of the canal over to the Panamanian government, arguing that because the United States had built it, it should retain ownership permanently. When so-called Panamanian strongman Manuel Noriega—who, we later learned, had been on the CIA payroll for years—began showing independence from Washington, he became a potential liability. The Bush administration then began portraying him as a criminal, drug trafficker, and thug—an evil man engaged in evil deeds. After an off-duty American serviceman was killed in Panama, Bush launched Operation Just Cause, an early-morning invasion of Panama, on December 20, 1989. The decisive action to topple Noreiga generated considerable public support. An ABC News poll reported on January 1, 1990, that 80 percent of the public approved of the president's actions. In Panama, as in Vietnam, the U.S. military worked hard to avoid reporting casualties, especially civilian deaths. Noreiga's military and communication headquarters was situated in the middle of a crowded Panamanian slum where thousands of people lived. The U.S. bombing of the headquarters put an enormous number of civilians at risk, yet casualty reports focused on the exact numbers of American soldiers killed and wounded and only occasionally mentioned small numbers of civilian casualties. On December 23, 1989, ABC News reported that 25 U.S. soldiers were killed, 241 were wounded, and 139 Panamanian soldiers were dead. News stories at the time of the invasion and well into January reflected careful management of estimates of civilian deaths. On December 21, at the start of the fighting, the government estimated that 220 civilians had died in the invasion; a week later, the estimate was 210 civilians. Some nongovernment sources were suggesting that there may have been 600 or even nearly 1,000 civilian deaths. On January 5, 1990, ABC reported, again from a nongovernmental source, that "as many as 500 civilians" had died. On January 9 government officials again estimated the number of civilian casualties at 220 but commented that the "estimate may be high" and might include some "rampaging Noriega loyalists" or "out of uniform PDF (Panamanian Defense Force) looters." Finally, on January 12, 1990, American and Panamanian authorities agreed on the official accounting of 202 civilian casualties.

Two months later, on March 20, 1990, ABC reported that an independent panel investigating the invasion was critical of the government's handling of media coverage of the invasion. Dr. Wise of Physicians for Human Rights reported that there were at least 300 civilian deaths, 100 more than the official count. The same news report quoted U.S. Commander Stone commending U.S. forces for an "outstanding job of limiting civilian casualties." But it was all a lie.

A year later, on the eve of the U.S. response to the Iraqi invasion of Kuwait, CBS's "Sixty Minutes" aired a report entitled "Victims of Just Cause," which interviewed workers in charge of unearthing mass graves in Panama. At least four thousand civilians had been killed, and many were buried secretly by U.S. military personnel. This information came too late and was seen by too few people to have a substantial effect on public opinion of Bush's handling of the invasion of Panama. The denial of the real human costs of U.S. actions by the government—facilitated in part by inadequate media coverage—and the denial of Americans who want to believe that the United States behaves justly, resulted in popular support for President Bush and a vast human tragedy.

Operation Desert Storm

The night before the January 15 deadline for the Iraqis to withdraw from Kuwait, PBS aired a round table discussion hosted by Fred Friendly. Among the participants were scholars Fouad Ajami, Gary Sick, and Edward Luttwak, several former diplomats, and such former military and intelligence officers as General John Wickham. The question posed for the participants was, should the U.S. launch an attack immediately after the midnight deadline or wait? And, if so, how long? The discussion was striking in two respects. First, until the very end of the debate, when Gary Sick intervened, none of the participants critically examined the way the question was posed. As Sick pointed out, the question assumed, first, that the United States would attack (although Massachusetts Senator Ted Kennedy, for one, had pointed out that the midnight deadline was only an authorization to use force, not a mandate); second, it assumed that the U.S. would be in position to launch the first strike. It was possible, Sick pointed out, that Saddam Hussein would either attack Israel before the midnight deadline or wait until just after the deadline to give the order to withdraw from Kuwait; he could then argue to his own people that he had stared down the alliance and made his point. The failure of any of the other participants in the discussion to reflect on the way in which the issue was framed reveals a certain cognitive rigidity, an assumption that the United States would attack first and would fight the war on its own terms.

An even more striking aspect of the discussion was the enthusiasm with which several of the participants anticipated a massive air attack on Iraq. General Wickham, for example, spoke with increasing breathlessness about "penetration" of Iraqi air space, about "owning" the air above Iraq, about "cleaning up" on the ground.[2] What was not mentioned, nor reflected in the tone of voice or facial expression of any of the participants, was the actual human consequences of "an air campaign, the likes of which no one has seen in modern times." The whole discussion sounded like nothing so much as a pregame warmup for the Super Bowl.

In August of 1990, many Americans had only a vague awareness of the existence of Kuwait. In response to the Iraqi invasion, the Bush administration created popular support for Operation Desert Shield by portraying Saddam Hussein as the next Hitler. President Bush appeared on national television, raised his fist, and warned Hussein: "A half century ago, our nation and the world paid dearly for appeasing an aggressor who should, and could, have been stopped. We are not going to make the same mistake again."[3] The media supported the portrayal with headlines proclaiming Hussein the "Baghdad Bully." In chapter 6 we saw how U.S. popular support for the use of military force against Iraq was aroused by portraying Iraqis as baby killers who ripped Kuwaiti infants from their incubators and left them to die. We also saw subsequent evidence that the story was exaggerated, or even fabricated, for public relations purposes.

There is no doubt that Saddam Hussein is anything but a humanitarian; yet the U.S. posture toward his regime did not always reflect that view of him. One of the great ironies of the Persian Gulf war, which was not dwelt on at the time by the Bush administration or by the media, was the extent to which the United States had armed Iraq. This foreign policy decision was apparently an attempt to achieve a balance of power against what was then perceived as the greater of two evils—the fundamentalist Islamic regime in Iran. Having armed Saddam Hussein, and having sent a message through the American ambassador to Baghdad that the United States had no interest in an Iraqi incursion against Kuwait, the Bush administration had to do an about-face and convince the American public that Hussein represented a clear danger.

In the immediate aftermath of the Iraqi invasion of Kuwait, the American public was told that Iraqi troops were massing along or, perhaps, only moving toward the Saudi Arabian border, threatening a key U.S. ally in the Gulf. The alleged troop movement provided a rationale for sending U.S. troops to Saudi Arabia. From that point on, the Bush administration enjoyed a distinct advantage; it is far more difficult to recall troops than to send them in the first place. Americans would probably have been unwilling to lose face by a futile, aborted military gesture reminiscent of both Vietnam and the Carter administration's failed attempt to rescue the hostages in Iran.

In crafting the international alliance against Iraq, Bush created the illusion, not only of clear good versus sheer evil, but of an overwhelming international consensus against that evil. None of the moral ambiguities involved received much attention in the press: for example, the fact that Kuwait was ruled by an oil-rich emir who invested heavily in the West and had dissolved his country's national assembly. Instead the American public was presented with a simple story of an innocent sovereign state preyed upon by its much larger neighbor, a dictatorship presided over by a bully.

Once the troops were in Saudi Arabia, the decision about supporting the use of military force in the Gulf was probably moot. It was unlikely that the Bush administration could offer the American public a plausible reason for the costs of sending them there, then bringing them home without taking any action. Nonetheless, Congress and the press discussed the decision at great length, although hardly anyone mentioned that the United States had overlooked numerous similar offenses elsewhere in the world. Access to Kuwaiti oil, the most immediate practical reason for sending troops to the Gulf, was barely discussed.

A seemingly minor, but fascinating, footnote to the Persian Gulf war concerns the ubiquitous yellow ribbons that symbolized support for our troops. As a nation, we seemed to be committed, to a person, to making sure that the troops knew that we would still want them when they came home. Perhaps the yellow ribbon fervor was a reaction to the shameful way we had treated the Vietnam veterans.

Over time, the media's reports of those symbolic ribbons in story after human-interest story helped perpetuate the phenomenon. Yellow ribbons appeared everywhere: on people's lapels and even in the form of decals on the windows of Boston trolley cars. The symbolism helped Americans deny the meaning and consequences of Operation Desert Storm and parochialize the war, focusing attention on the emotions of individuals rather than on the larger issues at stake. Wearing or displaying a yellow ribbon meant that one was righteously in support of "our men and women" in the armed forces. It produced the warm glow of in-group solidarity that effectively obscured the question of what we were doing in the Persian Gulf. Possession of a yellow ribbon comforted individuals and helped them believe their loved ones would come home safely and that ordinary life would resume without moral scars.

U.S. Department of Veteran Affairs psychiatrist Raymond Scurfield (1992) has commented on the "collusion of sanitization and silence" following the Persian Gulf War on the part of political leaders, the military, and the American public. In this, as in other wars, the unspoken agreement hid the human costs of war for both victors and victims.

Scurfield notes, however, that a new method of denial characterized Operation Desert Storm: "The grotesque obsession with body count . . . versus terrain objectives in Vietnam as the yardstick to measure battlefield success was resolved in ODS by an adamant refusal to give *any* body count estimates. Instead, the talk only was about 'ordnance,' and the scorecard of tanks, planes, and other military equipment destroyed. It's as if there weren't any people inside of or operating them" (p. 505). Scurfield points out that, of the tens of thousands of sorties flown, an estimated 80 percent were on target. No one ever mentioned the 100,000 to 200,000 Iraqis killed by the 20 percent that were not on target.

The Fruits of Military Adventure

There is good empirical evidence that similar means of creating such perceptions of a war do indeed promote public support for military action. Political scientists have consistently found that, in the days and weeks immediately following such military adventures, the American president enjoys an increase in popularity. This has been called the rally-round-the-flag effect.[4] It occurs whenever an acute crisis in foreign affairs involving a threat to U.S. security or interests is communicated directly to the public by the president, in a television speech or, in earlier days, in a live radio address. To produce the effect, the president must communicate the threat himself and take decisive action against it—usually in the form of military force. The crisis also has to be remote from the everyday experience of most Americans. When these conditions exist, the president's approval ratings increase markedly, and he enjoys a "halo" effect reflected in increased approval for other, unrelated policies.

We have seen how Bush portrayed Manuel Noreiga and, subsequently, Saddam Hussein, as evil men committing evil deeds. Doing so won him popular support for the invasion of Panama and for Operation Desert Shield. Bush's approval rating in February of 1989 was at 60 percent. A year later, in January of 1990, after the invasion of Panama, the rating hit 75 percent, only to drop to an all-time low of 58 percent by July of that year. However, within three weeks, between July and August of 1990, Bush's approval ratings rose nearly 20 percentage points to an all-time high of 77 percent—just after he ordered U.S. troops to Saudi Arabia in response to the Iraqi invasion of Kuwait.

The rally-round-the-flag effect is short-lived, as Bush learned in the 1992 campaign. In his case, domestic economic problems meant that, despite a seemingly successful war, he lost the presidency to Clinton. Before that, though, he had launched a war that won the approval of nearly 90 percent of the American public (*New York Times*, March 8, 1991).

Clinton and Haiti

In September of 1994, President Clinton had to deal with a situation in Haiti similar to the one Bush had faced in Panama. A military strongman, Raoul Cedras, had toppled a popularly elected civilian leader, Juan Bertrand Aristide and was challenging the United States to do something about it. After threatening action for months, Clinton finally had troops in the air on their way to an invasion of Haiti; but he aborted the military action in favor of a diplomatic settlement that potentially saved the lives of many U.S. military personnel and Haitians.

Clinton didn't take advantage of the rallying effect by choosing the highly dramatic alternative of military action, or by making use of evidence that Cedras, like Noriega, was involved in drug trafficking and thuggery. And he paid a price in public support. Instead of invading Haiti, as Bush had done in Panama, he sought the more complex path of negotiation and democracy-building. According to an ABC News report on September 26, 1994, his approval rating stood at 55 percent prior to the aborted invasion; it decreased to only 45 percent after he called off the invasion.

A comparison of Panama and Haiti show the risks a president takes when he tries not to deny the reality of the consequences of military actions, particularly for the innocent civilians who are so often the casualties. By avoiding the quick, simple, and, to the public, melodramatically satisfying use of military force against a demonized enemy, Clinton's popularity suffered. But lives were saved, and the pursuit of freedom and democracy was advanced.

The rally-round-the-flag effect suggests that the public can be seduced into war by political authorities who demonize the enemy and offer it the opportunity to displace anger onto despised out-groups. In the context of war and other acts of government-sanctioned violence, individuals can be induced, not only to support the use of military force, but also to participate in war, torture, and genocide. The foundation for the willingness to harm others in this context is, we believe, repressed feelings of rage, shame, and helplessness.

Participation in Government-Sanctioned Violence

How could the Nazis have freely slaughtered millions of Jews while the greater part of the German nation, as well as America and the other allies, stood by and allowed it to happen? It was the Nazis themselves, at Nuremberg, who gave us a clue to their own behavior: they claimed steadfastly that they had only been obeying orders. So did Lieutenant Calley and his men.

To understand why, and how, people can obey orders to injure others, social psychologist Stanley Milgram (1963) devised a set of now-famous studies. He recruited subjects through newspaper ads for a study of the "effect of punishment on human learning." They were assigned to work in pairs, with one person playing the role of the learner and the other the role of the teacher. In fact, the learner was an actor hired by Milgram to play the part of a 47-year-old accountant with a history of heart problems.

Subjects were instructed to administer increasingly severe electric shock, up to 450 volts, for each mistake the learner made on a test of recall for paired words. During the procedure, the learner was out of sight inside a closed cubicle. He was not actually shocked, but Milgram had prepared a tape recording of his voice so that when subjects pressed the switch to administer 120 volts, they heard the learner shout that the shocks were becoming too painful. At 150 volts, the learner demanded to be let out of the experiment; at 180 volts, he cried out that he could no longer stand the pain; at 300 volts, he screamed, refused to participate any further, and pounded on the wall of the cubicle to get out. Past 300 volts, the learner no longer responded at all; there was nothing but silence from the cubicle (remember that subjects had been led to believe that the learner suffered from a heart condition). In each instance the teacher was told to regard no reply at all as an incorrect response and, at intervals, to administer shocks up to 450 volts.

Before Milgram began the study, he surveyed a group of forty psychiatrists at a leading university medical school and asked them to predict how humans would behave in this situation. They conjectured that the average person would refuse to continue after administering a shock of 120 volts but acknowledged that a few "psychopathic" or "sadistic" people might go beyond that point. They believed that only a very small minority would actually administer 450 volts of electricity to a fellow human being. What Milgram actually found was that the majority of subjects, fully 65 percent, obeyed orders to administer 450 volts.

The subjects in Milgram's study were not threatened; nor were there any negative consequences for disobeying. They obeyed in spite of what Milgram described as obvious signs of emotional distress: they bit their lips, they sweated profusely, they wrung their hands—but they obeyed. Why? Variations of the original study have delineated the conditions under which most people will obey orders to harm another person. The key variable that predicts obedience is the presence of a legitimate authority figure; but the status of the authority figure is also important. Milgram obtained a higher level of obedience from a study conducted on the grounds of Yale university by an experimenter who was identified as a Yale professor and wore a white lab coat than when an unidentified researcher operated out of a storefront in Bridgeport, Connecticut. Milgram also found (1974) that obedience depended in part on the physical proximity of the teacher to the learner: when the victim was in clear view, subjects were more hesitant to obey. They were even less willing to obey when they had to hold the learner's hand down on a shock pad to administer the electric shock.

Milgram's research was important because it demonstrated just how far people will go—in a nonmilitary situation—toward harming another human being, and how little coercion is necessary to convince them to hurt him or her.

Replications of his study performed in a dozen countries around the world have shown that Germans are no more likely to be obedient toward authority than Americans, Italians, Jordanians, Spaniards, and many other national groups.[5] Although obedience rates in different countries vary somewhat, what seems most important is that, in all of the countries studied, key variations in the way the study is done produce comparable changes in behavior. For example, when a dissenting ally (an extra subject who refuses to obey) is present, rates of obedience decrease sharply in all the countries studied. This finding has important implications for breaking through denial (discussed in chapter 10); the support of just one other person makes it much more likely that an individual will resist obeying such orders. Moreover, in all the studies simply reminding subjects in advance of their personal responsibility—by telling them that the choice of the level of shock to administer is theirs, whatever the experimenter might tell them—has a dramatic effect: under these conditions virtually no one obeyed the order to deliver 450 volts. This reminder, it seems, reduces subjects' level of denial about what they are doing.

Milgram's findings are generally taken to mean that under the appropriate conditions many human beings will follow destructive orders. However, certain individuals are more susceptible to pressure than others. Elms and Milgram (1966) found that authoritarians are more likely than the average person to obey orders to harm another person, while Robert Altemeyer (1981) reported that, in a study similar to Milgram's, authoritarians playing the teacher role administered more intense shocks to a learner who made mistakes than nonauthoritarians did.

We have seen that authoritarians' denial of the pain of childhood abuse leads to glorification of the punitive parents and uncritical adoration of other authority figures. It is also likely to produce overreliance on external controls on behavior. According to Merelman (1969), children whose behavior is strictly controlled by external sanctions have no opportunity to develop their own internalized sense of morality. Authoritarians displace their anger toward parents onto substitute targets defined by the prejudices of parents and their society. Given Alice Miller's very convincing evidence of the severity and harshness of child rearing in Germany (though not limited to that nation), it is perhaps not surprising that Germans were able, psychologically, to stand by and do nothing when a previously stereotyped out-group, the Jews, were demonized and slaughtered.

Contemporary research documenting the correlates of authoritarianism is not encouraging when it comes to their willingness to obey orders to harm others or go along with governmental violence (Altemeyer 1988). In chapter 4, we reported on a study by Altemeyer and Hunsberger (1992) that found individuals who scored high on measures of authoritarianism more willing than nonauthoritarians to endorse a law outlawing radical political movements and to help the government track down, torture, and even execute radicals. The findings held even when the researchers controlled for subjects' educational levels.

Apparently individuals who are high on the authoritarianism scale are also not bothered by unjust or illegal acts committed by government officials; for example, many of them supported Richard Nixon despite Watergate. They are also more likely than nonauthoritarians to agree that "democracy gives people too much freedom" and to support repeal of the Bill of Rights. Further, the accumulated research has shown that authoritarians are much more accepting of a right-wing government abusing power than of a left-wing government doing so. American authoritarians condemn an act of aggression by the former Soviet Union against one of its neighbors more harshly than they condemn the same act committed by the American government; Russian authoritarians, not surprisingly, feel just the opposite.

Many authoritarians are "equal-opportunity bigots"—that is, they harbor prejudice against a wide range of groups, including African Americans, Hispanics, homosexuals, feminists, Japanese, Jews, and Arabs—and tend to support the myth of white supremacy. All this raises the disturbing possibility that authoritarians may be vulnerable to extreme forms of governmental violence aimed at other nations and groups.

Governmental Torture

Stanley Milgram (1963) argues that individuals who come from a family or social background that encourages obedience will follow the orders of an authority to hurt someone else if the rewards associated with obedience outweigh the stress of obeying. Such rewards might include social approval, economic gain, and status; the associated stress might be, for example, the emotional distress of causing another person physical pain.

Janice Gibson and Mika Haritos-Fatouras (1986) look at the effect of these factors and raise an issue that is clearly important for understanding the Holocaust and other instances of genocide and governmental violence: How can people take part in government-sanctioned actions in which they have to harm other people directly, face-to-face? We saw that Milgram's subjects were loath to obey an order to harm someone when they had to hold the person's hand down on a shock pad. His theory would predict, therefore, that hitting, shooting, or bayoneting another human being up close and witnessing the victim's agony would produce stress and that individuals would be less likely to obey authority under these conditions.

Gibson and Haritos-Fatouros shed some light on this question in a study of twenty-one soldiers in the Greek Army Police Corps (ESA) who were tried in Athens in 1975 when the military regime was overthrown. These men had been torturers in the military police from 1967 to 1974. The researchers relied for their conclusions in part on the soldiers' testimony at their trials and in part on interviews they conducted with sixteen of the twenty-one men.

Nothing in the background of these men suggested any propensity for violence; they had no history of previous psychiatric disorders or delinquent behavior. What distinguished the men chosen for the assignment of "warder," or torturer, was their physical strength (an obvious requirement) and their political beliefs. All were anticommunists and came from families with a rigid commitment to anticommunism. Beyond that, they were chosen from the larger pool of Army inductees for their ability to "keep your mouth shut" and be "their man"—meaning that the officers could trust them to obey blindly—characteristics associated with high levels of authoritarianism. The subsequent training the soldiers received was also an important part of their willingness to torture prisoners.

During the course of basic training, the soldiers were flogged, kicked, punched, cursed, and forced to run until they collapsed. At the end of the training, they were required to swear allegiance to their commander, on their knees. In another preparation for their assignment as torturers, the men were forced to watch as superiors beat prisoners and then to administer an occasional blow themselves. Finally, groups of recruits were required to participate in beating prisoners together.

There were powerful sanctions for disobeying orders to torture prisoners, including the threat that if they failed to inflict sufficient pain, they would themselves be tortured. Officers constantly harassed them and threatened them with punishment for disobedience as well as encouraging them to spy on fellow recruits and report any who disobeyed orders.

Simultaneously, the senior officers glorified the ESA, told initiates how lucky they were to be among the strongest, most important group supporting the regime, and let them know that they were essentially exempt from ordinary morality. In their roles as ESA soldiers they could act with impunity, even against a superior officer if they suspected he was disloyal to the regime.

The sense of belonging to a special, elite group was further encouraged by the language used in the ESA. In daily lectures on the dangers of communism, the men heard their victims referred to as "worms" that had to be "crushed." Various methods of torture were referred to with euphemisms: a "tea party" was an ordinary beating by a group of men using their fists; whereas a "tea party with toast" included the use of clubs to strike victims.

Finally, they were rewarded for their obedience. Members of the ESA were judged by a more relaxed set of standards than ordinary Army soldiers: they were allowed to wear their hair long, to leave camp without permission, to use military cars for their own purposes. They also received free restaurant meals and the promise of job placement after their military service was over.

Gibson and Haritos-Fatouros explain the ability of these men to torture other human beings, day in and day out for seven years, in terms of two elements of the training. First, they note that recruits were gradually introduced to the full horrors of torture. Second, their superiors made sure that the rewards associated with obedience outweighed the stress. Nonetheless, it seems hard to imagine that their membership in an elite group, relaxed discipline, free meals, and so forth could have been sufficient to overcome the strain of what these men had to do to victims every day.

The U.S. Marines

Gibson and Haritos-Fatouros point out that U.S. Marine recruits, like the Greek military police, are subjected to arduous basic training. They are completely isolated from families, friends, and society while being introduced to a new set of rules and values. They are subjected to constant harassment and verbal abuse, told that they are nothing, worthless, and so forth. They undergo brutal physical training including forced marches and runs that, combined with sleep deprivation, leave them too exhausted to think clearly about the values they are being taught. The slightest infraction is punished by additional hours of grueling calisthenics and loss of "privileges," such as food and sleep. They are taught to refer to "the enemy" with derogatory names and forced to scream chants and songs glorifying killing as they march or run.

Despite having been told over and over how worthless they are, recruits who survive the training are welcomed into a special, elite group. Their officers glorify the Marine Corps and make recruits feel special and above the law and ordinary morality because they have "made it"; that is, they have proven themselves by withstanding the abuse, which is made to seem an achievement, a sign of their worthiness and toughness.

We suspect that an important element, perhaps the key to creating a torturer, as well as a Marine, has to do with the systematic destruction of personal identity and self-esteem and their replacement by a new, heightened sense of self-esteem based on toughness. Recruits are, in effect, first broken and then offered a "better" self as a Marine or an ESA officer in exchange for their former identity. They are led to believe that they are acceptable within this elite society precisely because they were able to withstand the brutality of their initiation.

Exactly the same process was used to produce SS officers in the Third Reich. They were subjected to brutalization in the course of being socialized into the SS, required to pledge their personal loyalty to Hitler, and exempted from ordinary morality by becoming part of an elite based on hardness and obedience.

After the war, psychiatrists who had the opportunity of examining top SS officers involved in committing mass killings found no signs of mental disorder that might explain their behavior. What they did find was that most of the SS officers studied had been beaten frequently in childhood by authoritarian fathers. One study found that members of the SS scored significantly higher on a measure of authoritarianism than did regular German Army troops.[6]

All these examples of military training have parallels with the experiences of children in physically and or mentally abusive families. Such children are attacked, their wills broken, their self-esteem destroyed with blows, slaps, insults, and worse, by parents who value their own toughness and no-nonsense approach to discipline. Like the recruits, children are often required to deny the pain and grief they feel and to "toughen up," stop "whining" and come to believe that "it wasn't that bad." In adulthood, they often express admiration for their parents, along with a curious sense of pride in the amount of mistreatment they were able to withstand.

For a large segment of the world's population, childhood mistreatment is also a mode of initiation into an elite society: adulthood, specifically adult membership in a particular in-group based on ethnic or national identification, race, religion, and so forth. Adults raised this way can be insensitive to the harm they cause others because their sense of identity is based on their ability to be tough, unsentimental, and capable of surviving pain and mistreatment. They cannot empathize with their victims' suffering because they have to deny their own childhood suffering and its continued pain and grief. They cannot back away from treating others harshly because doing so would make them "soft," "soft on crime," "soft on communism," a weakling and therefore despicable to themselves. Their victims' pain is also bound to be a source of rage, because it reminds them of their own helplessness, the weak childhood self that was despised by their parents and has been disavowed. Hitler apparently understood this all too well. He once said, *"Der Jude sitzt immer in uns"* (loosely translated, "You are your own Jew").[7]

Children who are mistreated grow up to cling to the approval of authorities, who often enough provide them with both the opportunity and the rationalization for taking out their anger and self-hatred on others, particularly others who are perceived as weak and bad. In extreme cases, the result is genocide.

Eradication of the Sickness Within

According to Markusen (1991), ours has been the deadliest century in history. Besides the Holocaust, we have seen genocide perpetrated against the Armenians by the Turks, against the Tutsi by the Hutu, as well as "ethnic cleansing" among the peoples of the former Yugoslavia, and the mass murders of their own people by the Khmer Rouge.

Perhaps the single most influential theory of genocide was developed by psychologist Robert Jay Lifton.[8] In his model, Lifton sees genocide as the outcome of a process consisting of three steps: (1) psychohistorical dislocation, (2) totalistic ideological response, and (3) violent victimization. *Psychohistorical dislocation* occurs during periods when there is rapid breakdown of the social and political structures that have provided a group its sense of security. Such periods—whether of rapid social or economic change or of wartime—leave people angry, confused, and insecure. They attempt to cure this dislocating "illness" or meaninglessness with totalistic ideologies that promise to restore the lost sense of meaning and right their dislocated world. Such ideologies are invariably based in rigid, absolutist thinking. Although their content differs, such ideologies have certain features in common: for example, demands for purity within the group, reliance on pseudoscientific rationalizations for controlling others' behavior, and the premise that it is acceptable to eliminate those perceived as impure.

All these features are readily identifiable as characteristics of National Socialism, as well as of Stalinism. Hitler's notion of a cure for Germany's post–World War I woes involved the vision of a superrace of "pure" Aryans rationalized by pseudoscientific race theories. Stalin's campaign of mass murder, on the other hand, was based on the demand for ideological purity.

Genocidal killing as the "cure" for the illness of ideological impurity holds out the promise that, when the impure are no longer in our midst, old ways of understanding the world and feeling secure will be restored and revitalized. But, Lifton points out, the purification can never be complete; genocidal campaigns often take on a crazed fury in which more and more victims are sought and in which the category of appropriate victims continually expands.

The ever-expanding nature of genocide, as well as its tendency to become self-defeating, to turn back on and devour the very group it was intended to purify and protect, can be understood on an individual, psychological level as well as on a sociopolitical level. We argue above that socialization into denial requires individuals to endure pain and humiliation stoically and give up the true self for the promise of a better, exalted identity based on toughness. That socialization requires individuals to disavow their human needs for comfort, protection, and love, as well as human experiences of weakness, fear, and sadness. Such feelings and needs cannot, however, be simply eradicated by fiat; when they threaten to reemerge, they must be projected onto despised out-groups.

This is the mechanism, we believe, by which individuals come to see the "illness" or "cancer" threatening them as outside themselves and inside the groups despised by society. Projecting one's own disavowed feelings and needs offers the promise that a complete cure is possible simply by eradicating those groups. Yet, no matter how many Jews or Armenians or Tutsis die, the nagging feeling of illness remains, and so does the compulsion to go on killing. The reason is that the infection is within: it is nothing less than the despised childhood self. Just as individuals, in extreme cases, forfeit their lives through suicide in order to kill that despised self, nations engineer their own destruction to accomplish the same collective goal.

Genocide can be understood as an extreme form of governmental violence with multiple determinants. The systematic brutalization of children in the name of discipline, and the denial of that brutality, produces adults who carry within themselves residual rage, helplessness, humiliation, and despair that can be the seeds of mass destruction.

Denial of Governmental Violence

War and genocide often occur while the world community does nothing to stop them, in effect, denying their existence. Denial in this context may protect the world community from taking in a reality of massive destruction too overwhelming and painful to face. It may also blunt the impact of human tragedy in cases in which nations choose not to intervene. Denial in the aftermath of war and genocide functions to ward off pain, to protect nations from shame and guilt, and to serve political purposes. To illustrate some of these functions we examine three instances of denial of war and genocide in this century.

Genocide in Rwanda
In a little over three months in the late spring and early summer of 1994, eight hundred thousand Tutsi citizens—75 percent of the Tutsi population of Rwanda—were massacred by their Hutu compatriots (Gourevitch 1995). The genocide was orchestrated and encouraged by the government

after the president, who was a Hutu, was killed when the plane he was traveling in was shot down.

The ferocity and sadism of the killing is difficult to contemplate. In one province near the Tanzanian border, over a thousand Tutsis were rounded up and taken to a church where the killers hacked at them with machetes all day. In the evening the killers immobilized those who were still alive by severing their Achilles tendons and went home to have a meal and sleep before returning to finish off the survivors.

A number of reasons have been given for the genocide in Rwanda, including the traditional enmity between a privileged elite, the Tutsis, and a large oppressed majority, the Hutus. But there were apparently psychological reasons as well. Phillip Gourevitch quotes the vice-president of the Rwandan National Assembly, who described Rwandan culture as "a culture of fear" (p. 82). A Kigali lawyer noted that "Conformity is very deep, very developed here. . . . In Rwanda an order can be given very quietly" (p. 84). In some cases, the orders the Hutu population obeyed were anything but quiet or subtle. Radio announcers broadcast orders to kill and even "reminded listeners to take special care to disembowel pregnant victims" (p. 80).

Richard Mollica, a Boston psychiatrist who pioneered the treatment of Southeast Asian refugees with post-traumatic stress disorder, offers an even starker explanation. He claims that most atrocities in wartime and genocidal campaigns are committed by young males. Gourevitch quotes Mollica as saying that "Young males are really the most dangerous people on the planet, because they easily respond to authority and they want approval" (p. 84). In light of the research findings we reported in chapter 3, it is a disturbing thesis. We might refine it somewhat: young males who have themselves been the victims of brutality—in the form of childhood abuse, social and political oppression, and past atrocities—and who are socialized to deny the true source of their anger and direct it outward against a scapegoat, are the most dangerous people on the planet.

According to Gourevitch, in the aftermath of the killing, the Hutu majority denied the genocide, and the media colluded in that denial. In wire-service accounts of recent attacks by the current Tutsi government against Hutu forces, the former perpetrators of genocide are described as "Hutu rebels," according them the same moral status as the former "Tutsi rebels." The international community allowed the genocide in Rwanda to occur, despite the fact that, according to one western military source interviewed by Gourevitch, "a few thousand soldiers with tanks and big guns could have knocked out the radio, closed off Rwanda's main roads, and shut down the genocide in one or two days" (p. 92).

The Clinton administration, Gourevitch notes, joined in the refusal to acknowledge what was happening in Rwanda: "For a time, in June, 1994, as the killing continued in Rwanda, the Clinton Administration instructed its officials to avoid calling it a genocide, although the possibility that 'acts of genocide may have occurred' was acknowledged. 'There are obligations which arise in connection with the use of the term [genocide],' Christine Shelly, a State Department spokeswoman, explained at the time" (p. 91). The Clinton administration, it seems, would not call the slaughter of three-fourths of the Tutsi population genocide because it did not want to act to stop it. The avoidance of labeling the killings *genocide,* while admitting that 'acts of genocide may have occurred,' is another example of the use of language to serve the purposes of minimization and denial. How can "acts of genocide" occur in the absence of genocide? The most chilling passage in Gourevitch's account of the Rwandan genocide is a conversation he had with an American military intelligence officer in Rwanda (p. 91); the man's comments may be a clue to the failure of the international community to act.

"I hear you're interested in genocide," the man told Gourevitch. "Do you know what genocide is?"
I asked him to tell me.
"A cheese sandwich," he said. "Write it down. Genocide is a cheese sandwich."
I asked him how he figured that.
"What does anyone care about a year-old cheese sandwich?" he said. "Genocide, genocide, genocide. Cheese sandwich, cheese sandwich, cheese sandwich. Who gives a shit? . . . Hey, just a million Rwandans."

The failure of the international community to intervene in Rwanda raises the question of whether other nations ignore or deny the occurrence of genocide because of their own ethnocentrism or racism. In fact, the denial of the Holocaust that is rampant in some circles seems to be related to a desire to revive fascism as a support for the ethnocentric, anti-Semitic, and racist attitudes of the far right.

Denial of the Holocaust

Deborah Lipstadt, in her *Denying the Holocaust: The Growing Assault on Truth and Memory* (1993), documents the denial of the Holocaust occurring in America, Britain, France, and many other countries. This assault on truth is supported by increasingly sophisticated ploys to clothe denial in pseudointellectual garb and to claim for it the status of an "alternative viewpoint." As Lipstadt points out, when it comes to the Holocaust, there is no alternative viewpoint.

She argues that Holocaust denial has become a tool radical right–wing groups in a number of countries, including the United States and Britain, use to try to resurrect and whitewash fascism for their own purposes. If they can remove the stain of genocide from fascism, they can revive it as a viable political philosophy that supports their hatred of racial minorities within their own borders. There is, for example, a vigorous movement to deny the Holocaust within the American far right. David Duke, a former leader of the Ku Klux Klan, was elected to the Louisiana legislature in the late 1980s and went on to win 40 percent of the vote in a contest for the U.S. Senate. He has called the Holocaust a "historical hoax" and claimed that the greatest Holocaust was "perpetrated on Christians by Jews" seeking "tremendous financial aid" for the state of Israel and "immun[ity] from criticism" (Lipstadt, p. 5).

Doubt about the Holocaust, however, is not limited to the extreme far right. More mainstream American politicians have also voiced it. Lipstadt notes that in his syndicated column Patrick Buchanan argues, in her words, that "it was physically impossible for the gas chamber at Treblinka to have functioned as a killing apparatus because the diesel engines that powered it could not produce enough carbon monoxide to be lethal" (p. 6). The evidence he offers in support of this contention was the fact that passengers in a train stuck in a tunnel in Washington, D.C. in 1988 were not harmed, even though the train was emitting carbon monoxide fumes. Buchanan has also decried what he refers to as the "so-called Holocaust Survivor Syndrome," which involves "group fantasies of martyrdom and heroics" (p. 6). In 1992, during the Republican primary campaign, Buchanan refused to retract these comments and, Lipstadt argues, the American media largely declined to challenge him.

The "evidence" cited by Holocaust deniers is a thin tissue of lies, disingenuous twisting of the truth, and paranoid conspiracy theories. For example, Arthur R. Butz, a professor of electrical engineering at Northwestern University and author of *The Hoax of the Twentieth Century,* ingeniously explains the extensive documentation of the atrocities committed by the Nazis. Lipstadt wrote that he thinks that "the key to perpetrating the hoax was the forging of massive numbers of documents, an act committed with the complicity of Allied governments. . . . Hundreds of trained staff members were sent to Europe in the immediate aftermath of the war. . . . Without being discovered by anyone, they created reports by Einsatzgruppen commanders listing the precise cities in which massacres had been conducted and the exact numbers . . . who had been killed" (Lipstadt, p. 127). Earlier, another American "scholar," Austin J. App, a professor of English at LaSalle College, argued that the Holocaust was obviously a hoax because not all the Jews were exterminated. The legendary efficiency of the Nazis being what it was, had they decided to exterminate the Jews, "they would have done so—they had five years to do it in" (p. 93). The inanity of these arguments is exceeded only by the contention of American Nazi leader George Lincoln Rockwell that the six million Jews supposedly killed actually hid out in the United States and "later died happily and richly in the Bronx, New York" (p. 66).

Along with attempts to explain away the incontrovertible evidence, there is a curious tendency among those who deny the Holocaust to admire the perpetrators and deplore any sign of guilt or shame on their part. Lipstadt writes that Harry Elmer Barnes, once a respected historian, "found West Germany's relationship with the State of Israel particularly galling. He was nonplussed by a speech given by the president of the West German Bundestag in Israel in 1962 in which he acknowledged Germany's wrongdoings and asked for forgiveness for the Holocaust. Barnes characterized the speech as 'subserviency' and 'almost incredible grovelling'" (p. 80). This tendency to side with the strong and to glorify power and toughness is, of course, one of the primary characteristics of the authoritarian personality.

Holocaust deniers also blame its victims and exhibit a furious contempt for their suffering. Butz, Lipstadt notes, declares that it was the Germans and Austrians who were the Holocaust's real victims. In his book, he decries what he regards as the "hysterical yapping about the six million" human beings slaughtered, arguing that the gas chambers were nothing but "propaganda fantasies", "garbage", and "tall tales" (cited in Lipstadt, p. 125). There is a curiously aggrieved tone underlying much of this literature, a creeping note of self-pity and envy, along with cynicism about the extent of the Jews' suffering. As Lipstadt notes, many of the deniers complain that, while it is true Jews were held in Auschwitz and other camps, they lived there "'with all the luxuries of a country club,' including a swimming pool, dance hall, and recreational facilities" (p. 23). (Remember Patrick Buchanan's complaint about the "so-called Holocaust Survivor Syndrome" involving "group fantasies of martyrdom and heroics"?)

We have argued that genocide is fueled, in part, precisely by the psychological threat posed by the victims—the threat of becoming aware of one's own weakness and pain. Moreover, adults who have been brutalized and silenced in childhood—and whose protest has been bought off with a false sense of self-esteem based on being tough and stoic—are bound to feel aggrieved when they see victims, like those of the Holocaust, whose suffering is acknowledged and who are afforded the decency of being believed and taken seriously. The aggrieved, self-pitying tone of much of this literature sounds very much like a child demanding his own share of attention for the suffering he has experienced and being unwilling to allow others validation of their pain until his own is recognized.

It is tempting to dismiss the literature of Holocaust denial as too idiotic to pose a real threat. Yet, there are reasons to take it seriously. First, a lie does not have to be plausible or even rational to serve its primary purpose: in this case justification of the prejudices of neo-nazi and white supremacist groups. Further, as Lipstadt points out, Holocaust deniers have become more sophisticated in their approach, couching their denial in mock-intellectual and pseudoscientific trappings. For example, there is "engineer" Fred A. Leuchter, who conducted "tests" to detect residues of gas in the chamber at Auschwitz. In the anti-Semitism trial of Ernst Zundel in Canada, in which Leuchter testified for the defense, the prosecution established that Leuchter has a bachelor of arts, not sciences, from Boston University and that his lack of scientific qualifications is only equalled by his ignorance of history.

Nonetheless, Holocaust deniers have managed to gain ground by making a disingenuous appeal to "fairness" to gain a hearing for their fabrications. Lipstadt relates her own experience with television talk show producers who invited her to appear on their programs to debate their "alternative viewpoint" with Holocaust deniers.

Denial of the Vietnam War

Denial of the Holocaust is shocking in the brazenness with which its perpetrators lie, make up "facts," and insult and denigrate a people who were subjected to a campaign of genocide. Denial of the Vietnam war takes a more subtle form. In his *Lies My Teacher Told Me* (1995), James Loewen details the way in which recent problematic history disappears from the memory of a nation by excluding it from secondary school history textbooks. Whereas teenagers in German schools are required to study World War II, American teenagers receive very little education about Vietnam.

Comparing the books' treatments of the Vietnam war and the War of 1812, Loewen found that they devoted the same amount of space to both, even though "most textbook authors don't know what to make of the War of 1812 and don't claim any particular importance for it" (p. 235).

Loewen notes that high school history textbooks obscure Vietnam not only by devoting little space to it but also by excluding the most provocative and memorable photographic images of the war. They also ignore completely the issues involved—such as why the United States fought in Vietnam—and omit mention of some of the most troubling aspects of the war, such as the My Lai massacre. Publishers of these books choose inoffensive, bland photographs, such as the troops cheering President Johnson, and fail to include images that are widely familiar to those who lived through the war years: for example, the one showing a screaming, terrified little girl fleeing naked from a napalm attack or the one of a Buddhist monk protesting against the South Vietnamese government by incinerating himself on a Saigon streetcorner.

The authors of high school texts are equally cautious in treating conflicting views of how the war originated and how the United States became involved in it; in fact, they simply ignore those questions altogether.

One text Loewen reviewed noted only that, "Later in the 1950s, war broke out in South Vietnam" (p. 243). Frances FitzGerald, the journalist who wrote one of the most penetrating, detailed accounts of Vietnam, *Fire in the Lake* (1972), comments of the high school texts she reviewed, "Since it is really quite hard to discuss the war and evade all the major issues, their Vietnam sections make remarkable reading" (p. 242).

Loewen writes, "the [recent past] is our most important past, because it is not dead but living-dead. Its theft by textbooks and teachers is the most wicked crime schools perpetrate on high school students, depriving them of perspective about the issues that most affect them" (p. 246).

The Price of Governmental Violence

Government-sanctioned violence—whether war, genocide, torture, or the sort of excessive force used in the U.S. government's raid on the cult compound in Waco, Texas—carries a fearful price, not only for its victims, but also, ultimately, for the perpetrators.

These forms of governmental violence take their toll, in three principal ways: First, they cause trauma and its negative psychological consequences among both victors and victims. That trauma is transmitted to the next generation in the form of, for example, emotional disconnection and physical violence. Second, they model violence and implicitly sanction personal violence among citizens. Finally, they may radicalize segments of the population in violent opposition to the government, as seems to have been the case in the Oklahoma City bombing.

In the immediate aftermath of Vietnam, some writers claimed that the war produced fewer psychiatric casualties than any war fought by America in this century. This claim, it turned out, was another manifestation of denial, denial of the pain and long-term suffering that are always consequences of war.

Both combatants and civilians caught in a war do suffer.[9] More than 2.5 million American men and women served in Vietnam. The National Vietnam Veterans Readjustment Study (1988) estimated that 481,000 men (15 percent of those who served in Vietnam) and 716 women (10 percent of the women) suffered from combat-related post-traumatic stress disorder (PTSD). Moreover, 40 percent of those who served in Vietnam have, at some time in their lives, suffered from PTSD.

Civilians caught in the cross fire also suffer severe psychological consequences. Various psychiatric disorders have been found among Southeast
Asian refugees, Central Americans, and Holocaust survivors. Stevan
Weine and his colleagues (1995) found that Bosnian refugees in the
United States suffer high rates of post-traumatic stress disorder and depression. All but one of the Bosnian refugees in their sample reported
having experienced more than ten separate traumatic events, including
forced evacuations, starvation, the disappearance or death of family
members, and detainment in camps. Such a list cannot convey the horror
of what some of their subjects witnessed. One man interned in a concentration camp watched nightly as guards lined people up on the ground
and jumped on them from a distance of a meter and a half, killing them
instantly by breaking their chests. Another prisoner spent days on
crowded transport trains without food or water, watching the people
around her suffocate to death in the press of bodies.

Both veterans and civilian noncombatants with PTSD may suffer for
the rest of their lives from symptoms that include repeated intrusive memories of traumatic experiences and psychic numbing, an inability to respond emotionally.

Studies of Vietnam-era veterans also provide evidence of a long-term
effect of trauma that has potentially serious consequences for society as
a whole: difficulties in forming and maintaining intimate ties. Several investigators have found that Vietnam veterans are more likely than their
peers to experience isolation and alienation. Intimacy deficits among the
veterans are related both to combat exposure and to the intensity of combat. In a 1981 study, Penk and his colleagues found that combat veterans
reported significantly more difficulty getting along with people, forming
emotionally close relationships, expressing their feelings, and trusting
other individuals, governments, or institutions. Those who experienced
heavy combat had significantly more trouble than those exposed to light
combat in getting emotionally close to another person and in feeling and
expressing emotions. The study concluded that the difficulties with intimacy were not the result of psychological problems the veterans might
have had before the war.

Other studies link intimacy deficits among Vietnam veterans with post-
traumatic stress disorder.[10] In one study, Vietnam veterans with PTSD re-

ported having more problems of self-disclosure, expressiveness, physical aggression, and general adjustment to their partners than did veterans without PTSD or those with minimal or no combat exposure.

Combat veterans diagnosed with post-traumatic stress disorder are also physiologically overreactive to ordinary stressors that are reminiscent of combat—sudden loud noises, televised images of war, and so on. The danger is that combat veterans may without warning respond to relatively minor peacetime stressors as if they were life-and-death situations like those they faced in wartime. The combination of this physiological over-reactivity and the difficulties with trust and intimacy also put combat veterans at risk for behaving violently in their families. Returned veterans who have been traumatized by their war experiences have sometimes turned their anger on wives and children, thus handing on the trauma to the civilian population.

Judith Herman was the first to see the connection between the psychological casualties of war and neuroses among the civilian population. "Only after 1980," she wrote,

when the efforts of combat veterans had legitimated the concept of post-traumatic stress disorder, did it become clear that the psychological syndrome seen in survivors of rape, domestic battery, and incest was essentially the same as the syndrome seen in survivors of war. The implications of this insight are as horrifying in the present as they were a century ago: the subordinate condition of women is maintained and enforced by the hidden violence of men. There is war between the sexes. Rape victims, battered women, and sexually abused children are its casualties. Hysteria is the combat neurosis of the sex war. (Herman 1992, p. 32)

War and other forms of government-sanctioned violence have long-term effects that, ultimately, increase the likelihood of the next war or genocide. When governments sanction killing, civilians may feel more justified taking life. Wars produce trauma, both among the soldiers who fight them and the civilian populations whose lives are disrupted by them. Many of these individuals suffer severe long-term psychological consequences in the form of PTSD and other disorders that impair their ability to interact with others and increase their reactivity to stress. Each war, each episode of genocidal fury, simply exacerbates the trauma and deposits a new legacy of hatred for the atrocities committed, which fuels the next war. We have seen this most recently in the former Yugoslavia, where ancient enmities were fanned by political leaders and atrocities were justified by the memory of atrocities carried out during World War II. Now a new generation of Serbs, Croats, and Muslims has inherited memories of atrocities that, even if they do not lead to further violence, threaten to impair them psychologically and leave them as vulnerable to the manipulations of political leaders peddling hatred and exclusion as their parents' generation was.

Liberal Denial and Appeasement

Thus far, we have considered the way people can be seduced into war by an opportunity to displace their anger onto a despised out-group. But what of those who are mistreated in childhood and learn not to express their anger outward against others? We found in our own research (Milburn, Conrad, et al. 1995) that women with a history of severe childhood punishment tended to become more liberal, not more conservative. Does that mean that, to reduce violence, all we need to do is punish children severely and teach them through emotional socialization that anger is an unacceptable emotion? Unfortunately not. Miller has argued that women mistreated in childhood direct their anger toward themselves in the form of self-destructiveness. Hokanson and Edelman's (1966) research demonstrated yet another potentially negative effect of the way women are socialized in this and many other societies; women who were provoked with an electric shock chose not to retaliate aggressively but to become particularly friendly and generous toward their attacker.

This reaction suggests that there is a parallel to conservative punitiveness in the form of liberal appeasement. Moreover, men as well as women are susceptible to it. At Munich, liberal politicians chose to accept Hitler's assurances and, in effect, gave him carte blanche to invade Czechoslovakia and encouragement to go into Poland. More recently, the Clinton administration and the European Community stood back and took no action while a catastrophic war devastated Bosnia. For years, even in the face of ethnic cleansing, they did nothing. Liberal politicians at times deny the evidence of aggressive intent in others, fail to recognize the potential for catastrophic violence, and refuse to take decisive steps to forestall it. This statement is, of course, a generalization; still, the liberal tendency to denial must be taken into account, along with all the other factors that complicate any one instance of violence. In the case of Bosnia, for example, it is difficult to know whether decisive aggressive action would have prevented the slaughter. One might also argue that if human beings were not driven to conquest in order to assuage old hurts, there would be no necessity for preemptive violence. Given the reality of the world we live in, however, it may sometimes be necessary to use force to prevent massive violence or genocide. In such a case, liberal denial, which leads politicians to overlook clear signs of vicious intent and placate tyrants, is as dangerous as conservative denial of the anger within us.

Given the fact that government-sanctioned violence is so seductive to individuals who carry pain and anger from their own childhoods and from earlier wars and incidents of mass destruction, how can the cycle of violence be stopped? We address that question in chapter 10. First, however, we examine the role denial may play in contributing to environmental damage from pollution, global warming, and destruction of the ozone layer.

9

Denial and Environmental Destruction

Most people have heard of the hole in the ozone layer and the greenhouse effect, both of which, some scientists predict, will eventually result in global environmental catastrophes. Many are aware of these problems and see them as important environmental threats. In September of 1990 when a Harris poll asked people what aspect of environmental destruction worried them the most, 33 percent chose contamination of the rivers and oceans and 19 percent said air pollution. Destruction of the ozone layer was the greatest concern for 15 percent, while approximately 10 percent worried most about the greenhouse effect.

Many people may not be aware, however, that political ideology influences the debate over these scientific questions. In recent years, in fact, environmental issues have become a major focus of conservative denial. There are, of course, other reasons—particularly economic motives and political concerns—why some scientists and politicians vociferously deny the evidence of human contributions to worldwide environmental problems. We have no direct evidence of a relationship between childhood punishment and environmental attitudes, although future research may document this association. The research we describe below has shown, however, a clear connection between authoritarianism and opposition to environmental protection. The evidence we detail in chapter 3, which establishes the roots of punitive, authoritarian attitudes in experiences of childhood punishment, suggests that these experiences also play a role in authoritarians' denial of environmental destruction.

The relevance of denial to environmental issues was brought home to us when one of us (Milburn) took his car in for servicing because the air conditioning had stopped working. The mechanic discovered that there was a hole in bottom of the unit that held the freon gas and it had all leaked out. When Milburn expressed concern that he had contributed to damaging the ozone layer, the repair shop owner laughed and said not to worry, that he had read somewhere that the ozone layer was healing itself.

Milburn knew from earlier discussions that the owner held conservative political views. But now he became concerned that a person who worked with materials a consensus of the scientific community regards as environmentally destructive might be cavalier about the handling of these materials, simply because an article he had read fed into his capacity for denial. An even more troubling thought, and one that pointed to a very serious problem, was the possibility that the owner's political beliefs and denial of environmental dangers were widely shared.

The Ideology of Environmentalism

Two histories of American environmentalism have recently been published: Mark Dowie's *Losing Ground: American Environmentalism at the Close of the Twentieth Century* (1995) and Philip Shabecoff's *A Fierce Green Fire: The American Environmental Movement* (1993). Both works suggest that there have been three waves of environmentalism over the past century and a half, the first beginning in the mid-nineteenth century. The early conservation movement was inspired by the writings of John James Audubon (1785–1851), the ornithologist and artist, and was primarily concerned with the efficient management of resources promoted by Theodore Roosevelt's Secretary of the Interior, Gifford Pinchot. Advocates of the more radical preservationist thinking of John Muir (1838–1914), founder of the Sierra Club, worked to protect the environment from the effects of human exploitation and preserve wilderness. Early conservationists tended to be wealthy white men who saw the wilderness as a place of recreation and renewal for people like themselves. (Some early national parks were posted "whites only.") The conservation movement tended to be politically conservative.

The second wave of American environmentalism began in 1962 with the publication of Rachel Carson's *Silent Spring,* which decried the damage to the environment wrought by the pesticide DDT. Alternatively, some see the first Earth Day demonstration on April 22, 1970, as the birthdate of environmental activism. The energy of this wave of activism resulted in several important pieces of environmental legislation but was sapped by the Reagan administration's opposition in the 1980s. Dowie and Shabecoff agree that the third wave was launched at the beginning of the Bush administration in 1988. Dowie (1995) notes that since that date, public financial support for environmental groups has declined markedly and that public-opinion polls reflect a somewhat lessened concern about environmental issues.

The environmental movement has been attacked from both the left and the right. Marxists were initially very critical of the early environmental movement. In his *Roots of Modern Environmentalism* (1984), David Pepper observes that Marxists viewed environmentalism as a conservative movement in which the middle classes and capitalists were striving to protect their economic interests. They criticized Dennis Meadows's popular *Limits to Growth* (1972), which predicted shortages of many natural resources, because it failed to place the issue of shortages in an economic and social context. According to Dowie, "Many leftists, particularly new leftists of the early 1970s, were outrightly hostile to environmentalism, deriding enviros as apolitical bourgeois romantics and anti-urban, elitist, utopian Luddites who believed, as Pogo did, that 'the enemy is us.' Such thinking, leftists believed, shifted responsibility for pollution away from the real polluter, corporate capitalism, just as certainly as the population-control zealots at the Rockefeller Foundation shifted the industrial North's attention away from the real problem in the third world—economic and cultural imperialism" (p. 239).[1]

As the environmental movement grew during the 1970s and 1980s, and began questioning the assumption of unlimited growth that underlies entrepreneurial capitalism, conservatives allied with corporations and large economic interests attempted to mobilize opposition to environmental protection. The advent of the Green party, first in Germany, and later in the United States, incited various conservatives to paint environmentalism with the broad brush of fascism. Ben Bolch (1993) has even suggested that there were many environmental extremists in the Nazi party.

Attitudes toward the environment range from *ecocentrism,* a lack of faith in technology and the belief that ecological laws should define human morality; to *technocentrism,* a faith in science and technology and the belief that economic growth and scientific progress will generate sufficient resources for the world's growing population. Political scientist Lester Milbrath's *Environmentalists: Vanguard for a New Society* (1984) argues that attitudes toward the earth represent a new dimension of public opinion different from the traditional right-left orientation historically used to characterize political belief systems and ideology. Milbrath sees the two ends of this dimension as reflecting two different belief paradigms. First, there is the New Environmental Paradigm (NEP), which promotes a high valuation of nature, argues that there are limits to growth, and advocates careful planning to avoid environmental degradation. The current Dominant Social Paradigm (DSP), by contrast, emphasizes the benefits of technology, exults in human domination of nature, and recognizes no limits on growth.[2]

To avoid being criticized from both the left and the right, most Green party members dissociate themselves from all existing parties. This lends some credence to Milbrath's argument that the left-right dimension is an inappropriate tool for interpreting environmental attitudes. Nonetheless, recent research in the United States supports the conclusion that concern for the environment is correlated with more liberal attitudes; and that antipathy toward the environment and environmentalism is often associated with the punitive, authoritarian attitudes we see as the result of high levels of childhood punishment and denial.

Antienvironmentalism and the Authoritarian Personality

Faith in the power of human ideas and technology to triumph over environmental problems is a central element of the ideology of antienvironmentalists. The accompanying belief in the right of human beings to dominate, and even destroy, nature may in fact be the ultimate expression of denied rage. These themes of power and toughness, which are central to the authoritarian personality, appear to underlie many segments of the antienvironmental movement.

Studies have indicated that individuals who score high on measures of authoritarianism have much more negative attitudes toward the environment and environmental protection than those with low scores. Psychologists Peterson, Doty, and Winter (1993) found that individuals who hold authoritarian attitudes express hostility toward the environmental movement, rather than toward polluters. In a study of university undergraduates, these researchers found that authoritarianism (as measured by Altemeyer's right-wing authoritarianism [RWA] scale) predicted agreement with statements such as: Environmental problems are "blown out of proportion by sentimental people" and environmental problems are "exaggerated by special interest groups." Another item measured the authoritarian focus on power and toughness related to environmentalism: "The environmental movement will reduce this country to a second-rate power." Agreement with this statement was significantly correlated with authoritarianism.

In two studies of the relationship of authoritarianism and environmental attitudes, psychologists Schultz and Stone (1994) also found people high in authoritarianism to be low in concern for the environment. These researchers assessed the attitudes of individuals in the audience at a Planning Board meeting considering the building of a coal-fired power plant on the Penobscot River in Maine. Schultz and Stone distributed questionnaires that assessed authoritarianism—using items from Altemeyer's right-wing authoritarianism scale—and environmentalism—as measured by statements such as, "Fines aren't enough, it's time we told every polluter, 'if you poison our water, you will go to jail and your money will be spent to clean up the mess.'" Authoritarians, who are normally high in punitiveness toward individuals who break laws, were much more forgiving in their attitudes toward polluters; they were significantly less likely than people low in authoritarianism to feel that individuals who pollute the environment should be severely punished. In their second study, Schultz and Stone found that opponents of the New Environmental Paradigm were significantly higher in authoritarianism than its supporters.

One could argue that opposition to environmentalism is not rooted in authoritarianism but results from an underlying belief in free-market capitalism, which authoritarians also support. This criticism suggests that the correlation between authoritarianism and antienvironmentalism is spurious. To argue this, however, is to suggest that belief in a free market "causes" authoritarian attitudes. The available evidence on the roots of

authoritarianism indicates that childhood experiences, rather than economic philosophy, exert the causal influence. It is true, however, that there
is an element of authoritarianism in rigid, uncompromising support for
free markets. A belief in the importance of power and toughness and
"survival of the fittest" is very much a part of laissez-faire capitalism; and
this belief is also an underlying element of authoritarianism. It is thus
most likely that authoritarian beliefs underlie both antienvironmentalism
and uncompromising support for the free market.

As we suggested in the opening of this chapter, two issues that have
become a focus for conservative opposition to the public-policy initiatives
of the environmental movement are the hole in the ozone layer and the
hypothesized greenhouse effect. An examination of the science and politics surrounding these issues reveals how they have become a focus of
conservative denial.

A Hole in the Ozone Layer?

The ozone layer is a layer of gas that lies eight to thirty miles above the
earth. It protects us from ultraviolet light (UV), primarily UVB, one of
the two types of ultraviolet radiation relevant to the discussion of ozone
depletion. The ozone layer does not filter out the other type, UVA radiation. Ozone is created when intense sunlight reaches the earth's atmosphere and breaks molecules of oxygen gas into two oxygen atoms. Most
of these atoms reassemble, not as common oxygen but as a molecule of
ozone, containing three oxygen atoms.

If the ozone layer is depleted worldwide, increased amounts of ultraviolet radiation can reach the earth and, scientists predict, lead to increased
rates of skin cancer, the death of certain microorganisms, and crop failures. It is calculated that for each 1 percent decrease in total ozone,
2 percent more UVB will reach the earth's surface and cause 4 percent
more cases of skin cancer (Firor 1990). Lyman (1991) notes that children
born during the next decade will be at the greatest risk from the effects
of increased ultraviolet radiation.

The power of ultraviolet radiation to change biological material implies
that almost any living tissue exposed to it suffers some effect (Firor 1990).
Franck and Brownstone (1993) quote Margaret Kripke, an immunologist
at the M. D. Anderson Cancer Center in Houston, on the effects of expo-

sure on the human immune system: "We already know that ultraviolet light can impair immunity to infectious diseases in the animals. We know that there are immunological effects in humans, though we don't yet know their significance" (p. 61). Ultraviolet radiation can cause mutations in DNA leading to skin cancers, including the deadly melanoma. According to Lemonick (1992), a one-half of 1 percent depletion of atmospheric ozone would mean an extra six thousand cases of cancer per year. Ultraviolet radiation can also cause the lens of the eye to cloud up with cataracts that, if not treated, lead to blindness.

The increased UV radiation resulting from a decrease in atmospheric ozone would also hurt animals and plants, especially aquatic life and food crops. UVB penetrates scores of meters below the surface of the oceans and can kill phytoplankton (one-celled plants) and krill (tiny shrimplike animals that are at the bottom of the oceanic food chain). If organisms at the bottom of the food chain are destroyed, the bigger fish and aquatic mammals that eat them will die off as well. High doses of UV radiation can also reduce the yield of important crops such as soybeans (Lemonick 1992).

So, we know about all these negative effects, but do we know that there is a problem from UV radiation *because* of ozone depletion? Concern began in 1974 when Mario Molina and Sherwood Rowland published their calculations that chlorofluorocarbons (CFCs) were putting chlorine, which destroys ozone, into the stratosphere. Chlorofluorocarbons contain carbon, fluorine, chlorine, and sometimes hydrogen and have been used as aerosol-spray propellants and as refrigerants. In 1973 the annual worldwide production of CFCs reached a million tons. At the time, CFC emissions were thought to be harmless; and between 1973 and 1986, according to Lyman (1991), they increased at an annual rate of 5 to 7 percent a year worldwide.

According to Rowland and Molina's calculations, at 1973 levels, between 7 and 13 percent of the ozone layer would be depleted within about a hundred years. This is a large enough depletion to seriously alter life on earth. As significant production of CFCs began only in the 1960s, in 1973 actual damage to the ozone layer wasn't yet apparent. Because they ascend gradually, most of the CFCs released since the 1930s, when they were first manufactured, had not yet reached the mid-stratosphere where the reactions take place. Even though we see no discernible damage from ozone depletion today, the CFCs already in the stratosphere will lead to increased damage in the future (Fisher 1990). Peak levels of ultraviolet radiation will not occur until 2010 or 2020 (Lyman 1991); thus, the full impact of atmospheric ozone depletion may not be evident for several decades.

Much of the world regards the evidence for human-caused ozone depletion as very compelling. Molina and Rowland were awarded the Nobel prize in chemistry in 1995 for their work on the ozone layer. As Molina said in a CBS News interview on November 23, 1995, scientists no longer debate whether or not ozone depletion is a problem. A recent report in the prestigious journal *Nature* concludes that the ozone layer over Antarctica has thinned measurably over the past ten years. Figure 9.1, which is reprinted from the Jones and Shanklin article (1995), combines their data with previously published data to demonstrate the ozone depletion that has occurred in the past forty years. The evidence of a significant problem with the ozone layer is hard to deny.

Why, then, is there resistance to warnings about ozone depletion? A number of economic, political, and psychological considerations are involved with the public policy issue of whether to accept the scientific findings and, if so, to act on them. Denial of the seriousness of this problem, again, appears to be related to political conservatism.

The Politics of Ozone Depletion   In 1980, when the Reagan administration came to power, the director of the Environmental Protection Administration (EPA), Anne Burford, believed that the ozone hole was nothing more than a scare issue. Roan reports (1989) that "In the 1980s, ozone depletion was considered so unimportant that a Washington environmentalist had to beg his friends to show up at an EPA meeting on it." Reagan officials treated the question with minimal concern, even derision. Yet, in spite of conservative opposition, the United States signed, first the 1987 Montreal Protocol to cut the use of CFCs in half by 1999, and, in 1990, the London Agreement calling for the ban of CFC production by the year 2000.

Prior to the Republican revolution in the 1994 congressional elections, the United States was moving forward in dealing with the problem of

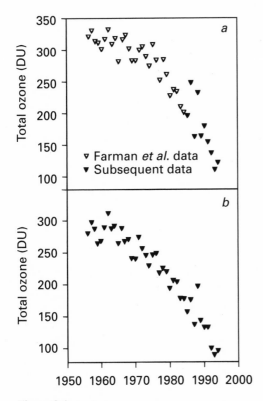

Figure 9.1.
(a) October mean total ozone observed over Halley, Antarctica from 1956 to 1994. (b) Lowest daily value of total ozone observed over Halley in October for the years between 1956 and 1994. Figure reprinted from Jones and Shanklin (1995) with the permission of the authors and the publishers of *Nature*.

ozone depletion. In 1992, by a 96 to 0 vote, the Senate found the evidence alarming enough to justify a faster phaseout of CFCs. Twenty-four American states already have laws limiting or banning CFC production, and Germany has passed a law banning production after 1995. In 1995 the ozone-damaging chemical halon was also banned by Australia, Sweden, and Norway, while Canada has banned production of CFCs after 1997 and of methyl chloroform (another danger to ozone) after the year 2000.

Then, in 1994, Newt Gingrich and the freshman class of Republicans took over key congressional committees with jurisdiction over the environment and began hearings aimed at stopping progress. Representative Dana Rohrabacher (R-Calif.) chair of a House Subcommittee on Energy and the Environment, referred to restrictions on CFC production as a product of "liberal arrogance" and the misuse of science. Representative Thomas DeLay (R-Texas)—as reported by CBS News on November 23, 1995—referred to ozone depletion as "just a theory." The unscientific basis for the effort to stall environmental protection efforts is remarkable for its level of denial.

The Backlash against Environmental Protection   Several books attacking the environmental movement have been published in the last few years. Although they are ostensibly based on scientific information, their authors' motivations appear to be conservative political ideology, not scientific argument. These books include: *Trashing the Planet* (1990) and *Environmental Overkill* (1993), both by Dixie Lee Ray, head of the Atomic Energy Commission under Ronald Reagan, and Lou Guzzo; *Apocalypse Not* by Ben Bolch and Harold Lyons, professors of business and chemistry, respectively, at Rhodes College in Memphis; and *Eco-Scam* by Ronald Bailey. Bolch and Lyons's book was published by the conservative Cato Institute, which also supported Bailey while he was writing his book.

The essence of their attack on the environmental movement is the argument that, because the jobs of professional environmentalists depend on the public belief that environmental crises are imminent and ongoing, they use scare tactics. Professors and scientists are willing partners in this deception because, as Bolch and Lyons write, "Scientists, especially academic scientists, are easily flattered with cocktail parties and press conferences, and can be counted on for a steady stream of new ideas" (p. 23). Along with conservative talk show hosts like Rush Limbaugh, these authors paint the picture of a broad conspiracy of liberal politicians, scientists, and environmentalists who, in cooperation with the mass media, are deceiving the public into believing that the environment faces threats from technology. These books are loaded with undocumented statements, misinterpretations of research, and factual errors—all reflecting the effects of denial on thinking processes we discussed in earlier chapters.

Rush Limbaugh, who has called proponents of the ozone-hole theory "dunderhead alarmists," stated that he obtained his information from Ray and Guzzo's *Trashing the Planet*, which he calls the most thoroughly documented book he has ever read. Gary Taubes, in the June 1993 issue of *Science,* carefully details many of the errors and misrepresentations that fill this and other books on the subject. Taubes notes that most of Ray and Guzzo's information about ozone depletion comes from Fred Singer and Rogelio Maduro (who holds a bachelor of science degree in geology). Maduro edits a magazine called *21st Century Science & Technology,* which is published by supporters of libertarian politician Lyndon LaRouche—currently in jail for tax evasion. In her book, Ray cites extensively from Maduro and Schauerhammer's *The Holes in the Ozone Scare* (1992). According to Taubes, atmospheric scientists who have read all or parts of the Maduro and Schauerhammer book found it to be based on a selection of out-of-date studies and bad research.

One of the influential arguments Maduro makes against the theory of ozone depletion is repeated by Ray and Guzzo, Bailey, and Rush Limbaugh. It states that numerous natural sources of ozone-depleting chemicals (such as chlorine from volcanic eruptions) emit far greater quantities of these substances than CFCs do, and that the ozone layer has nonetheless survived intact for billions of years. It turns out, however, that such natural sources of chlorine are water soluble; so, because they are washed out of the lower atmosphere by rain, they never reach the stratosphere, where they would damage the ozone layer (Taubes 1993). CFCs, by contrast, are not water soluble and are thus able to reach the upper atmosphere and release the chlorine molecules that initiate the chemical reactions thought to deplete the ozone layer.

Fred Singer (1989), whom Ray and Guzzo cite in support of their rejection of the ozone problem, disputes Maduro's argument about natural sources of chlorine. Although he once believed that such natural sources have a greater impact on the ozone layer than do manufactured chemicals, Singer has since concluded, on the basis of published evidence, that CFCs are the primary source of danger (Begley 1993).

Ozone Depletion and Skin Cancer   We explained earlier in our discussion that denial can take the form of either outright disbelief in some unpleasant reality or of minimization—in which a reality is acknowledged but claimed to be unimportant. The books by Ray and Guzzo and Bailey, which both downplay the importance of increases in skin cancer from ozone-layer depletion, are revealing examples of environmental denial and minimization.

Ray and Guzzo state first, without documentation, that most melanomas begin on areas of the body that are not often exposed to sunlight and that no research evidence links UVB exposure to melanoma, only UVA radiation (pp. 40, 41). As the ozone layer filters out only UVB radiation, they concluded, a decline in ozone levels could not possibly result in increased melanoma rates. Aaron Wildavsky (1995), a prominent conservative political scientist makes the same claim. When we checked his footnotes, however, we found that he references only one 1992 paper claiming that UVB has no relationship to melanoma. His other statements minimizing the risks of melanoma are also ungrounded.

It turns out, however, that a major predictor of developing melanoma is having bad sunburns as a child. Since UVB is primarily responsible for sunburns, it is obvious that UVB has some connection with melanoma. In a 1993 article on the causes of melanoma, Dr. Koh and his colleagues at the Skin Oncology Program of the Boston University Medical Center state that the available evidence, albeit imperfect, indicates that development of melanoma is associated with exposure to sunlight, particularly to UVB radiation, the type of radiation the ozone layer screens out. UVA and UVB radiation appear to interact with each other in causing melanoma. The claim that melanomas typically occur on areas not exposed to sunlight is contradicted by the finding that 90 percent of malignant tumors of the skin are localized in areas often exposed to sunlight, usually in men on their backs and in women on their legs.[3]

Bailey's *Eco-Scam* also contains several examples of minimization. Instead of researching the issue of ozone-layer depletion and skin cancer, Bailey interviewed just two dermatologists. His book implies that non-melanoma cancers—basal-cell carcinomas and squamous-cell carcinomas—are unimportant; he quotes one doctor as saying (p. 131) that it is hard to die from them (the death rate is about 1 percent). But, of course, there are other effects of these cancers; if they occur on the eyelid or nose or ears, they can become significant cosmetic or functional problems. Moreover, the incidence of these types of cancer may increase dramatically as the ozone layer is depleted. An article in the *British Journal of Dermatology* (Jones 1992) estimates that a 10 percent loss of atmospheric ozone would result in an increase in basal and squamous-cell carcinomas of between 30 and 50 percent.

Bailey also dismisses the effect of ozone depletion on melanoma (p. 131), simply saying that the main risk factor for melanoma is severe sunburns in childhood, rather than frequent exposure to UVB radiation. Nonetheless, the research indicates clearly that exposure to the sunburn-causing UVB radiation the ozone layer screens out is associated with the development of melanoma, and there are strong indications that ozone depletion will increase UVB radiation. But Bailey seems oblivious of this and to the fact that children, who are significantly less careful about avoiding sunburns than adults, will obviously be at great risk of exposure to the UVB radiation associated with melanoma.

Economic Costs   Some ozone skeptics are also concerned about the economic costs of banning CFCs. Bailey, for example, argues that they will be enormous. He also claims that, because of the likelihood of food spoilage from inadequate refrigeration, many people, particularly in the developing world, will go hungry. These claims, like many of his arguments, are simply wrong. A *Business Week* article in July 1995 reports that the availability of recycled CFCs means that conversion to non-CFC chemicals—a number of which have already been developed—need not take place immediately. In addition, Carey (1995) points out that, because non-CFC building air-conditioning units are more energy efficient, the long-term economic results of the ban may be positive.

It must be said, however, that some uncertainties about the effects of ozone depletion remain. Complete evidence to support the ozone theory is still not available, and more research must be done. For example, it has not yet been demonstrated that ozone depletion has led to increases in ultraviolet radiation at the ground level. One of the only studies available on ground UV-level was conducted by Joseph Scotto et al. (1988a). Their measurements at eight locations in the United States found no increase in ultraviolet radiation, and perhaps a slight decrease between 1974 and 1985. The equipment they used, however, was not designed to measure annual trends. Additionally, William Grant of the California Institute of Technology's Jet Propulsion Laboratory, in a response to Scotto's *Science* article, noted that the measurements were taken primarily in urban centers with increasing populations. Because such areas have increasing levels of tropospheric ozone (smog), which filter out ozone, Scotto's findings may underestimate the ultraviolet radiation reaching the earth. Scotto et al. (1988b) responded that they "share the concern that UVB exposures and skin cancer incidence are likely to increase with further depletion of the ozone layer" (p. IIII).

In 1993 an article debunking the ozone-hole theory written by science-fiction writer James Hogan was published in *Omni*, a popular science magazine with a circulation of one million. Hogan drew extensively on the writings of Maduro, raising the same arguments and citing the same evidence that purports to cast doubt on the problems some scientists hypothesize will result from thinning of the ozone layer. In a companion article, however, fellow science-fiction writer Frederick Pohl countered with what has been called the precautionary principle: "If the consensus of most scientists is wrong, and there is, after all, no danger to the ozone layer, then doing what that consensus suggests will unnecessarily cost us all some money and inconvenience. *But if the scientists are right and we do nothing, it will cost us a great deal more money, a great deal more inconvenience, and a very great deal of suffering and human lives*" (p. 36, emphasis added).

The Greenhouse Effect
There is a wide consensus among scientists around the world that the average temperature on the earth is rising and that it will continue to increase because of human-produced emissions of greenhouse gases; these include carbon dioxide, methane, nitrous oxides, CFCs, and tropospheric ozone (smog). Scientists predict various consequences of global warming, including higher sea levels, severe heat waves, and increases in infectious diseases. In January of 1990, as reported by *Science News*, seven hundred scientists, including forty-nine Nobel prize winners, petitioned the White House to take quick action to forestall increases in global temperature so that "future generations will not be put at risk" (p. 95).

Nonetheless, a vocal minority of scientists against governmental action was reportedly influential during the Bush administration (Hempel 1993), and no action was taken. Although the Clinton administration is more inclined to action on this issue than the Reagan and Bush administrations, the Republican capture of Congress in November of 1994 is likely to slow down government activity on global warming.

For example, when, on Thursday, November 16, 1995, the House held hearings on the issue, Patrick J. Michaels, an environmental science professor at the University of Virginia, was a prominent witness. He contended that global warming is an insignificant problem and that the media should "go find another issue" (quoted in Allen 1995). His statement reflects the predominant opinion voiced at these hearings. One might guess from the prevalence of this view that the scientific community had reconsidered its conclusions about global warming.

It hadn't. Just two weeks later, an international UN-sponsored conference in Madrid reiterated that global warming is a real phenomenon and that evidence indicates that such human activities as burning coal and oil are responsible for it. The final report (as summarized in the *Boston Globe*, November 30, 1995) drew on the work of twenty-five hundred scientists around the world and called for a worldwide effort to reduce the production of greenhouse gases. It concluded that, "The balance of evidence suggests a discernible human influence on global climate" (p. 67).

On October 24, 1995, a report by the Intergovernmental Panel on Climate Change (IPCC), an international scientific body, predicted that by the year 2100 global warming would cause an increase in global temperature of between 1 and 3.5 degrees Celsius; as a consequence, sea levels could be expected to rise by between six and thirty-seven inches. The report, to which one thousand scientists contributed, noted that 46 million people currently live in areas susceptible to catastrophic flooding; an increase in sea level of a half a meter would bring those potentially affected to 90 million; a thirty-nine-inch increase in the sea level would mean that 118 million people could experience devastating floods (Utility Environment Report 1995).

The report also indicated that world temperature increases would result in more intense and frequent droughts, and heat waves. The report emphasized that "climate change is likely to have wide-ranging and mostly adverse impacts on human health, with significant loss of life" (p. 1). These impacts would include deaths caused by heat waves and increased transmission of such infectious diseases as yellow fever, malaria, and viral encephalitis. How could U.S. congressional representatives be so out of touch with the world scientific community?

Conservative ideologues like Dixie Lee Ray and others have labeled the greenhouse effect, like ozone depletion, an unproven environmental threat. Their primary claim is that climatic changes are not well understood. Ray and Guzzo (1990, 1993) argue that the computer simulation models that predict global warming cannot explain climate changes in the past and do not take into account factors such as the temperature changes of the oceans. They also allege that naturally produced greenhouse gases are more prevalent than those produced by human activity.

A handful of skeptical academic scientists have added weight to these criticisms. Besides Patrick J. Michaels, Richard Lindzen, a meteorology professor at MIT; Robert Balling, a climatologist at Arizona State University; Dr. Sherwood Idso; and Dr. Fred Singer have all testified repeatedly that concern for global warming is misplaced. Given their credentials and their arguments that global warming is a myth, how could an international conference conclude so decisively that it is a real phenomenon and that steps to reverse the trend must be taken? Here again, as in the case of ozone depletion, economic and psychological forces are operating to produce a level of denial that threatens future generations.

Money is at stake, of course—a lot of money. Coal and oil corporations stand to lose billions of dollars from the lowered consumption of their products that would be necessary to reduce carbon dioxide emissions. Journalist Ross Gelbspan, writing in the December 1995 issue of *Harpers,* documents the enormous amounts oil and coal companies have spent in recent years to influence public opinion on climate change. The Global Climate Coalition, a leading oil-industry public relations firm, spent more than a million dollars in a year and a half to minimize the threat of global warming; and the National Coal Association spent over $700,000 in 1992 and 1993. The American Petroleum Institute paid $1.8 million to a public relations firm, in part to help defeat a proposed tax on fossil fuels intended to reduce the generation of greenhouse gases.

It also turns out that some of the substantial amounts spent to protect oil and coal company profits end up in the pockets of the scientists who are skeptical about global warming. According to Gelbspan, Michaels received more than $115,000 from energy and coal interests in the four years between 1991 and 1995; and the Western Fuels Association, a $400-million consortium of coal-using utilities and suppliers, funds his journal, *World Climate Review,* which regularly downplays concern about global climate changes. Balling has received more than $200,000 from European oil and coal companies, and he and Sherwood Idso have received funds from the mining company Cypress Minerals, which also funds militant antienvironmental groups such as People for the West. Lindzen receives consulting fees of $2,500 per day from coal and oil companies; the costs of his trip to testify before the Senate in 1991 were paid by Western Fuels.[4]

Many of these skeptics argue that global climate studies are inadequate and that more research needs to be done before public policies are changed. Their criticisms (e.g., Ray and Guzzo 1993) focus on the models (GCMs) that produce computer simulations of the world's climate and cast doubt on the calculations showing increases in average global temperatures. In 1995, however, new research emerged that supports the global-warming proponents and addresses some of the issues the skeptics raise. For example, in the April 7, 1995, issue of *Science,* David Thomson presents the results of his elaborate time-series analyses of temperature changes and greenhouse-gas accumulation over the past century. Utilizing measurements from all around the world, Thomson concludes that the 0.6-degree Celsius increase in temperature in the past one hundred years correlates significantly with increases in greenhouse gases.

Greenhouse Politics   In June 1992 at the Earth Summit in Rio de Janeiro, more than eighty countries signed a climate treaty, setting the target date of the year 2000 for developed countries to stabilize their emissions of greenhouse gases at 1990 levels. The conference and agreement were met with derision by Republican presidential candidates such as Patrick Buchanan. Buchanan declared that, "This is a shakedown of the American taxpayer to provide another income transfer to Third World socialist thugs." He also ridiculed the conference sponsors as "Sandals and Beads International" (Robinson in *Boston Globe* April 15, 1992). In response to this pressure from within his own party, President Bush refused to set a target date for the United States.

President Clinton has pledged to meet the treaty's dates for reduction of emissions. Republican control of Congress, however, is now jeopardizing this goal. Under Clinton, the EPA allocated funds to stimulate businesses like the American Express Company to install energy-efficient lighting. The company cut its electricity use by 40 percent, which resulted in lowered consumption of coal and oil to generate electricity and, therefore, lower emissions of greenhouse gases—an annual reduction of 3,300 tons in New York and five other cities. According to a *New York Times* report, however, the Republican Congress plans to cut funds for this project by at least 40 percent, making the Rio targets far more difficult to reach. Conservative denial about global warming is reflected by the words of Republican Rohrabacher of California, chair of a House Subcommittee on Energy and the Environment; he calls global warming "unproven at best and liberal claptrap at worst" (quoted in Wright 1995, p. 6).

We can respond to concerns about global warming in a number of ways. These might include: (1) doing nothing; (2) promoting regional efforts to respond to the effects of climate changes with such countermeasures as new seawalls to keep back rising sea levels; (3) attempting to absorb increases in carbon dioxide through reforestation; and (4) reducing the generation of greenhouse gases by switching to carbon-free fuels. Some environmentalists argue that setting strict limits on emissions for different countries at this time is counterproductive and that establishing effective information gathering and communication systems are essential first steps to setting strict targets that can succeed. Virtually all scientists agree, however, that human activities are contributing to global warming and that only an international effort can effectively address the problem.

Conclusion

One of the Republican politicians leading the attack against the environmental movement is Texas Representative DeLay, a former bug exterminator who calls the EPA "a Gestapo organization." He also believes that ozone depletion is not a threat and labeled the Nobel prize committee that awarded Rowland and Molina the Nobel prize in chemistry for their work identifying the danger to the ozone layer "a bunch of Swedish environmental extremists." He has assembled more than a hundred business lobbyists into Project Relief, a group whose goal is elimination of federal government regulation of business. The many political-action committees associated with Project Relief donated more than $10.3 million in campaign contributions to House members during 1993–94 (Ivins 1995).

Some Republicans in Congress have become concerned that efforts to gut funding for EPA and other environmental initiatives will result in their being portrayed as antienvironmentalist in the November 1996 elections. To counter that impression, an October 1995 memo from the House Republican Conference urged members to try to "counteract the environmentalist lobby and their extremist friends in the eco-terrorist underworld" who "have been working overtime to define Republicans and their agenda as anti-environment, pro-polluter and hostile to the survival of every cuddly critter roaming God's green earth" (quoted in Kenworthy and Lee 1995). And what did the memo urge members to do? Participate in Earth Day celebrations, tree plantings, and highway-cleanup programs. In other words, emphasize symbolic actions that do little or nothing to protect the environment from the conservative antienvironmental agenda.

Republicans' belittling of people whose weakness produces concern about "cuddly critters" rings with the authoritarian emphasis on power and toughness. As discussed in earlier chapters, harsh child rearing results in displaced anger and denial and forms the foundation of punitive, authoritarian political attitudes. This kind of toughness, and the belief that human beings are meant to dominate nature with no limits, pervade the antienvironmentalist movement. It may be that predictions of environmental catastrophe and death are actually very disturbing to authoritarians and evoke a need to deny their own potential weakness.

This speculation that environmental denial among conservative authoritarians is in part a reaction to a fear of death is supported by the results of experimental studies on authoritarianism. Greenberg et al. (1990) asked individuals high in authoritarianism to think about their own deaths. The result was that high authoritarians subsequently expressed significantly higher levels of punitiveness toward social deviants, while low authoritarians' expressions of punitiveness did not increase. A similar study by Greenberg et al. (1992) found an increased dislike for dissimilar others in conservatives—but not liberals—who thought about their own death.

There is also an internal contradiction in the arguments of conservatives who, like Dixie Lee Ray, attack the environmental movement and the integrity of scientists. On the one hand, they believe fervently in the ability of technology to improve the quality of life for those on this planet; such technologies are, obviously, a result of scientific advances made by pure scientists. At the same time, however, Ray implicitly suggests, and Rush Limbaugh explicitly argues, that there is a conspiracy of self-

interested scientists around the world to promote false visions of apocalypse as a way to obtain research funds. Now, either scientists are, by and
large, honest, or they are not. You can't have it both ways. Suggesting that
only Nobel prize–winning chemists and most atmospheric scientists are
dishonest, while the few scientists who are antienvironmental critics are
honest, strains credulity.

What is fascinating, and disturbing, about the ozone issue is how conservative ideologues start with a particular viewpoint and then ignore the
evidence, and the vast consensus of scientists, that contradict it. For example, in 1995 the House of Representatives held hearings on a bill,
sponsored by House Majority Whip DeLay, to repeal the ban on U.S.
production of CFCs specified in the Montreal Protocol. The hearing testimony was reported in the November 1995 issue of *Dermatology World,*
the journal of the American Academy of Dermatology. If, as some antienvironmentalists might argue, dermatologists were primarily motivated by
economic self-interest, they would ignore the problem of the ozone layer,
as increases in cancer would mean more business for them. Nevertheless,
Dr. Margaret Kripke, who has conducted research on the effects of ultraviolet radiation for twenty years, testified that UVB plays a role in the
onset of both melanoma and nonmelanoma skin cancers. Subcommittee
chair Rohrabacher challenged her testimony. He simply claimed, despite
testimony to the contrary by other physical and biological scientists, that
there were no negative health effects from ozone depletion. It is clear that
Rohrabacher's capacity for denial is very high indeed.

The claim that there is a conspiracy among scientists—of course, it
would have to be a worldwide conspiracy—to keep the ozone problem in
the forefront for the sake of headlines and cocktail parties would be
laughable if conservatives in Congress were not threatening to undo much
environmental progress while expressing the same view. One can point
out, as many environmentalists do, that opponents of the ozone theory
have ties to industries that incur considerable costs because of environmental regulations. Yet there must be something else involved too: a capacity for denying unpleasant realities. The same conservative politicians
fighting to eviscerate the EPA and sneering at the possibilities of the ozone
hole and the greenhouse effect support a whole range of punitive welfare
and prison legislation. Their capacity for denial—and acceptance of cam-

paign contributions from antienvironmental groups and industrial polluters—threatens serious damage to the global environment. Unfortunately, these conservatives have real political power in Congress and the ability to reverse many of the advances in protecting and cleaning up the environment we have made in the past twenty years.

10

Conclusion

The last few years have seen increasing support for punitive public policies in the United States. In response to fears about crime, the public and politicians have advocated the death penalty, tough sentencing laws, and even a return to chain gangs and corporal punishment in prisons. The same punitive spirit also appears in calls to reinstitute corporal punishment in schools, reduce benefits for children and the poor, abolish affirmative action, and withhold services from legal immigrants.

Our research documents the influence that harsh child-rearing practices have on support for such policies. Many people who were physically and psychologically abused as children, as adults developed hostile attitudes toward others and denial of past and present reality. We found them more likely to identify themselves as politically conservative and to hold conservative attitudes toward abortion, the use of military force, and the death penalty.

A study of the transmission of political attitudes from parents to children in Israel offers strong support for the view that methods of child rearing substantially influence adult political attitudes (Liebes, Katz, and Ribak 1991). In Israel, the ability of "dovish" parents to "reproduce" their ideology in their children depended on their educational level; better-educated doves were more likely to have dovish children than less-educated parents. The ability of "hawkish" parents to reproduce their ideology in their offspring, was not, however, related to educational level. Parents who were hawks were more likely to have children whose political views matched theirs than were dovish parents. Moreover, hawkish parents who scored high on authoritarianism were the most likely to pass on their beliefs.

We argue throughout this book that denial distorts politics and public policy in ways that have negative consequences for American society. To the extent that our political process is dominated by a handful of issues like the death penalty and abortion—issues that stir powerful emotions and may activate residual childhood rage, helplessness, and a desire for retribution—we will not as a nation be able to address issues that could promote a higher quality of life. As long as we continue to define and debate the same issues in emotional terms, they will remain sources of divisiveness and resist solution. As a nation, therefore, we need to move beyond the politics of denial. How do we accomplish this? One man's experience may be instructive.

A Neo-Nazi's Change of Heart

In 1989, Ingo Hasselbach, a young East German drifter and punk who had been in trouble with the police for various petty offenses, was elevated to the status of a future "führer figure" of the East German right wing by Michael Kuhnen, head of the neo-Nazi movement in West Germany. The story of Hasselbach's path to prominence in the movement illustrates the way that an abusive upbringing can contribute to development of a punitive, right-wing ideology. It also gives hope of the individual's capacity to break through denial and destructive hostility.

According to his memoirs (1996), Hasselbach's conversion to neo-Nazism was strikingly nonideological. He said he knew little of the history or literature of the movement. Growing up in East Germany he learned only a limited and skewed version of twentieth-century history. His gradual conversion to neo-Nazism seems to have been a way of rebelling against his father and of protesting against the repressive East German state.

Hasselbach's father, a radio announcer and later director of Radio-G.D.R., was a committed Communist and vehemently anti-Nazi. As Hasselbach put it, "My father's voice *was* the state" (p. 39). His father had lost both his parents in World War II, his father in combat and his mother in an Allied air raid. After the war he was imprisoned for his activities in the Communist party and, when released, went over the wall to East Germany. There he was lionized as a heroic fighter against fascism. While married with five children, he had a brief affair with a young East German woman, Hasselbach's mother.

Hasselbach knew his father as Uncle Hans, a man who occasionally visited during his childhood. In early childhood, the boy also saw little of his mother, who was often away on press assignments; he mostly lived with his mother's parents, "the least ideological people I knew" (p. 38). His grandfather had refused to hang out a swastika during the Nazi era and was similarly unimpressed with the Communist government. When the boy was three years old, his mother remarried and the family moved out of the grandparents' apartment into one of their own. Hasselbach's stepfather took to beating him with coat hangers; by the age of twelve he was already staying away from home as much as possible.

He first became involved with a group of "hippies" who were camping out in his grandmother's building, then with street punks who initiated him into gang fighting. He describes these fights, "in which you'd beat up everyone who was dressed differently from you" (p. 39). A variety of protest groups—hippies, punks, and skinheads—fought each other, but their real enemy was the state.

Hasselbach dropped out of school, and, at sixteen, he and a friend were picked up by police for petty theft. The police took exception to his friend's mohawk haircut, which was dyed in the colors of the East German flag, and "beat the hell" out of both of them. Hasselbach was given a choice of prison or going to live with his father. His father forbade him to see his friends or to visit his mother; when Hasselbach met his mother secretly, his father threw him out on the street. There followed further petty acts of defiance—public drunkenness, disrupting a festival to "honor the Soviet troops," and so forth—for which Hasselbach ended up in prison, in solitary confinement. Later, when he was moved into the regular prison population, he learned to suppress all human feeling and remain aloof in order to avoid being raped: "Feelings were an invitation to abuse. Only the hard and the cold were left alone. I think that this attitude, acquired in prison, was ideal for my later life in the neo-Nazi scene. Prison was a kind of school that prepared you for a life in a community without scruples" (p. 41).

In prison, his hatred of the Communist regime grew, and he met and came to admire several Nazi war criminals who were imprisoned with him. One of them, "the butcher of Oradour," had been in charge of the extermination of Jews in that French town. Hasselbach's conversion to neo-Nazism seems to have had quite a lot to do with the denial and hypocrisy of the Communist state that had imprisoned him: "If you're going to worship power, why not admit it? At least the Nazis had been straightforward in their brutality. These people insisted that they were beating you and locking you up for your own edification and for the sake of universal brotherhood" (p. 40).

Once released from prison, Hasselbach became deeply involved with West German and American neo-Nazis and was eventually elevated to head of a neo-Nazi party in East Germany. He and his friends distributed hate literature and stockpiled explosives to use in attacks against gypsy and refugee shelters.

Hasselbach's story is fascinating, not only because of the extent to which personal motives, rather than political ideology, fueled his conversion to neo-Nazism, but also because of his subsequent repudiation of the movement. His disillusionment seems to have been triggered by two events: he became sickened by the killing of refugees in a neo-Nazi arson attack; and he met someone, for perhaps the first time in his life, who valued him as an individual and was able to hold up a mirror in which Hasselbach saw himself clearly for the first time.

That man, a German filmmaker living in France, approached Hasselbach with a proposal to make a film about neo-Nazis. Hasselbach liked him and was intrigued by his apparent sincerity. As the filmmaker followed him to neo-Nazi meetings, Hasselbach began to see his comrades and himself in a new light. In one meeting, a neo-Nazi named Heinz Reisz "described how he would personally erect concentration camps for Jews, fags, and the Jew-influenced politicians in Bonn. . . . Then he sipped his beer and sang a little anti-Semitic song, jumping up and down in his seat, his huge potbelly and walrus mustache jiggling. . . . I began to feel ashamed to be associated with these hate-filled, drunken pigs" (p. 52). The final blow to Hasselbach's right-wing activism came when, for the first time, he read carefully some texts denying that the Holocaust ever happened, texts he had previously accepted unthinkingly. Their "shoddy" evidence and reasoning shocked him, and he was able to break through the denial that had controlled his life.

The Costs of Denial

Hasselbach's story, and the findings of the research on outcomes of harsh parental discipline we have presented throughout this work, confirm that the denial inevitably produced by punitive child rearing has heavy costs for individuals and society. Some might argue, of course, that there is nothing wrong with these effects of punishment. Children need to learn to obey, and if physical punishment is the only way to teach them, fine. If, in addition, people end up holding conservative political views, all the better. The trouble is that there are numerous other serious, undesirable consequences of using physical means to enforce obedience. For individuals, receiving frequent corporal punishment is associated with a higher likelihood of suicidal thoughts, depression, drug addiction, and child and spousal abuse. It is also associated with a tendency toward aggressive behavior, tolerance of violence, and the support of its use. Denial appears to put people at risk for health problems, to impair their ability to cope with problems and think clearly, and to contribute to the intergenerational transmission of violence.

On the social level, we saw that punitive child rearing is connected with prejudice and intolerance toward minority groups. Our discussion of the Religious Right documents the long tradition of severe physical punishment in Protestant fundamentalist families. The ideological perspective toward child rearing Alice Miller calls "poisonous pedagogy"—whose history she traces in eighteenth-century child-rearing manuals—is alive today in James Dobson's advice to parents to abolish "defiance" in children. The religious right's militant and sometimes violent opposition to abortion and to homosexual rights, and the documented link between right-wing militia groups and fundamentalist beliefs, are extreme manifestations of the dangerous link between extensive childhood punishment and authoritarian political views. Moreover, we have seen that the punitive social and political attitudes underlying the fundamentalists' social program are increasingly reflected in the national political agenda.

Further societal consequences of punitiveness are evident in the schools and the criminal justice system: in California, there is a movement to allow corporal punishment in the schools, and in prisons individuals are brutalized by guards and other inmates. Alabama has reinstituted chain gangs, while in several states, proposals to allow the beating of prisoners have been discussed. Penologists and former prisoners agree that the increased punitiveness advocated is likely to have the opposite of the intended effect. Rather than reforming prisoners, such harsh policies, particularly when implemented with young, first-time offenders, are likely to produce rage and the desire for revenge that will be acted out in the community.

In a few states, some politicians have begun to realize the economic cost of punitiveness in the justice system. Wisconsin Republican Governor Tommy Thompson has declared he will not support more prison construction; Pennsylvania secretary of corrections Martin Horn has calculated that at the current rate of increase in incarceration—particularly of nonviolent drug offenders—the state will need a new prison every two to three months, which would cost up to $10 billion over the next twenty years. Some Republicans are balking at this expense. State representative Jerry Birmelin, chair of the Pennsylvania legislature's Judiciary Committee, argues that "It's really not in our best interest to build more prisons and lock up more people. I'm not saying put them out on the streets with no supervision. But if they're not rapists, murderers, or violent criminals, we can have electronic monitoring and alternative sentencing. The key is making restitution" (Jackson 1996, p. 11).

Perhaps the most disturbing effect of denial and displaced punitive attitudes is in the political arena. Using emotionally compelling themes dramatized in simplistic media images, politicians can win office by manipulating residual rage and fear among the electorate. Evidence that dramatic media images erode the ability to remember and process information in the news suggests that such images used in campaign ads have a similar negative effect on people's ability to assess the claims and qualifications of candidates. George Bush successfully defined his 1988 campaign around two sensational issues, flag burning and prison furloughs, by using such a dramatic technique, the Willie Horton tape, to exploit the public's fear of crime. In the meantime, both parties in the election ignored the catastrophic consequences of the savings-and-loan deregulation debacle. Political leaders also use melodramatic images of evil enemies to gain public support for using military force against other nations; and there is evidence that the perceptions created by such images have exactly the intended effect.

For children, the political consequences of punitive child rearing and the denial that surrounds it are often victimization. Marian Wright Edelman, president of the Children's Defense Fund, assessed the cuts in welfare proposed by the Republican Congress in an interview with Calvin Tomkins (1996): "They're proposing to cut two hundred and fifty billion dollars from programs for poor children, poor families, disabled children—and it's not even to balance the budget! It's to give a two-hundred-and-forty-five-billion-dollar tax cut to the non-needy. . . . I have never seen less attention paid to facts or the truth" (p. 24). Edelman's open letter to President Clinton, published in the *Washington Post* in November 1995, urged him to respond to this crisis. He has, although somewhat belatedly, promised to veto legislation that would have negative consequences for children.

Edelman voiced her frustration to Tomkins: "I don't think I've ever seen more people who are aware that something fundamental has come loose in this country. What in the world has happened to us, that we've become so numb, so spiritually dead? Our children are dying like flies. A child dies from guns every ninety-eight minutes in this country, and from poverty every fifty-three minutes, and from child abuse every seven hours. Is there one shred of evidence that punishing children will change the behavior of parents? I am sick and tired of begging people not to hurt children" (p. 26).

Evidence that there is a childhood basis for the current distortion of the political process by conservative politicians, from Patrick Buchanan to Newt Gingrich, seems overwhelming. Historically, conservative politicians have tended to protect and advance the interests of wealthy individuals and large corporations. As only a small percentage of the voting public falls into these categories, conservatives seek to persuade citizens to vote against their own self-interests by marrying simplistic economic policies to emotional issues involving power, toughness, and retribution. Richard Nixon, for example, successfully characterized George McGovern's candidacy as favoring, "Amnesty, Acid, and Abortion," distracting attention from the destructiveness of the Vietnam War, the Watergate burglary, and McGovern's populist economic proposals.

One might argue that the 1996 election will be different, since the seemingly emotionally neutral topic of a "balanced budget" is such a central issue. The notion of a balanced budget, which suggests old-fashioned fiscal restraint on the part of candidates, has often proved to be an illusion. Ronald Reagan campaigned in 1980 for a balanced budget and then presided over unbalanced budgets that tripled the national debt. The current balanced-budget debate is not so much about economic responsibility as it is about economic choices, about how the government should spend money. Conservatives derided programs in Clinton's crime bill—for example, a minor expenditure for midnight basketball to provide constructive alternatives for young people—and labeled them pork-barrel spending. Instead they called for more money to be spent on prisons and military weapons systems. In fact, research (Embry 1996) has demonstrated that having organized sports activities available to youths significantly decreases violence in schools.[1]

The denial of racism is one more political consequence of displaced emotion. At a time when highly publicized cases such as the Rodney King trial and the O. J. Simpson verdict should serve as a wake-up call to political leaders and the public alike about the broad gulf between the perceptions of black and white Americans, we are seeing a revival of the old divisive, and largely spurious, issue of racial differences in intelligence. Books such as *The Bell Curve,* by implying or stating that differences in achievement between blacks and whites are attributable to genetic causes, deny the consequences of racism in America and perpetuate racism. In doing so, they scapegoat African Americans and other people of color, setting them up as targets for displaced anger. Politicians can exploit negative images of minorities, including immigrants, to gain office. Focusing public anger against these groups allows politicians to neglect genuine, broader systemic issues that desperately need to be addressed; for example, how America can forge a new national identity that includes the diversity of its population, or how to reduce crime and drug dependence.

Scapegoating of despised minority groups has led in this century to repeated episodes of genocide, against Jews, Armenians, Cambodians, Tutsi, and others. It is our belief that punitive child rearing can serve as the foundation for genocide when other factors, such as psychosocial dislocation, are also present. Punitive child rearing is linked with obedience to orders to harm others and leaves individuals with feelings of shame, weakness, and self-hatred that—when projected onto minority groups—can fuel the wish to eradicate an entire people.

Authoritarianism, with its roots in punitive, harsh treatment of children, is also significantly related to opposition to environmental protection. The politicians who currently control the U.S. Congress, and who disregard the evidence of ozone depletion and global warming, are re-enacting the practice of science in the Stalin era; that is, finding the few scientists who espouse beliefs they want to promulgate and then trumpeting their findings and opinions while disregarding the opposing broad scientific consensus. Politicians who can deny, without evidence, the conclusions reached by a worldwide scientific community are capable of a dangerously high level of denial and should be voted out of office.

The negative consequences of punishment, in the form of cognitive rigidity, prejudice, and so on, far outweigh the small benefits. Moreover, punitiveness doesn't work, whether it is used in the family, in schools, in prison, or as the basis of public policy. It simply fuels greater levels of both denial and punitiveness.

Breaking Through Denial

The system and modes of denial found in the United States are a result of the way children have been raised and the political system that has evolved in that context. Consequently, there are no easy, instant fixes to this problem. The eventual solution depends on change at a variety of levels, beginning with individuals and extending to the social and political arenas.

On the Individual Level

Individuals can begin to counter the effects of denial on their thinking and their political and social attitudes by thinking and talking about their childhood experiences with others. Often we take for granted experiences that, if they had happened to someone else, might seem shocking or abusive. As our research has indicated, simply recalling these events seems temporarily to reduce the displacement of emotions onto political attitudes. Research also suggests that talking and writing about traumatic experiences, including childhood abuse, has very significant benefits over a longer term. Pennebaker and Beall (1986) found that, while writing about a traumatic experience produced a temporary increase in blood pressure and negative mood immediately thereafter, it also resulted in a significant decrease in the number of doctor visits over the next six months.

Individuals can also examine their social and political attitudes, particularly those they feel most emotional about, and attempt to identify the roots of that emotion. Are such attitudes based on reasoned political thinking, discussions and evidence, or some other foundation? We can become aware of when retribution serves as the basis of our political attitudes. One example of such a reaction occurred in many individuals in the wake of the Oklahoma City bombing. Many people publicly voiced the desire for retribution against the perpetrators and called for the death penalty for those responsible. It is easy to understand the desire for revenge in this instance. But it is also possible to feel the sorrow and rage of the victims and their families and still separate those emotions from the question of how this event could have happened and how we can prevent such events from happening again. We are not likely to answer these questions or solve these problems by executing the bombers but, instead, by attempting to understand how individuals are attracted to violence as a means of protest.

Developing higher levels of *emotional intelligence,*—a term made popular by clinical psychologist Daniel Goleman (1995) to describe awareness of one's emotions and the ability to manage them—is an important component of breaking through denial. Goleman documents how emotional illiteracy, an aspect of denial, contributes to higher divorce rates, conflict in the workplace, physical illness, and to aggressiveness, drug abuse, and depression resulting from punishment and abuse in childhood. According to Goleman, emotional relearning is necessary for many people to overcome the trauma, abuse, or emotional damage done to them during childhood. Psychotherapy can provide such an emotional tutorial.

There are, however, other avenues for emotional relearning, including powerful resources located within communities. Ingo Hasselbach's conversion from the hate-driven ideology of neo-Nazism occurred when a man who seemed to value him as a person reflected his actions back to him on film. We have seen too that the presence of one dissenting ally in the replications of Stanley Milgram's study of obedience to orders to harm another sharply decreases rates of obedience. Both examples suggest that the support of just one other person can help us resist pressures toward conformity—particularly conformity to cultural values that support toughness and stoicism rather than compassion and cooperation. Individuals therefore need to seek out others and find or build a community of people to whom they can speak about their experiences and emotions without being disparaged.

For Parents

Those who are parents or plan to become parents can investigate ways to teach and discipline children without using physical punishment. Many resources are available. With young children, simple behavior-modification techniques can be enormously effective, particularly with the right type of reward. A student and single mother in one of our classes a few years ago told us she needed to use her belt to discipline her nine-year-old son because he kept getting into trouble in school, and nothing else seemed to work. Yet he continued to get into trouble in school, and her emotional relationship with him was suffering. Clearly the belt wasn't working either. We suggested setting up a chart and pasting gold stars on it each day he didn't get into trouble. We also recommended that she ask her son what reward he would like for each week he managed not to get into trouble, for each month, and so on. Children often feel rewarded with far less than we might think. This mother found that one of the best rewards was simply spending time with her son, going on picnics and other outings. At the end of the semester she reported that her son was no longer getting into trouble at school and that family life was happy and peaceful for the first time in a long time. Reward succeeded where punishment had failed, miserably.

It is important, however, not to overuse behavior modification. Psychologist Thomas Gordon (1975), in his *P.E.T.: Parent Effectiveness Training*, observes that this method of solving conflict between parents and children still means that the parent "wins," and the child "loses." Gordon advocates an alternative, that is, negotiating a win-win solution in which both parents' and child's needs are met. It takes more time but the payoffs, in terms of developing more responsible children and in the quality of the parent-child relationship, are immense. Goleman and Gordon both see childhood as a "window of opportunity" for the development of emotional intelligence. Helping children to decode their emotional states, reflecting back to them what they are feeling, a technique Thomas Gordon called "active listening," is crucial. Avoiding ridicule and blame ("Look what you've done!") and instead communicating our own experiences and emotions ("I feel frightened when you do that") helps children develop the capacity for empathy.

Political Choices

In the political arena, individuals can begin to counter the negative effects of denial by being wary of politicians who offer simplistic solutions, particularly ones based on intolerance and scapegoating. Instead we can vote for candidates who have demonstrated their ability to compromise and who propose long-term solutions to such intractable problems as crime. Political leaders, for their part, need to identify counterproductive policies based on retribution, work strenuously to change them, and resist pressures to use such issues to gain votes. Responsible political leaders need to use their public position to argue for an end to the use of violence in the home and in the schools.

Necessary Changes in Public Policy

The danger we see in advocating particular policies is that many of the most serious problems that face America are long-standing, chronic problems with no one simple solution. The only way to counter denial in the long term is for political leaders and the public to commit themselves firmly to giving up violence at all levels of society and, equally firmly, to targeting resources where evidence suggests they can produce the greatest long-term benefits: in prevention and early remediation. Specific policies would include changes in schools, prisons, courts, and the way we address the problem of drug dependency.

Many changes need to made in our schools. We must begin by outlawing corporal punishment. We must pay teachers more and require that they have excellent training, not only in their subject and in education, but also in child psychology and social work. We need to hire many more teachers and provide them with the opportunity to consult with experts in their fields and with child development and education specialists who can keep them up to date on the latest scientific findings. Our educational practices should be based on empirical research about what works in the schools, rather than on impressionistic ideas or popular fads.

We also need to institute school programs in child development and child rearing. There is a national consensus that all children should graduate from high school knowing geometry and American history; they also need systematic and thorough training in such skills as conflict resolution, negotiation, management of emotions, and child rearing. Goleman proposes expanding the current mission of schools, instituting programs in emotional and social skills, and supporting teachers to develop their capacity to teach emotional awareness, empathy, and the management of emotions. Such programs could be combined in innovative ways with community-building by locating community day-care facilities in secondary schools. Such facilities could be expertly staffed and serve as training sites for high school students, both male and female, who would be required to augment their study of child development with practical, supervised experience.

Child-abuse prevention programs in schools have come under attack by conservatives, particularly religious fundamentalists. These programs must be maintained and strengthened by focusing them on teaching children to protect themselves. Because so many young children see violence in their everyday life—in their families or in their neighborhoods—schools also need to institute programs to heal children who have been exposed to violence.

Above all, the dramatic shift toward punitiveness in our society must be reversed. Mandatory sentencing should be eliminated, giving judges the necessary discretion to let the punishment fit the crime. Much greater use of alternative sentencing, with less reliance on prisons, is essential. Research has shown (e.g., Van Stelle, Mauser, and Moberg 1994) that alternative treatment programs for substance-abusing offenders reduce recidivism and are more cost effective than incarceration. The death penalty must be abolished, so that the United States can join those nations that—unlike Iraq, Iran, and a few other nations—are attempting to move beyond revenge. The tremendous drain of tax dollars, in the massive shift of funds away from schools and public assistance and toward the prison system, must stop.

We should seriously consider one proposal to address this issue: the decriminalization and regulation of drugs. People will use drugs whether they are legal or illegal. The effect of criminalizing them has been to create a "tax" on drugs—in prison time and lawyers fees—that some individuals, such as those in organized crime, are willing to pay. This tax on suppliers results in a substantial increase in the cost to individual users and produces the need for some to engage in other criminal activity, such as robbery, to support their habits.

The effect of the so-called War on Drugs has been to incarcerate thousands of nonviolent drug offenders and to brutalize many of them without substantially reducing the drug problem. A better approach would be to make drug treatment and therapy available to all who want them, and to make it, in fact, a condition for parole. There are currently long waiting lists for treatment programs, which have been shown to reduce the likelihood that a convict will commit additional crimes after being released (Treaster 1995).

Prison rape must be stopped. Several steps can be taken to accomplish this, including separating nonviolent offenders from violent ones and giving guards more training.[2]

Repairing the damage that the politics of denial has done to our society will not be easy, on a practical level or on an emotional level. Overcoming denial as a nation ultimately begins with the individual, and the personal costs of relinquishing it are high. Part of that price is confronting complex problems for which there are no easy answers—a distressing prospect. Hasselbach (1996) discovered that when he left the neo-Nazi movement, "It was as though I'd stepped out of a cartoon universe into real life and was seeing it before me in its staggering complexity. Where before I'd seen everything in terms of certainties, now I saw it as an endless string of questions" (p. 54).

Another part of the price of giving up denial is pain. The first step in breaking through denial is recognizing the punitive treatment one has been subjected to and the residual anger resulting from it. But recognizing, feeling, and expressing anger are not enough. Many individuals in our society who have recognized that their parents, teachers, and others mistreated them, still seem perpetually angry and unhappy. For them, anger serves, ultimately, as a way of avoiding feelings of loss and grief; until those feelings too are confronted, they cannot move to the next level.

The hopeful message is that there is another level. Individuals and society both use large amounts of energy maintaining denial. When denial is no longer necessary to protect us from the pain of our experiences in a punitive society, individuals, and the nation, too, will have access to that energy for creatively solving problems. The first step, we are convinced, is to develop empathy for one's own suffering; those who can empathize with themselves can begin to have empathy and compassion for others too.

Appendix

Results of 1988 Harris Survey on Spanking

1. Correlations

Males were spanked significantly more often than females ($r = .09^{**}$), and those with higher education were spanked significantly less often ($r = -.26^{**}$). Having been spanked or hit as a child predicted approval of the use of spanking ($r = .18^{**}$) and actual use of spanking as a parent ($r = .26^{**}$).

NOTE: $^{**} = (p < .01)$; $^{*} = (p < .05)$.

2. Regression Results

Dependent Variable: OKPARSPK (OK for parents to spank their children)

Independent variables

1	....	BLACKDUM (Race)
2	....	AGE
3	....	EDUCATION
4	....	WERESCH (were spanked in school)
5	....	WERESPK (were spanked)
6	....	INCOME
7	....	JOB

Multiple R	0.27446
R square	0.07533
Adjusted R square	0.06569
Standard error	0.57492

Analysis of Variance

	DF	Sum of squares	Mean square
Regression	7	18.08299	2.58328
Residual	672	221.96781	0.33054

F = 7.81539; Signif F = .0000

Variables in the Equation

Variable	B	SE B	Beta	T	Sig T
BLACKDUM	0.035839	0.068886	.020168	0.520	0.6031
AGE	0.018173	0.010150	.069816	1.790	0.0738
EDUC	−0.063465	0.016379	−.178699	−3.875	0.0001
WERESCH	−0.035979	0.033640	−.042797	−1.070	0.2852
WERESPK	−0.108160	0.031261	−.139135	−3.460	0.0006
INCOME	−0.013942	0.015765	−0.036956	−0.884	0.3768
JOB	−0.007099	0.010560	−0.029988	−0.672	0.5016
(Constant)	3.027415	0.184925	——	16.371	0.0000

Results of 1968 Harris Survey No. 1887 (Adult Sample)

1.   Correlations

Strict child rearing

1. What young people need most of all is strong discipline by their parents (r = .11**).

Rigidity of thinking

1. Everything changes so quickly these days that I often have trouble deciding which are the right rules to follow (r = .11**);

2. People were better off in the old days when everyone knew just how he was expected to act (r = .06*).

3. Sex criminals deserve more than prison, they should be publicly whipped or worse (r = .09**). (This is a question used on the original F-scale designed to measure the authoritarian personality [Adorno et al. 1950].)

Support for violence

1. When a boy is growing up, it is important for him to have a few fist fights (r = .15**).

2. Groups have the right to train their members in marksmanship and underground warfare tactics in order to help put down any conspiracies that might occur in the country (r = .10**).

3. In dealing with other countries in the world, we are frequently justified in using military force (r = .04+).

4. Any man who insults a policeman has no complaint if he gets roughed-up in return ($r = .07^*$).

Tolerance of violence in politics

1. Some politicians who have had their lives threatened probably deserve it ($r = .07^*$).

2. Human nature being what it is, there must always be war and conflict ($r = .10^{**}$).

3. If people go into politics, they more or less have to accept the fact that they might get killed ($r = .07^*$).

4. Politicians who try to change things too fast have to expect that their lives may be threatened ($r = .05+$).

5. A lot more people in government and politics will probably be assassinated in the next few years ($r = .08^*$).

Attitude toward federal government

1. "The government in Washington is the enemy, not the friend, of people like me ($r = .07^*$)."

NOTE: $^{**} = (p < .01)$; $^* = (p < .05)$; $+ = (p < .10)$.

2. Analyses of Covariance in Support for Death Penalty

by   GOTSPANK (spanked as a child)

         SEX

with   EDUCATION

       ECONLEVEL

Source of Variation	Sum of squares	DF	Mean square	F	Sig of F
Covariates	0.099	2	0.049	1.458	0.233
EDUC	0.090	1	0.090	2.659	0.103
ECONLEV	0.001	1	0.001	0.044	0.834
Main effects	0.571	3	0.190	5.636	0.001
GOTSPANK	0.210	2	0.105	3.105	0.045
SEX	0.317	1	0.317	9.392	0.002
Two-Way interactions	0.067	2	0.034	0.994	0.371
GOTSPANK SEX	0.067	2	0.034	0.994	0.371
Explained	0.737	7	0.105	3.116	0.003
Residual	27.730	821	0.034	——	——
TOTAL	28.466	828	0.034	——	——

NOTE: 1,175 cases were processed; 346 cases (29.4 percent) were missing.

3.   Analyses of Variance in support for (composite measure of authoritarian/punitive items)

NEWAUTH
by   GOTSPANK (spanked as a child)
       SEX
with   EDUCATION
       ECONLEVEL

Source of variation	Sum of squares	DF	Mean square	F	Sig of F
Covariates	28.641	2	14.321	117.808	0.000
EDUC	25.230	1	25.230	207.554	0.000
ECONLEV	0.771	1	0.771	6.345	0.012
Main effects	1.746	3	0.582	4.789	0.003
GOTSPANK	1.246	2	0.623	5.124	0.006
SEX	0.590	1	0.590	4.853	0.028
Two-Way interactions	0.423	2	0.211	1.738	0.177
GOTSPANK SEX	0.423	2	0.211	1.738	0.177
Explained	30.810	7	4.401	36.208	0.000
Residual	102.230	841	0.122	——	——
TOTAL	133.040	848	0.157	——	——

NOTE: 1,175 cases were processed; 326 cases (27.7 percent) were missing.

Notes

Notes to the Introduction

1. *Washington Post,* February 24, 1995, p. 4, reported a January poll conducted by Peter D. Hart Research Associates sponsored by the Death Penalty Information Center. See Radelet et al. (1992) on wrongful convictions in capital cases.

2. Jennings and Niemi (1968) reported a correlation of .20 between parents' political attitudes and their children's political attitudes, and a correlation of .47 between parents' party identification and their children's party identification.

Pearson's *r*, called a *correlation coefficient,* is the statistic used in many social scientific studies to express the nature and degree of the relationship between two variables, or two factors such as adults' political attitudes and their children's political attitudes. The question psychologists address in such studies is whether, for example, one set of attitudes can be predicted from the other. Pearson's *r* can take on any value between −1 and +1. An *r* of +1 (a positive correlation) would mean that the two variables are perfectly correlated; that is, that it is possible to predict the child's attitude on some issue with complete accuracy if you know the parent's attitude and vice versa. A correlation coefficient of −1 (a negative correlation) also implies the ability to predict one variable from the other perfectly; the only difference is that the variables are inversely related—as scores on one variable increase, scores on the other decrease. So, for example, we have found that there is a negative correlation between an individual's use of denial and his or her experience with therapy. Those who have not had therapy are apt to show higher levels of denial. While the sign associated with *r* indicates whether the relationship is a direct or inverse one, the numerical value of *r* indicates how strongly associated the two variables are or how well scores on one variable can be predicted by scores on the other. An *r* of 0 means that there is no relationship between the two variables. In psychology, correlation coefficients above .3 or .4 are considered evidence of a fairly strong relationship between the variables.

It is important to note that a correlation between two variables does not imply that one causes the other. All we can say is that the two factors are related. We will address this issue in more detail in chapter 3.

3. In his *Persuasion and Politics: The Social Psychology of Public Opinion* (1991), Milburn discusses a variety of factors that affect the development and expression of political attitudes.

Notes to Chapter 1

1. Freud (1936), p. 246. Anita Eckstaedt (1989) cites and discusses Freud's example of the king's denial.

2. See Forchuk and Westwell (1987) for a discussion of Freud's early use of the term.

3. Anna Freud describes children's use of denial in fantasy, word, and action. She later refined and extended the concept of denial in a series of conversations with fellow analysts reported in Freud and Sandler (1985).

4. Levin (1969a, 1969b) addresses the denial of shame; Zetzel (1943), the denial of anxiety; Altschul (1969), the denial of grief, and Emerson and Harrison (1990) the denial of anger.

5. Strauss, Gelles, and Steinmetz (1980) reported a national survey asking about kicking, biting, punching and beating up children. The estimate that 1.4 million children are abused annually is from Gelles and Cornell (1985). The 1993 Department of Health and Human Services estimate of 2.9 million children abused and neglected was reported in the *Boston Globe,* December 4, 1995, as was the fact that child abuse is the number one cause of death for children under four. The report that 84 percent of parents regularly use physical punishment on children is from Gelles (1979).

6. Among the organizations which have called for an end to the use of physical punishment are the Committee for Rights and Legal Matters of the American Academy of Child and Adolescent Psychiatry (1988); the Governing Council of the American Public Health Association (1980); and the American Academy of Pediatrics (1983, 1991). Morris, Johnson, and Clasen (1985) and McCormick (1992) report, however, that the majority of health-care professionals continue to support its use.

7. Freudian theory of identification with the aggressor as a rationale for physical punishment is discussed by Greven (1991).

8. The Cambridge-Somerville Youth Study is reported in McCord (1983, 1988) and cited in Volavka (1995). See also Becker (1964), Bongiovanni (1979), Eron (1982), and Larzelere (1986), who have all documented higher levels of aggression resulting from spanking.

9. See Herzberger (1983) and Hoffman and Saltzstein (1967).

10. See Bongiovanni (1979) and Dubanoski, Inaba, and Gerkewicz (1978).

Notes to Chapter 2

1. See Morse and Flavin (1992); Fuller (1988); and Dufour and Fe Caces (1993).

2. See Bowlby (1980); Parkes (1975); Langer (1994); and Kubler-Ross (1975).

3. See Lowery (1991) for a review of the evidence on the relationship between denial and emotional distress in heart patients.

4. Parsons, Fulgenzi, and Edelberg (1969), Cohen (1975), Scarpetti (1973), and Weinberger et al. (1979) report that denial is associated in some individuals with higher levels of physiological reactivity to stress. See also Shedler, Mayman, and Manis (1993) and Weinberger (1990).

5. See Friedman and Ulmer (1984); Krantz and Glass (1984); Williams et al. (1980); Williams, Barefoot, and Shekelle (1985); and Wood (1986).

6. Friedman and Ulmer (1984), p. 216, quoted in Hassett and White (1989).

7. See Rosenzweig and Leiman (1989) for a review of the research on stress and immune functioning.

8. See Suls and Fletcher (1985) for a review and metaanalysis of studies of the relative effectiveness of denial as opposed to other coping strategies.

9. Melanie Klein (1934, p. 282) called this *scotomization,* the denial of all feelings, and considered it to be the basis of the most severe psychopathology.

10. Zeanah and Zeanah (1989) suggest that Bowlby's (1969/1982, 1973, 1980) theory of attachment can be used to explain the process of transmission of abuse from one generation to the next. Bowlby argues that an individual, beginning in infancy, develops cognitive structures Bowlby calls a *working model,* which contains representations of the self and important others that guide responses in social interactions. See Zeanah and Zeanah (1989) for a discussion of research showing a relationship between childrens' behavior and their parents' models of attachment.

11. Main et al. (1985) found a 76 percent agreement between ratings of infants and their mothers, even though the mothers were measured five years after the child. A measurement closer in time would probably have yielded a greater correspondence. Eichberg (1987) found an 82 percent agreement between the Strange Situation assessment of an infant and the Adult Attachment Interview classification of the mother; and Grossman et al. (1988) found that 86 percent of mothers classified as secure (either "positive," or "non-defensive" in their attachment orientation) had infants who were classified as secure.

12. Bandura, Ross, and Ross (1963b) and Bandura, Ross and Ross (1963c). See also Kaufman and Zigler (1987) for a review of evidence for the transmission of abuse from parents to children.

13. See Aronson (1995) for a detailed discussion of these points.

Notes to Chapter 3

1. Lasswell (1930/1960). The concept of displacement, as Laswell uses it, originated with Freud: e.g., (1930/1961), p. 43.

2. See Sanford (1971) on this point; and Milburn (1991) and Stone, Lederer, and Christie (1993) for contemporary views of the relationship between authoritarianism and political conservatism.

3. See Milburn (1991) and Corbett (1991) for discussions of independent issue domains.

4. For the relationship of authoritarianism with these political issues, see Byrne and Przybyla (1980); Hanson (1981, 1989); Bailes and Guller (1970); Granberg and Corrigan (1972); Izzett (1971); and Karabenick and Wilson (1969). The quotation on the origins of authoritarianism is from Stone et al. (1993), p. 240. Hopf (1993) comments on the relationship between authoritarianism and the denial of problems originating in early experience.

5. Tomkins (1964, 1965, and 1987).

6. Weiss, Dodge, Bates, and Pettit (1992) and Quiggle, Garber, Panak, and Dodge (1992).

7. Research psychologists distinguish among the various types of evidence that can be brought to bear to support a theoretical hypothesis, such as our hypothesis that childhood punishment contributes to punitive adult political attitudes. In some sense, theory itself can be considered a form of evidence, or at least a form of argument. One could deduce from Freudian theory, for example, that individuals are likely to use defense mechanisms such as displacement to handle threatening emotions, including anger toward one's parents. In this case, the strength of the argument would depend on the internal consistency of the theory, its economy, and so forth. In contemporary psychology, however, we place more value on evidence that is empirical: evidence that is gathered in the world by observing how people actually behave. One can gather empirical evidence in a variety of ways, including, in clinical settings, by paying close attention to what patients say, their accounts of dreams, their behaviors, and even their small gestures. The problem with such evidence is that there is a danger that therapists who already have a tentative idea of the reasons for their patients' difficulties will come to see and hear what they expect, and the data gathered will be biased in favor of therapists' expectations. Also, individuals seeking therapy may not be representative of the general adult population.

For this reason, psychologists value most highly empirical evidence that is gathered in the course of deliberately constructed research studies that employ various safeguards against bias. We take up several approaches to the design of research studies later in this chapter.

8. See Neapolitan (1983); Harris (1973); Vidmar (1974); and Ellsworth and Ross (1976).

9. See Hoffman (1977) on differences between girls and boys in empathy. For

two literature reviews of gender differences in aggression, see Frodi, Macaulay, and Thome (1977) and Eagly and Steffen (1986).

10. The first study we conducted was a correlational one, that is, it measured two variables—the severity of childhood punishment and the punitiveness of adult political attitudes—at the same time. This type of design allows one to conclude that there is a correlation between the two variables—literally, whether they "co-relate" or go together—but not that one variable causes the other. An old classic example used in psychology courses dramatically illustrates the logic: it happens that there is a strong, positive correlation between the amount of ice cream consumed in a specific geographical area during a given time period and the homicide rate in that area during the same period. Most of us feel fairly certain that neither variable causes the other: eating ice cream doesn't raise your blood sugar level to the point that you feel a need to go murder someone; nor does murder normally stimulate a craving for ice cream. In fact, it is a third variable which predicts both ice cream consumption and the homicide rate: air temperature. In the summer, when it is hot, people eat more ice cream and there are more murders, in part because heat is a significant stressor that is related to aggression in humans.

11. An experiment is one of the two types of research studies, the other being a correlational study. In an experiment, the researcher manipulates one factor or variable that is of interest while holding all other factors constant, and observes the effect of the manipulation on behavior, thus establishing that there is a *causal* relationship.

12. See also Schachter (1957).

13. Levine found that men were significantly more politically conservative than women ($r = .23$) and that individuals reporting high levels of childhood punishment were significantly more conservative in their attitudes than subjects reporting low levels of punishment ($r = .25$). Both correlation coefficients reported are statistically significant at the level of $p = .05$, that is, there is less than a 5-percent probability that correlations of this size could occur purely by chance.

14. The correlation between severity of childhood punishment and anger was $r = .34$, which is statistically significant at $p = .01$, meaning there is less than a 1-percent chance of such a result occurring by chance. The correlation between experimental condition and heart rate was $r = -.43$ ($p < .001$), meaning that subjects who first recalled their childhood punishment and then expressed their political attitudes had significantly lower heart rates than subjects who answered the political-attitude items first.

15. *Boston Globe,* December 1, 1995, p. 27.

Notes to Chapter 4

1. Wuthnow and Lawson (1994); and *U.S. News and World Report* (1994).

2. Greven (1991) citing Matthew 18:3–6, p. 51; Matthew 18:10, 14, p. 51; and Proverbs 13:24, p. 48.

3. For a discussion of this phenomenon, see Minkowsi (1958).

4. See Harding (1994) and Kierulff (1992).

5. See Putnam (1989) on dissociation and its relation to childhood abuse, Spiegel and Cardena (1990) on dissociation in relation to self-hypnosis, and Terr (1994) for case studies of adults who used dissociation to cope with childhood abuse.

6. See Wylie and Forest (1992); Edgington and Hutchinson (1990); and Altemeyer and Hunsberger (1992).

7. Swomley (1995), p. 5.

8. The account of Randall Terry's antiabortion activism is based on Ginsburg (1993); all the quotations cited from that source.

Notes to Chapter 5

1. Irwin Hyman and other scholars have published extensively on the prevalence of school punishment: see, for example, Hyman (1978, 1987, 1990, and 1995), and Rose (1984). Barnhart (1972), Greven (1977, 1991), and Wiehe (1990) have found religious differences in the use of physical punishment; and Jones (1993), Richardson and Evans (1992), and Hyman (1995) document racial and class differences. Information on types of injuries sustained by children is from Hyman (1995), p. 115.

2. Quoted in Greydanus, Pratt, Greydanus, and Hoffman (1992).

3. Many studies document negative effects of punishment; see Hyman and Wise (1979); National Institute of Education (1978); Hyman (1990); and Pynoos and Eth (1985). For evidence of the escalation of punishment to physical abuse, see Hyman (1990); Feshbach 1980; Kadushin and Martin, (1981).

4. See Princeton Survey Research Associates (1994).

5. White and Zimbardo (1973), italics added.

6. Extensive information about prison rape is presented in Donaldson (1993, 1995a, and 1995b).

7. See Appendix for specific statistical results.

8. Survey results from the Harris Poll (September 1990); *Los Angeles Times* poll (September 20, 1995); Roper Center (1995); and American Viewpoint (1994). Immigration information is from Rayner (1996) and poll data on immigration from a *Times-Mirror* poll (1995).

9. McCann and Stewin (1990); and Doty, Peterson, and Winter (1991).

10. We should note that, because of the limited variability in the Harris measurement of punishment, it is more limited in its explanatory power than the measure discussed in our research presented in chapter 3. In the latter, we looked at a range of different situations in which respondents might have been punished by their parents; so there was much wider range in the variable, which increases the likeli-

hood of uncovering a significant relationship. When researchers measure a greater range of responses, statistical techniques are more likely to identify a relationship, if one in fact exists.

11. The reliability of this new variable, roughly speaking the accuracy with which the concept is measured, was high (Cronbach's alpha $= .79$; perfect reliability would be 1.0); correlation with spanking was $r = .16**$.

12. Significantly more support for the death penalty existed when the person reported a high level of spanking ($r = .07*$).

Education correlated negatively with the composite variable measuring punitiveness ($r = -.44**$); a person's education was negatively correlated with having been spanked ($r = -.15**$); and income was negatively correlated with having been spanked ($r = -.09**$).

Notes to Chapter 6

1. Helm (1990); and Beam (1994).

2. Information about Silber's background is from Epstein (1989); Butterfield (1990); and Barron (1990).

3. Cannon (1991) provides excellent information on Reagan's background.

4. Lane (1996) and Buchanan's 1988 autobiography discuss his beliefs and history at length.

5. Articles by Martinez (1994) and Lesher (1993) document Dornan's behavior and family situation.

6. See, for example, Eysenck (1954); Eysenck and Wilson (1978); and Rokeach (1954, 1960).

7. Manheim (1994); and Livingston and Dorman (1994).

Notes to Chapter 7

1. For additional documentation of the sexual abuse of female slaves, see Bourne (1837) and Child (1973).

2. Hartz is an important source of information about southern denial and intellectual history; see pp. 8, 153, 195.

3. For extensive critiques of Herrnstein and Murray, see Jacoby & Glauberman (1995) and Fraser (1995). Gould's analysis of *The Bell Curve* was originally published in *The New Yorker* (November 28, 1994) and has been reprinted in both the above anthologies. See the work of M. D. Storfer (1990). See also Hanushek and Kain (1972) for a critique of the type of statistical analysis used in *The Bell Curve*.

4. See Leonard (1990), p. 62 and Leonard (1984).

Notes to Chapter 8

1. Herr provides one of the most evocative journalistic accounts of the war. Expressions commonly used by soldiers and by the military command referred to in this account all appear in his book, *Dispatches,* with one exception. "Don't mean nothin'" is quoted by Edelman (1985) in his introduction to a collection of letters home from Vietnam.

2. When he was chief of staff of the Army, Wickham named James Dobson, author of *The New Dare to Discipline* (1992), chairman of the U.S. Army Family Initiative. See discussion of conservative child rearing in chapter 1.

3. Bush's statement, and those of other government and military officials quoted at the time of Operation Desert Storm are from Jaynes (1991).

4. This discussion of the rally-round-the-flag effect is from Mueller (1973) and Bowen (1989). Public approval ratings for the Bush administration from 1989 to 1990 are based on polls reported by the *New York Times,* August 22, 1990.

5. See Smith and Bond (1994) for a discussion of the cross-cultural replications of Milgram's work.

6. See Staub (1989), p. 130; Dicks (1972); and Steiner (1980).

7. Alford (1990), p. 13.

8. Lifton's views on genocide are summarized in Markusen (1992).

9. See Camacho, Bowen and Hunt (1991) for estimates of the number of Vietnam veterans diagnosed with post-traumatic stress disorder.

For accounts of post-traumatic stress disorder among civilian populations, see Mollica, Wychak, de Marneffe, Khuon, and Lavalle (1987); Chodoff (1963); Krupinski, Stoller, and Wallace (1973); Kinzie, Frederickson, Ben, Fleck, and Karls (1984); and Lopez, Boccelari, and Hall (1988).

10. Herman (1992) describes the long-term symptoms of PTSD, including intrusive memories and psychic numbing. See Egendorf, Kadushin, Laufer, Rothbart, and Sloan (1981) for evidence that Vietnam veterans are more apt to experience isolation and alienation from their peers. Intimacy deficits among Vietnam veterans have been reported in Penk, Robinowitz, Roberts, Patterson, Dolan, and Atkins (1981); Carroll, Rueger, Foy, and Donahoe (1985); and Roberts, Penk, Gearing, Robinowitz, Dolan, and Patterson (1982). Shalev et al. (1993) have documented the physiological overreactivity to ordinary stressors of combat veterans with PTSD. See Jordan et al. (1992), Reilly et al. (1994), Hiley-Young et al. (1995) and Maloney (1988) for documentation of domestic violence among combat veterans.

Notes to Chapter 9

1. For Marxist critiques of environmentalism and Meadows et al., see Sandbach (1978) and Burgess (1978).

2. See O'Riordan (1981) and Milbrath (1984); for the origins of the NEP, see Dunlap and Van Liere (1978). Taylor (1992) also writes about the Green party.

3. For scientific findings on melanoma, see Lew et al. (1983); Rauterberg and Jung (1993); Koh, Sinks, Geller, Miller, and Lew (1993); and Friedman et al. (1991).

4. For an analysis of money involved in antienvironmental testimony, see Gelbspan (1995), pp. 33–34. Interested readers may also want to consult *The Greenpeace Guide to Anti-environmental Groups*.

Notes to Chapter 10

1. Embry 1996, personal communication.

2. For more information, contact Stop Prison Rape, Inc., Stephan Donaldson, President. The address is Stop Prisoner Rape, Inc.; P.O. Box 2713; Manhattanville Station; New York, NY 10027–8817.

References

ABC/*Washington Post* Poll. 1981. September 14, 1981. Roper Center accession no. 0007975.

Adorno, T. W., Frenkel-Brunswik, E., Levinson, D. J., and Sanford, A. N. 1950. *The authoritarian personality.* New York: Harper & Row.

Ainsworth, M. D. S., Belhar, M., Waters, E., et al. 1978. *Patterns of attachment: A psychological study of the strange situation.* Hillsdale, NJ: Lawrence Erlbaum.

Alford, C. F. 1990. The organization of evil. *Political Psychology* 11(1):5–27.

Alford, J. D., Mahone, C., and Fielstein, E. M. 1988. Cognitive and behavioral sequelae of combat: Conceptualization and implication for treatment. *Journal of Traumatic Stress* 1(4):489–501.

Allen, S. 1995. Global warming debate joined. *Boston Globe,* November 17, 1995, p. 20.

Allgeier, A. R., Allgeier, E. R., and Rywick, T. 1981. Orientations toward abortion: Guilt or knowledge? *Adolescence* 16:272–280.

Allport, G. W., and Ross, J. M. 1967. Personal religious orientation and prejudice. *Journal of Personality and Social Psychology* 5:432–43.

Altemeyer, B. 1981. *Right-wing authoritarianism.* Winnipeg: University of Manitoba Press.

Altemeyer, B. 1988. *Enemies of freedom: Understanding right-wing authoritarianism.* San Francisco: Jossey-Bass.

Altemeyer, B., and Hunsberger, B. 1992. Authoritarianism, religious fundamentalism, quest, and prejudice. *International Journal for the Psychology of Religion* 2(2):113–33.

Altheide, D. L. 1987. Format and symbols in TV coverage of terrorism in the United States and Great Britain. *International Studies Quarterly* 31:161–76.

Altschul, S. 1969. Denial and ego arrest. *This Journal* 16:301–18.

American Academy of Child and Adolescent Psychiatry. 1988. Corporal punishment in schools. A policy statement. AACAP: Washington, D.C.

American Academy of Pediatrics, Committee on Psychological Aspects of Child and Family. 1983. The pediatrician's role in discipline. *Pediatrics* 72:373–74.

American Academy of Pediatrics, Committee on School Health. 1991. Corporal punishment in schools. *Pediatrics* 88:173.

American Viewpoint. 1994. American Viewpoint Poll, April 1994. Roper Center accession no. 0229480.

Archer, D., and Gartner, R. 1978. Peacetime casualities: The effects of war on the violent behavior of noncombatants. In *Violence: Perspectives on murder and aggression,* ed. I. L. Kutash, S. B. Kutash, and L. B. Schlesinger, pp. 219–32. San Francisco: Jossey-Bass.

Archer, D., and Gartner, R. 1984. *Violence and crime in cross-national perspective.* New Haven: Yale University Press.

Arendt, H. 1965. *Eichmann in Jerusalem: A report on the banality of evil.* New York: Viking Press.

Aronson, E. 1995. *The social animal,* 7th ed. New York: W. H. Freeman.

Atlas, J. 1990. Understanding the correlation between childhood punishment and adult hypnotizability as it impacts on the command power of modern "charismatic" political leaders. *The Journal of Psychohistory* 17:309–18.

Bailes, D., and Guller, I. 1970. Dogmatism and attitudes toward the Vietnam War. *Sociometry* 33:140–46.

Bailey, R. 1993. *Eco-scam: The false prophets of ecological apocalyse.* New York: St. Martin's Press.

Bailey, W. C., and Peterson, R. D. 1989. Murder and capital punishment: A monthly time-series analysis of execution publicity. *American Sociological Review* 54:722–43.

Bandura, A., Ross, D., and Ross, S. 1963a. Imitation of film-mediated aggressive models. *Journal of Abnormal and Social Psychology* 66: 3–11.

Bandura, A., Ross, D., and Ross, S. 1963b. A comparative test of the status envy, social power, and secondary reinforcement theories of identificatory learning. *Journal of Abnormal and Social Psychology* 67:527–34.

Bandura, A., Ross, D., and Ross, S. 1963c. Vicarious reinforcement and initiative learning. *Journal of Abnormal and Social Psychology* 67:601–607.

Bandura, A., and Walters, R. H. 1959. *Adolescent aggression: A study of the influence of child-training practices and family interrelationships.* New York, Ronald Press.

Barnhart, J. 1972. *The Billy Graham religion.* Philadelphia: The Pilgram Press.

Barron, J. 1990. The 1990 Campaign: Man in the news, outspoken newcomer: Dr. John Robert Silber. *New York Times,* September 20, 1990. p. A16.

Batson, C. D. 1971. Creativity and religious development: Toward a structural-functional psychology of religion. Unpub. Ph.D. diss., Princeton University.

Batson, C. D., and Raynor-Prince, C. 1983. Religious orientation and cognitive complexity. *Journal for the Scientific Study of Religion* 22:38–50.

Beam, A. 1994. Three gentlemen from Texas: Exploring the Lone Star state of mind. *Boston Globe,* January 23, 1994, p. 67.

Becker, W. C. 1964. Consequences of different kinds of parental discipline. In *Review of child development research,* ed. M. L. Hoffman & L. W. Hoffman. New York: Russell Sage Foundation.

Begley, S. 1993. Is the ozone hole in our heads? *Newsweek* October 11, 1993.

Bennett, W. L. 1996. *News: The politics of illusion,* 3rd ed. White Plains, N.Y.: Longman.

Bernstein, W. M. 1984. Denial and self-defense. *Psychoanalysis and Contemporary Thought* 7:423–57.

Bissinger, H. G. 1995. *The Killing Trail. Vanity Fair,* February 1995.

Blanchard, E. B., Kolb, L. C., Pallmeyer, T. P., et al. 1982. A psychophysiological study of posttraumatic stress disorder in Vietnam veterans. *Psychiatric Quarterly* 54:220–29.

Bolch, B. and Lyons, H. 1993. *Apocalypse not: Science, economics, and environmentalism.* Washington D.C.: Cato Institute.

Bongiovanni, A. F. 1979. An analysis of research on punishment and its relation to the use of corporal punishment in schools. In *Corporal punishment in American education: Readings in history, practice, and alternatives,* ed. I. A. Hyman and J. H. Wise. Philadelphia: Temple University Press.

Bourgois, P. 1995. *In search of respect: Selling crack in El Barrio.* Cambridge: Cambridge University Press.

Bourne, G. 1837. Slavery illustrated in its effects on woman and domestic society. Boston: Isaac Knapp.

Bowen, G. L. 1989. Presidential action and public opinion about U.S. Nicaraguan policy: Limits to the "rally 'round the flag" syndrome. *Political Science & Politics* 22(4):793–98.

Bowlby, J. 1969/1982. *Attachment.* New York: Basic Books.

Bowlby, J. 1973. *Separation.* New York: Basic Books.

Bowlby, J. 1980. *Loss.* New York: Basic Books.

Brecht, B. 1957. *Brecht on theater: The development of an aesthetic.* New York: Hill and Wang.

Buchanan, P. J. 1988. *Right from the beginning.* Boston: Little, Brown.

Burgess, R. 1978. The concept of nature in geography and Marxism. *Antipode* 10:1–11.

Burns, H. 1973. Can a black man get a fair trial in this country? In *Race, creed, color, or national origin,* ed. Robert Yin. Itasca, Ill.: F. E. Peacock.

Burnstein, J. 1995. *Where's the payoff?* Washington D.C.: Economic Policy Institute.

Butterfield, F. 1990. Boston educator offers a bold campaign style. *New York Times,* April 6, 1990, p. A14.

Butterfield, F. 1995. *All God's children: The Bosket family and the American tradition of violence.* New York: Knopf.

Butz, A. R. 1975. *The hoax of the twentieth century.* Richmond, England: Historical Review Press.

Byrne, D., and Przybyla, D. P. J. 1980. Authoritarianism and political preferences in 1980. *Bulletin of the Psychonomic Society* 16:471–72.

Camacho, P. R., Bowen, K. J., and Hunt, D. 1991. *From a troubled past to an uncertain future: Vietnam veterans, a community at risk.* University of Massachusetts at Boston: William Joiner Center.

Cannon, L. 1991. *President Reagan: The role of a lifetime.* New York: Simon and Schuster.

Carey, J. 1995. Why business doesn't back the GOP backlash on the ozone. *Business Week,* July 24, 1995, p. 47.

Carroll, E. M., Rueger, D. B., Foy, D. W., and Donahoe, C. P. 1985. Vietnam veterans with post-traumatic stress disorder: Analysis of marital and cohabiting adjustment. *Journal of Abnormal Psychology* 94:329–37.

Carson, R. 1962. *Silent spring.* Cambridge: Houghton Mifflin.

Carver, C. S., Scheier, M. F., and Weintraub, J. K. 1989. Assessing coping strategies: A theoretically based approach. *Journal of Personality and Social Psychology* 56(2):267–83.

Cassirer, E. 1953–1957. *The philosophy of symbolic forms.* Ralph Manheim, trans. New Haven: Yale University Press.

CBS/*New York Times* poll. August 1986. Roper Center accession no. 0017891.

Child, L. M., ed. 1973. *Linda Brent: Incidents in the life of a slave girl.* New York: Harcourt Brace Jovanovich.

Chodoff, P. 1963. Late effects of the concentration camp syndrome. *Archives of General Psychiatry* 8:323–33.

Christie, R. 1993. Some experimental approaches to authoritarianism: II Authoritarianism and punitiveness. In W. F. Stone, G. Lederer, and R. Christie eds. *Strength and weakness: The authoritarian personality today.* New York: Springer-Verlag.

Coccaro, E. F. 1993. Heritability of impulsive-aggressive behavior: A study of twins reared together and apart. *Psychiatry Research* 48:229–42.

Cohen, B., Eden, R., and Lazar, A. 1991. The efficacy of probation versus imprisonment in reducing recidivism of serious offenders in Israel. *Journal of Criminal Justice* 19:263–70.

Cohen, D. B. 1975. Eye movements during REM sleep: the influence of personality and presleep conditions. *Journal of Personality and Social Psychology* 32: 1090–93.

Coleman, J. S., Campbell, G. Q., Hobson, C. J., McPartland, J., Mood, A. M., Weinfeld, F. D., and York, R. L. 1966. *Equality of Educational Opportunity,* 2 vols. Washington, D.C.: U.S. Government Printing Office, OE-38001.

Collins, D. L., Baum, A., and Singer, J. E. 1983. Coping with chronic stress at Three Mile Island: Psychological and biochemical evidence. *Health Psychology* 2(2):149–66.

Conrad, S. D., Casimira, P. S., and Milburn, M. A. Dissociative effects of violent news on person perception and the capacity for intimacy. Unpubl. manuscript. University of Massachusetts/Boston.

Corbett, M. 1991. *American public opinion: Trends, processes, and patterns.* White Plains, N.Y.: Longman.

D'Souza, D. 1995. *The end of racism.* New York: The Free Press.

Davis, A. Y. 1981. *Women, race, and class.* New York: Random House.

Davis, J. A., and Smith, T. W. 1994. *General Social Survey, 1972–1991* [machine-readable data file]. Chicago National Opinion Research Center. Chapel Hill, N.C.: Institute for Research in Social Science (distributor).

Dermatology World. 1995. Protection of ozone layer under fire in Congress. November 1995, p.1.

DeSantis, J. 1994. *The new untouchables: How America sanctions police violence.* Chicago: The Noble Press.

Dicks, H. V. 1972. *Licensed mass murder: A sociopsychological study of some SS killers.* New York: Basic Books.

Dimsdale, J. E., and Hackett, T. P. 1982. Effect of denial on cardiac health and psychological assessment. *American Journal of Psychiatry* 139:1477–80.

Dobson, J. 1992. *The new dare to discipline.* Wheaton: Ill.: Tyndale House.

Dodge, K. A., Bates, J. E., and Pettit, G. S. 1990. Mechanisms in the cycle of violence. *Science* 250:1678–83.

Dollinger, S. J., and Cramer, P. 1990. Children's defensive responses and emotional upset following a disaster: A projective assessment. *Journal of Personality Assessment* 54(1&2):116–27.

Donaldson, S. 1993. The rape crisis behind bars. *The New York Times,* December 29, 1993.

Donaldson, S. 1995a. Can we put an end to inmate rape? *USA Today* magazine. May 1995.

Donaldson, S. 1995b. Stop Prison Rape World Wide Web site: http://www.igc.apc.org/spr/.

Doty, R., Peterson, B., and Winter, D. 1991. Threat and authoritarianism in the United States, 1978–1987. *Journal of Personality and Social Psychology* 61:629–40.

Dowie, M. 1995. *Losing ground: American environmentalism at the close of the twentieth century.* Cambridge: MIT Press.

Dubanoski, R. A., Inaba, M., and Gerkewicz, K. 1978. Corporal punishment in schools: Myths, problems, and alternatives. *Child Abuse and Neglect* 7:195–99.

Dufour, M. C., and FeCaces, M. 1993. Epidemiology of the medical consequences of alcohol. *Alcohol Health & Research World* 17(4):265–271.

Dunlap, R. E., and Van Liere, K. 1978. The New Environmental Paradigm. *The Journal of Environmental Education* 9:10–19.

Eagly, A. H., and Steffen, V. J. 1986. Gender and aggressive behavior: A meta-analytic review of the social psychological literature. *Psychological Bulletin* 94:100–31.

Eckstaedt, A. 1989. Ego-syntonic object manipulation: The formation of a submissive relationship. *International Journal of Psychoanalysis* 70:499–512.

Edelman, B., ed. 1985. *Dear America: Letters home from Vietnam.* New York: Pocket Books.

Edelman, M. 1971. "Information and cognition." In his *Politics as Symbolic Action: Mass Arousal and Quiescence.* New York: Academic Press.

Edgington, T. J., and Hutchinson, R. L. 1990. Fundamentalism as a predictor of cognitive complexity. *Journal of Psychology and Christianity* 9(1):47–55.

Egendorf, A., Kadushin, C., Laufer, R., Rothbart, G., and Sloan, L. 1981. *Legacies of Vietnam: Comparative adjustment of veterans and their peers.* Washington, D.C.: U.S. Government Printing Office.

Ehrenreich, B. 1992. Cauldron of anger: Domestic issues that stirred our emotions. *Life,* January 1, 1992, p. 62.

Eichberg, C. 1987. Quality of infant-parent attachment: Related to mother's representation of her own relationship history. Paper presented to Biennial Meeting, Society for Research in Child Development, Baltimore, 1987.

Ellison, C. G., and Musick, M. 1993. Southern intolerance: A fundamentalist effect? *Social Forces* 72(2): 379–98.

Ellison, R. 1964. *Shadow and act.* New York: Random House.

Ellsworth, P., and Ross, L. 1976. Public opinion and judicial decision making: An example of research on capital punishment in the United States. In *Capital Punishment in the United States,* ed. H. Bedau and C. Pierce. New York: AMS Press.

Elms, A. C., and Milgram, S. 1966. Personality characteristics associated with obedience and defiance toward authoritative command. *Journal of Experimental Research in Personality* 2:282–89.

Embry, D., and Malfetti, J. L. 1982. Safe playing. Final report on process field test. AAA Foundation for Traffic Safety. August 1982. Washington, D.C.

Emerson, C. S., and Harrison, D. W. 1990. Anger and denial as predictors of cardiovascular reactivity in women. *Journal of Psychopathology and Behavioral Assessment* 12(4):271–83.

Engdahl, B. E., Speed, N., Eberly, R. E., and Schwartz, J. 1991. Comorbidity of psychiatric disorders and personality profiles of American World War II prisoners of war. *Journal of Nervous and Mental Disease* 179(4):181–87.

Epstein, H. 1989. Crusader on the Charles. *New York Times Magazine*, May 28, 1989, p. 10.

Erlanger, H. 1974. Social class and corporal punishment in child-rearing: A reassessment. *American Sociological Review* 39:68–85.

Eron, L. D. 1982. Parent-child interaction, television violence and aggression of children. *American Psychologist* 37:197–211.

Etheredge, L. S. 1975. Personality and foreign policy. *Psychology Today* 9:37–42.

Eysenck, H. J. 1954. *The psychology of politics*. London: Routledge & Kegan Paul.

Eysenck, H. J., and Wilson, G. D. 1978. *The psychological basis of ideology*. Baltimore: University Park Press.

Fairbanks, J. D. 1982. Reagan, religion, and the New Right. *Midwest Quarterly* 23(3):327–45.

Faludi, S. 1989. Where did Randy go wrong? *Mother Jones*, November 1989, pp. 22–28, 61–64.

Feshbach, N. 1980. Physical punishment: The fraternal twin of child abuse. In *Children and Violence, Proceedings of the International Symposium on Violence*, ed. R. Barren. Stockholm: Akademi Litteratur.

Festinger, L. 1957. *A theory of cognitive dissonance*. Stanford: Stanford University Press.

Fick, P. 1995. *The dysfunctional president*. New York: Birch Lane Press.

Firor, J. 1990. *The changing atmosphere*. New Haven: Yale University Press.

Fisher, D. E. 1990. *Fire and ice, the greenhouse effect, ozone depletion and nuclear winter*. New York: Harper & Row.

FitzGerald, F. 1972. *Fire in the lake: The Vietnamese and the Americans in Vietnam*. New York: Vintage.

Fitzhugh, G. 1854. *Sociology for the South; or, The failure of a free society*. Richmond, Va., A. Morris.

Fitzhugh, G. 1857. *Cannibals all! or, Slaves without masters*. Richmond, Va.: A. Morris.

Fivush, R. 1989. Exploring sex differences in the emotional content of mother-child conversations about the past. *Sex Roles* 20:675–91.

Flowers, R. B. 1988. *Minorities and criminality.* New York: Greenwood Press.

Flynn, J. R. 1987. Massive IQ gains in fourteen nations: What IQ tests really measure. *Psychological Bulletin* 101:171–91.

Foa, E. B., and Kozak, M. J. 1986. Emotional processing of fear: Exposure to corrective information. *Psychological Bulletin* 99:20–35.

Fogel, R. W., and Engerman, S. L. 1974. *Time on the cross: The economics of American negro slavery.* Boston: Little Brown.

Forchuk, C., and Westwell, J. 1987. Denial. *Journal of Psychosocial Nursing* 25(6):9–13.

Franck, I., and Brownstone, D. 1993. Ozone. In *The green encyclopedia,* pp. 231–32. New York: Prentice Hall.

Fraser, S. 1995. *The bell curve wars: Race, intelligence, and the future of America.* New York, N.Y.: Basic Books.

Frenkel-Brunswik, E. 1954. Further explorations by a contributor. In *Studies in the scope and method of the authoritarian personality,* ed. R. Christie and M. Jahoda. Glencoe, Ill.: Free Press.

Freud, A., 1946, 1966. *The ego and the mechanisms of defense,* rev. ed. New York: International Universities Press.

Freud, A., and Sandler, J. 1985. *The analysis of defense: The ego and the mechanisms of defense revisited.* New York: International Universities Press.

Freud, S. 1930/1961. *Civilization and its discontents,* trans. J. Strachey. New York: Norton.

Freud, S. 1936. A disturbance of memory on the Acropolis. An open letter to Romain Rolland. In *The standard edition of the complete psychological works of Sigmund Freud,* ed. J. Strachey, vol. 22. London: Hogarth Press.

Freud, S. 1955/1985. Studies in Hysteria. In *The standard edition of the complete psychological works of Sigmund Freud,* ed. J. Strachey, vol. 1. London: Hogarth Press.

Friedman, M., and Ulmer, S. 1984. *Treating Type A behavior and your heart.* New York: Knopf.

Friedman, R. J., Rigel, D. S., Kopf, A. W., Harris, M. N., and Raker, J. W. 1991. *Cancer of the skin.* Philadelphia: W. B. Saunders.

Frodi, A., Macaulay, J., and Thome, P. R. 1977. Are women always less aggressive than men? A review of the experimental literature. *Psychological Bulletin* 84:634–60.

Fuller, R. K. (1988). Validity of self-report in alcoholism research: Results of a Veterans Administration cooperative study. *Alcoholism: Clinical and Experimental Research* 12(2):201–205.

Gallup Poll. 1988. Attitudes toward the public schools. April 8, 1988. Roper Center accession no. 0045153.

Gallup Poll. 1996. February 1996. Roper Center accession no. 0252616.

Gallup/*Newsweek* Poll. 1988. December 1988. Roper Center accession no. 0050323.

Gardner, H. 1983. *Frames of mind: The theory of multiple intelligences.* New York: Basic Books.

Gelbspan, R. 1995. The heat is on: The warming of the world's climate sparks a blaze of denial. *Harper's Magazine,* December 1995, pp. 31–37.

Gelles, R. J. 1979. Violence toward children in the United States. In his *Family violence* (1987). Newbury Park, Calif.: Sage.

Gelles, R. J., and Cornell, C. P. 1985. *Intimate violence in families.* Beverly Hills, Calif.: Sage.

Genovese, E. D. 1974. *Roll, Jordan, roll: The world the slaves made.* New York: Pantheon.

Genovese, E. D. 1988. *The world the slaveholders made: Two essays in interpretation.* Middletown, Conn.: Wesleyan University Press.

George, C., Kaplan, N., and Main, M. 1984. The Adult Attachment Interview. Unpublished. Department of Psychology, University of California at Berkeley.

Gibbs, N., and Tumulty, K. 1995. Master of the House. *Time,* December 25, 1995–January 1, 1996, pp. 54–83.

Gibson, J. T., and Haritos-Fatouras, M. 1986. The education of a torturer. *Psychology Today* 20:50–58.

Ginsburg, F. 1993. Saving America's souls: Operation Rescue. In *Fundamentalisms and the state: Remaking polities, economies, and militance,* ed. Martin E. Marty and R. Scott Appleby, vol. 3, the Fundamentalism Project. Chicago: University of Chicago Press.

Glock, C. Y., and Stark, R. 1966. *Christian beliefs and anti-Semitism.* New York: Harper and Row.

Godwin, R. 1996. The exopsychic structure of politics. *Journal of Psychohistory* 23:252–59.

Goldman, P., and Fuller, T. 1985. *The quest for the presidency 1984.* New York: Bantam Books.

Goleman, D. 1995. *Emotional intelligence.* New York: Bantam Books.

Goodwin, D. K. 1995. Taking his measure: Five historians weigh Newt on the scales of time—and against other leaders. *Time,* December 25, 1995–January 1, 1996, p. 98.

Gordon, L. 1988. *Heroes of their own lives: The politics and history of family violence.* New York: Viking Penguin.

Gordon, T. 1975. *P.E.T.: Parent effectiveness training.* New York: New American Library.

Gould, S. J. 1981. *The mismeasure of man.* New York: W. W. Norton.

Gould, S. J. 1994. Curveball. *New Yorker,* November 28, 1994.

Gourevitch, P. 1995. Letter from Rwanda: After the Genocide. *New Yorker,* December 18, 1995, pp. 78–94.

Governing Council, American Public Health Association. 1980. Corporal punishment of children in schools and institutions. *American Journal of Public Health* 70:308–309.

Granberg, D., and Corrigan, G. 1972. Authoritarianism, dogmatism, and orientations toward the Vietnam War. *Sociometry* 35:468–76.

Grant, W. B. 1988. Letter commenting on Scotto et al., "Global stratospheric ozone and UVB radiation." *Science,* November 25, 1988, p. iiii.

Grasmick, H. G., Bursik, R. J., Jr., & Kimpel, M. (1991). Protestant Fundamentalism and attitudes toward corporal punishment of children. *Violence and Victims, 6,(4),* 283–298.

Grasmick, H. G., Davenport, E., Chamlin, M. B., Bursik, R. J., Jr. 1992. Protestant Fundamentalism and the retributive doctrine of punishment. *Criminology, 30 (1),* 21–45.

Grasmick, H. G., Morgan, C. S., & Kennedy, M. B. 1992. Support for corporal punishment in the schools: A comparison of the effects of socioeconomic status and religion. *Social Science Quarterly, 73,* 177–187.

Greenberg, J., Pyszczynski, T., Solomon, S., and Rosenblatt, A. 1990. Evidence for terror management theory II: The effects of mortality salience on reactions to those who threaten or bolster the cultural worldview. *Journal of Personality and Social Psychology* 58:308–18.

Greenberg, J., Simon, L., Pyszczynski, T., Solomon, S., and Chatel, D. 1992. Terror management and tolerance: Does mortality salience always intensify negative reactions to others who threaten one's worldview? *Journal of Personality and Social Psychology* 63:212–20.

Greer, S. 1983. Cancer and the mind. *British Journal of Psychiatry* 143:535–43.

Greider, W. 1991. The politics of diversion: Blame it on the blacks. *Rolling Stone,* September 5, 1991, pp. 32–33, 96.

Greven, P. 1977. *The Protestant Temperament: Patterns of child-rearing, religious experience, and the self in early America.* New York: Knopf.

Greven, P. J. 1991. *Spare the child: The religious roots of punishment and the psychological impact of physical abuse.* New York: Vintage.

Greydanus, D. E., Pratt, H. D., Greydanus, S. E., and Hoffman, A. D. 1992. Corporal punishment in schools: A position paper of the Society for Adolescent Medicine. *Journal of Adolescent Health* 13:240–46.

Groh, L. S. 1981. Primitive defenses: Cognitive aspects and therapeutic handling. *International Journal of Psychoanalytic Psychotherapy* 8:661–83.

Grossman, K., Fremmer-Bombik, E., Rudolf, J., and Grossman, K. E. 1988. Maternal attachment representations as related to patterns of infant-mother attachment and maternal care during the first year. In *Relationships within families:*

Mutual influences, ed. R. A. Hinde and J. Stevenson-Hinde. Oxford: Clarendon Press.

Gutman, H. G. (1976). *The black family in slavery and freedom, 1750–1925.* New York: Pantheon.

Hackett, T. P., and Cassem, N. H. 1974. Development of a quantitative rating scale to assess denial. *Journal of Psychosomatic Research* 18:93–100.

Hammond, P. E., Shibley, M. A., and Solow, P. M. 1994. Religion and family values in presidential voting. *Sociology of Religion* 55(3):277–90.

Hanson, D. J. 1981. Authoritarianism and candidate preference in the 1980 presidential election. *Psychological Reports* 49:326.

Hanson, D. J. 1989. Authoritarianism and candidate preference in the 1988 presidential election. *Psychological Reports* 64:914.

Hanushek, E. A., and Kain, J. F. 1972. On the value of *Equality of Educational Opportunity* as a guide to public policy. In *On equality of educational opportunity,* ed. F. Mosteller and D. P. Moynihan. New York: Random House.

Harding, S. 1994. Imagining the last days: The politics of apocalyptic language. In *Accounting for fundamentalisms,* ed. M. E. Marty & R. S. Appleby, vol. 4, the Fundamentalism Project. Chicago: University of Chicago Press.

Harris, L. 1968. Harris Survey no. 8817. Harris Data Archive, Institute for Research in the Social Sciences, University of North Carolina, Chapel Hill.

Harris, L. 1973. *The Harris Survey.* New York: Lou Harris and Associates.

Harris, L. 1988. Harris Survey no. 884019. Harris Data Archive, Institute for Research in the Social Sciences, University of North Carolina, Chapel Hill.

Harris Poll. 1990. Harris Poll, July 8, 1990. Roper Center accession no. 0059016.

Harris Poll. 1990. Harris Poll, September 7, 1990. Harris Survey no. 902041. Harris Data Archive, Institute for Research in the Social Sciences, University of North Carolina, Chapel Hill.

Hartz, L. 1955. *The liberal tradition in America.* New York: Harcourt, Brace & World.

Hasselbach, I., with Reiss, T. 1996. How Nazis are made. *New Yorker,* January 8, 1996.

Hasselbach, I. 1996. *Führer-Ex: Memoirs of a former neo-Nazi.* New York: Random House.

Hassett, J., and White, K. M. 1989. *Psychology in perspective,* 2nd ed. New York: Harper & Row.

Havik, O., and Maeland, J. G. 1988. Verbal denial and outcome in myocardial infarction patients. *Journal of Psychosomatic Research* 32(2):145–57.

Hawkins, H., and Thomas, R. 1991. White policing of black populations: A history of race and social control in America. In *Out of order?: Policing black people,* ed. E. Cashmore and E. McLaughlin. London: Routledge.

Haywood, T. W., and Grossman, L. S. 1994. Denial of deviant sexual arousal and psychopathology in child molesters. *Behavior Therapy* 25:327–40.

Helm, S. 1990. Voter fury shakes Massachusetts. *The Independent,* October 30, 1990, p. 10.

Hempel, L. C. 1993. Greenhouse warning: The changing climate in science and politics. *Political Research Quarterly* 46:213–39.

Herman, J. L. 1981. *Father-daughter incest.* Cambridge: Harvard University Press.

Herman, J. L. 1992. *Trauma and recovery.* New York: Basic Books.

Herr, M. 1977. *Dispatches.* New York: Avon.

Herrnstein, R. J., and Murray, C. M. 1994. *The bell curve: Intelligence and class structure in American life.* New York: Free Press.

Herzberger, S. D. 1983. Social cognition and the transmission of abuse. In *The dark side of families: Current family violence research,* ed. D. Finkelhor, R. J. Gelles, G. T. Hotaling, & M. A. Straus. Beverly Hills, Calif.: Sage.

Hiley-Young, B., Blake, D. D., Abueg, F. R., Rozynko, V., and Gusman, F. D. 1995. Warzone violence in Vietnam: An examination of premilitary, military, and postmilitary factors in PTSD in-patients. *Journal of Traumatic Stress* 8(1):125–41.

Hilgard, J. 1970. *Personality and hypnosis: A study of imaginative involvement.* Chicago: University of Chicago Press.

Hinojosa, M. 1995. Will harsher sentencing laws deter crime? Morning Edition (National Public Radio), December 11, 1995.

Hoffman, M., and Saltzstein, H. D. 1967. Parent discipline and the child's moral development. *Journal of Personality and Social Psychology* 5:45–57.

Hoffman, M. L. 1977. Sex differences in empathy and related behaviors. *Psychological Bulletin* 84:712–22.

Hogan, J. P. 1993. Ozone politics: They call this science? *Omni* 15:34–42, 91.

Hokanson, J. E., and Edelman, R. 1966. Effects of three social responses on vascular processes. *Journal of Abnormal and Social Psychology* 3:442–47.

Hopf, C. 1993. Authoritarians and their families: Qualitative studies on the origins of authoritarian dispositions. In *Strength and weakness: The authoritarian personality today,* ed. W. F. Stone, G. Lederer, and R. Christie. New York: Springer-Verlag.

Hunsberger, B., Pratt, M., and Pancer, S. M. 1994. Religious fundamentalism and integrative complexity of thought: A relationship for existential content only? *Journal for the Scientific Study of Religion* 33(4):335–46.

Hyman, R. A. 1978. A social science review of evidence cited in litigation on corporal punishment in schools. *Journal of Child Clinical Psychology* 7:195–200.

Hyman, R. A. 1987. Psychological correlates of corporal punishment and physical abuse. In *Psychological maltreatment of children and youth,* ed. M. Brassard, S. Hart & B. Germain. Elmsford, N.Y.: Pergamon Press.

Hyman, R. A. 1990. *Reading, writing and the hickory stick: The appalling story of physical and psychological abuse of American school children.* Lexington, Mass.: Lexington Books.

Hyman, R. A. 1995. Corporal punishment, psychological maltreatment, violence, and punitiveness in America: Research, advocacy, and public policy. *Applied and Preventive Psychology* 4:113–30.

Hyman, R. A., and Wise, J. 1979. *Corporal punishment in American education.* Philadelphia: Temple University Press.

Ivins, M. 1995. Something rotten in the GOP's eco-proposals. *Boston Globe,* December 12, 1995, p. 17.

Izzett, R. 1971. Authoritarianism and attitudes toward the Vietnam war as reflected in behavioral and self-report measures. *Journal of Personality and Social Psychology* 17:145–48.

Jackson, D. 1996. We're prisoners of bad thinking about punishment. *Boston Globe,* January 3, 1996, p. 11.

Jacoby, R., and Glauberman, N. 1995. *The* Bell Curve *debate: History, documents, opinions.* New York: Times Books.

Jaynes, G. 1991. Into the storm. *Life* 14(3):41–82.

Jennings, M. K., and Niemi, R. G. 1968. The transmission of political values from parent to child. *American Political Science Review* 62:169–84.

Johnson, S. L. 1983. Race and the decision to detain a suspect. *Yale Law Journal* 93:214.

Jones, A. E., and Shanklin, J. D. Continued decline of total ozone over Halley, Antarctica, since 1985. *Nature* 376 (August 3, 1995):409–11.

Jones, L. 1993. Why are we beating our children? *Ebony* (March).

Jones, R. R. 1992. Ozone depletion and its effects on human populations. *British Journal of Dermatology* 127:2–6.

Jordan, B. K., Marmar, C. R., Fairbank, J. A., Schlenger, W. E., Kulka, R. A., Hough, R. L., and Weiss, D. S. 1992. Problems in families of male Vietnam veterans with posttraumatic stress disorder. *Journal of Consulting and Clinical Psychology* 60(6): 916–26.

Kadushin, A., and Martin, J. 1981. *Child abuse: An interactional event.* New York: Columbia University Press.

Kagan, J. 1994. *Galen's prophecy.* New York: Basic Books.

Karabenick, S., and Wilson, W. 1969. Dogmatism among war hawks and peace doves. *Psychological Reports* 25:419–22.

Karlin, E. 1995. An abortionist's credo. *New York Times Magazine,* March 19, 1995, p. 32.

Kaufman, L. 1994. Life beyond God. *New York Times Magazine,* October, 16, 1994.

Kaufman, J., and Zigler, E. 1987. Do abused children become abusive parents? *American Journal of Orthopsychiatry* 57(2):186–92.

Kellstedt, L., and Smidt, C. 1991. Measuring fundamentalism: An analysis of different operational strategies. *Journal for the Scientific Study of Religion* 30(3): 259–78.

Kenworthy, T., and Lee, G. 1995. Divided GOP falters on environmental agenda. *Washington Post,* November 24 1995, Section A, p. 1.

Kierulff, S. 1992. Armageddon theology and the risk of global war: The limits of religious tolerance in the nuclear age. *Journal of Humanistic Psychology* 32(4):92–107.

Kinzie, J. D., Frederickson, R. H., Ben, R., Fleck, J., and Karls, W. 1984. Posttraumatic stress disorder among survivors of Cambodian concentration camps. *American Journal of Psychiatry* 141:645–50.

Kirkpatrick, L. 1993. Fundamentalism, Christian orthodoxy, and intrinsic religious orientation as predictors of discriminatory attitudes. *Journal for the Scientific Study of Religion* 32(3):256–68.

Klein, M. 1934. A contribution to the psychogenesis of manic-depressive states. In her *Contributions to psychoanalysis, 1921–1945,* pp. 282–310. London: Hogarth, 1948.

Koh, H. K., Sinks, T. H., Geller, A. C., Miller, D. R., and Lew, R. A. 1993. Etiology of melanoma. *Cancer Treatment Research* 65:1–28.

Kranish, M. 1994. Gingrich's rise: Long, costly, calculated: Backers' millions helped him realize a vision. *Boston Globe,* November 20, 1994, p. 1.

Krantz, D. S., and Glass, D. C. 1984. Personality, behavior patterns, and physical illness: Conceptual and methodological issues. In *Handbook of behavioral medicine,* ed. W. D. Gentry, pp. 38–86. New York: Guilford.

Krupinski, J., Stoller, A., and Wallace, L. 1973. Psychiatric disorders in East European refugees now in Australia. *Social Science Medicine* 7:31–49.

Kubler-Ross, E. 1975. *Death: The final stage of growth.* Englewood Cliffs, N.J.: Prentice-Hall.

Lane, C. 1996. Daddy's boy. *New Republic,* January 22, 1996, pp. 15–25.

Langer, K. G. 1994. Depression and denial in psychotherapy of persons with disabilities. Special Section: Psychotherapy and physical disability. *American Journal of Psychotherapy* 48(2):181–94.

Larzelere, R. E. 1986. Moderate spanking: Model or deterrent of children's aggression in the family? *Journal of Family Violence* 1:27–36.

Lasswell, H. D. 1930/1960. *Psychopathology and politics.* New York: Viking Press.

Lechner, F. J. 1989. Fundamentalism revisited. *Society* 26(2):51–59.

Lee, V. E., and Loeb, S. 1995. Where do Head Start attendees end up? One reason why preschool effects fade out. *Educational Evaluation and Policy Analysis* 17:62–82.

Lehigh, S., and Phillips, F. 1990. Poll finds Weld leading Silber. *Boston Globe,* September 29, 1990, p. 24.

Lemonick M. D. 1992. The ozone vanishes. *Time,* February 17, 1992, pp. 60–63.

Leonard, J. S. 1984. Anti-discrimination or reverse discrimination: The impact of changing demographics, Title VII and affirmative action on productivity. *Journal of Human Resources* 19:145–74.

Leonard, J. S. 1990. The impact of affirmative action regulation and equal employment law on black employment. *Journal of Economic Perspectives* 4:47–63.

Lesher, D. 1993. "I take full blame": Sallie Dornan says a longtime drug addiction drove her to falsely accuse her husband of abuse. *Los Angeles Times,* June 24, 1993, p. 1.

Levin, S. 1969a. A common type of marital incompatibility. *This Journal* 17:421–36.

Levin, S. 1969b. Further comments on a common type of marital incompatibility. *This Journal* 17:1097–1113.

Levine, J., Warrenburg, S., Kerns, R., Schwartz, G., Delaney, R., Fontana, A., Gradman, A., Smith, S., Allen, S., and Cascione, R. 1987. The role of denial in recovery from coronary heart disease. *Psychosomatic Medicine* 49(2):109–17.

Levine, R. 1996. Childhood punishment, emotion, and political ideology. Unpubl. Sr. honors thesis, University of Massachusetts/Boston.

Lew, R. A., Sober, A. J., Cook, N., Marvell, R., and Fitzpatrick, T. B. 1983. Sun exposure habits in patients with cutaneous melanoma: A case control study. *Journal of Dermatological Surgery and Oncology* 9(12):981–86.

Liebes, T., Katz, I., and Ribak, R. 1991. Ideological reproduction. *Political Behavior* 13(3):237–52.

Lifton, R. J. 1968. *Revolutionary immorality: Mao Tse-tung and the Chinese Cultural Revolution.* New York: Random House.

Lifton, R. J. 1973. *Home from the war: Vietnam veterans—neither victims nor executioners.* New York: Simon and Schuster.

Lifton, R. J. 1982. *Death in life: Survivors of Hiroshima.* New York: Random House.

Lifton, R. J. 1986. *The Nazi doctors: Medical killing and the psychology of genocide.* New York: Basic Books.

Linebaugh, P. 1995. The farce of the death penalty. *Nation,* August 14, 1995, p. 165.

Lipset, S. M. 1959. Democracy and working-class authoritarianism. *American Sociological Review* 24:482–501.

Lipstadt, D. 1993. *Denying the Holocaust: The growing assault on truth and memory.* New York: Free Press.

Livingston, S., and Dorman, W. A. (1994). News and historical content: The establishment phase of the Persian Gulf policy debate. In *Taken by storm: The media, public opinion, and U.S. foreign policy in the Gulf war,* ed. W. L. Bennett and D. L. Paletz, pp. 63–81. Chicago: University of Chicago Press.

Loewen, J. W. 1995. *Lies my teacher told me: Everything your American history textbook got wrong.* New York: New Press.

Logan, R. 1970. *The betrayal of the Negro.* New York: Macmillan.

Longres, J. F. 1991. An ecological study of parents of adjudicated female teenage prostitutes. *Journal of Social Service Research* 14:113–27.

Lopez, A., Boccelari, A., and Hall, K. 1988. Post-traumatic stress disorder in a Central American refugee. *Hospital Community Psychiatry* 39:1309–11.

Los Angeles Times poll. 1995. September 20, 1995. Roper Center accession no. 0242514.

Loth, R. 1986. The Silber agenda. *Boston Globe Magazine,* December 14, 1986, pp. 22–24, 33–37, 49–56, 59.

Lowery, B. J., 1991. Psychological stress, denial and myocardial infarction outcomes. *Image: Journal of Nursing Scholarship* 23(1):51–55.

Lyman, F. 1991. As the ozone thins, the plot thickens. *American Journal* 13:21–30.

MacArthur, John R. 1992. *Second front: Censorship and propaganda in the Gulf war.* New York: Hill and Wang.

Maduro, R. A., and Schauerhammer, R. 1992. *The holes in the ozone scare.* Washington D.C.: 21st Century Science Association.

Main, M., Kaplan, N., and Cassidy, J. 1985. Security of attachment in infancy, childhood, and adulthood: A move to the level of representation. In *Growing points in attachment theory and research,* ed. I. Bretherton and E. Waters. Society for Research in Child Development Monographs 49(6), no. 209.

Maloney, L. J. 1988. Post-traumatic stresses on women partners of Vietnam veterans. *Smith College Studies in Social Work* 58(2):122–43.

Manheim, J. B. 1994. Strategic public diplomacy: Managing Kuwait's image during the gulf conflict. In *Taken by storm: The media, public opinion, and U.S. foreign policy in the Gulf war,* ed. W. L. Bennett and D. L. Paletz, pp. 131–48. Chicago: University of Chicago Press.

Maraniss, D. 1995. *First in his class: A biography of Bill Clinton.* New York: Simon and Schuster.

Maret, S. M. 1984. Attitudes of fundamentalists toward homosexuality. *Psychological Reports* 55:205–206.

Marks, R. 1995. An overview of skin cancers: Incidence and causation. *Cancer* 75:607–12.

Markusen, E. 1991. Genocide, total war, and nuclear omnicide. In *Genocide: A critical bibliographic review,* vol. 2. New York: Facts on File.

Markusen, E. 1992. Comprehending the Cambodian genocide: An application of Robert Jay Lifton's model of genocidal killing. *Psychohistory Review* 20(2):145–69.

Martinez, G. 1994. Dornan challenges foe's claims of spousal abuse. *Los Angeles Times,* October 26, 1994, p. 1.

McCann, S. J., and Stewin, L. L. 1990. Good and bad years: An index of American social, economic, and political threat (1920–1986). *Journal of Psychology* 124:601–17.

McCord, J. 1983. A longitudinal study of aggression and antisocial behavior. In *prospective studies of crime and delinquency,* ed. K. T. Van Dusen and S. A. Mednick, pp. 269–75. Boston: Kluwer-Nijhoff.

McCord, J. 1988. Parental aggressiveness and physical punishment in long-term perspective. In *Family abuse and its consequences: New directions in research,* ed. G. T. Hotaling, D. Finkelhor, J. T. Kirkpatrick, et al. pp. 91–98. Newbury Park, Calif.: Sage.

McCormick, K. F. 1992. Attitudes of primary care physicians toward corporal punishment. *Journal of the American Medical Association* 267(23):3161–65.

McFarland, S. G. 1989. Religious orientations and the targets of discrimination. *Journal for the Scientific Study of Religion* 28(3):324–36.

Mead, F. S. 1965. *Handbook of denominations in the United States,* 4th ed. New York: Abingdon Press.

Meadows, D. H., Meadows, D. L., Randers, J., and Behrens, W. 1972. *The limits to growth.* London: Earth Island.

Merelman, R. M. 1969. The development of political ideology: A framework for the analysis of political socialization. *American Political Science Review* 63: 750–67.

Milbrath, L. W. 1984. *Environmentalists: Vanguard for a new society.* Albany: SUNY Press.

Milburn, M. A. 1991. *Persuasion and politics: The social psychology of public opinion.* California: Brooks/Cole.

Milburn, M. A., Conrad, S. D., Sala, F., and Carberry, S. 1995. Childhood punishment, denial, and political attitudes. *Political Psychology* 16(3):447–78.

Milburn, M. A., Luster, L., and Fine, J. 1994. Television news, emotional arousal, and cognitive complexity. Paper presented at the 17th annual meeting of the International Society of Political Psychology, Santiago de Compostela, Spain, July 13, 1994.

Milburn, M. A., and McGrail, A. B. 1992. The dramatic presentation of news and its effects on cognitive complexity. *Political Psychology* 13:613–32.

Milburn, P. B. 1995. Personal communication. (Milburn is a dermatologist in private practice in Brooklyn.)

Milgram, S. 1963. Behavioral study of obedience. *Journal of Abnormal and Social Psychology* 67:371–78.

Milgram, S. 1974. *Obedience to authority: An experimental view.* New York: Harper & Row.

Miller, A. 1983. *For your own good: Hidden cruelty in child-rearing and the roots of violence.* New York: Farrar, Straus, & Giroux.

Miller, A. H., and Wattenberg, M. P. 1984. Politics from the pulpit: Religiosity and the 1980 elections. *Public Opinion Quarterly* 48:301–17.

Minkowsi, E. 1958. Findings in a case of schizophrenic depression. In *Existence: A new dimension in psychiatry and psychology,* ed. R. May, E. Angel, & H. F. Ellenberger. New York: Simon and Schuster.

Mitchell, M. 1936. *Gone with the Wind.* Toronto: Macmillan.

Molina, M. J., and Rowland, F. S. 1974. Stratospheric sink for chlorofluoromethanes: Chlorine atom-catalysed destruction of ozone. *Nature* 249:810.

Mollica, R. F., Wychak, G., de Marneffe, D., Khuon, F., and Lavalle, J. 1987. Indochinese versions of the Hopkins Symptom Checklist-25: A screening instrument for the care of refugees. *American Journal of Psychiatry* 144:497–500.

Mooney, B. C. 1990. Survey shows Silber, Kerry leading, tax rollback losing. *Boston Globe,* October 23, 1990, p. 1.

Morin, R. 1995. A distorted image of minorities: Poll suggests that what whites think they see may affect beliefs. *Washington Post,* October 8, 1995, p. A1.

Morison, S. E. 1942. *Admiral of the ocean sea.* Boston: Little Brown.

Morison, S. E. 1955. *Christopher Columbus, mariner.* Boston: Little Brown.

Morris, J. L., Johnson, C. F., and Clasen, M. 1985. To report or not to report. Physicians' attitudes toward discipline and child abuse. *American Journal of Diseases of Children* 139:194–97.

Morse, R. K., and Flavin, D. K. 1992. The definition of alcoholism. *Journal of the American Medical Association* 268:1012–14.

Mueller, J. E. 1973. *War, presidents, and public opinion.* New York: Wiley.

National Abortion Federation. (October, 1990). Women who have abortions. National Abortion Federation Fact Sheet. Washington, D.C.: National Abortion Federation.

National Institute of Education. 1978. *Violent schools–safe schools: The safe school study report to the Congress.* Washington, D.C.: Superintendent of Documents.

National Vietnam Veterans Readjustment Study (NVVRS): Description, current status, and initial PTSD prevalence. Research Triangle Park, NC: Research Triangle Institute 1988.

Neapolitan, J. 1983. Support for and opposition to capital punishment. Some assorted social-psychological factors. *Criminal Justice and Behavior* 10:195–208.

Nel, E., Helmreich, R., and Aronson, E. 1969. Opinion change in the advocate as a function of the persuasibility of his audience: A clarification of the meaning of dissonance. *Journal of Personality and Social Psychology* 12:117–24.

Nyhan, D. 1995. Bumper-sticker prison reform. *Boston Globe,* December 6, 1995, p. 23.

Obligato, C. 1994. Facts against the death penalty. *Boston Globe,* June 25, 1994, p. 15.

O'Brien, T. 1994. The Vietnam in me. *New York Times Magazine,* October 2, 1994.

Ogletree, C. J., Prosser, M., Smith, A., and Talley, W. 1995. *Beyond the Rodney King story: An investigation of police conduct in minority communities.* Boston: Northeastern University Press.

Orentlicher, D. 1992. Corporal punishment in schools. *Journal of the American Medical Association* 267:3205–08.

Oreskes, M. 1990. Confrontation in the Gulf: Bush regains record rating in crisis. *New York Times,* August 22, 1990, p. 13.

O'Riordan, T. 1981. Environmentalism and education. *Journal of Geography in Higher Education* 5:3–18.

Otto, M. 1996. Running on religion. *Charlotte Observer,* March 3, 1996, p. 1C.

Painter, N. I. 1995. Soul murder and slavery: Toward a fully loaded cost accounting. In *U.S. history as women's history: New feminist essays,* ed. L. K. Kerber, A. Kessler-Harris, and K. Kish Sklar, pp. 125–146. Chapel Hill: University of North Carolina Press.

Parkes, C. M. 1975. Psycho-social transitions: Comparison between reactions to loss of a limb and loss of a spouse. *British Journal of Psychiatry* 127:204–10.

Parsons, O. A., Fulgenzi, L. B., and Edelberg, R. 1969. Aggressiveness and psychophysiological responsivity in groups of repressors and sensitizers. *Journal of Personal and Social Psychology* 12:235–44.

Penk, W. E., Robinowitz, R., Roberts, W. R., Patterson, E. T., Dolan, M. P., and Atkins, H. G. 1981. Adjustment differences among male substance abusers varying in degree of combat experience in Vietnam. *Journal of Consulting and Clinical Psychology* 49(3):426–37.

Pennebaker, J. W., and Beall, S. K. 1986. Confronting a traumatic event: Toward an understanding of inhibition and disease. *Journal of Abnormal Psychology* 95:274–81.

Pepper, D. 1984. *The roots of modern environmentalism.* London: Croom Helm.

Perry, J. C., and Cooper, S. H. 1986. What do cross-sectional measures of defense mechanisms predict? In *Empirical studies of ego mechanisms of defense,* ed. G. E. Vaillant. Washington, D.C.: American Psychiatric Press.

Peterson, B. E., Doty, R. M., and Winter, D. G. 1993. Authoritarianism and attitudes toward contemporary social issues. *Personality and Social Psychology Bulletin* 19:174–84.

Piaget, J. 1951. *Play, dreams and imitation in childhood*. London: Heinemann.

Pines, D. 1986. Working with women survivors of the Holocaust: Affective experiences in transference and countertransference. *International Journal of Psycho-Analysis* 67:295–307.

Pitman, R. K. 1988. Post-traumatic stress disorder, conditioning, and network theory. *Psychiatric Annals* 18(3):182–89.

Pohl, F. 1993. Ozone realities. *Omni*, June 1993 pp. 15, 36.

"Primetime," January 25, 1995.

Princeton Survey Research Associates. 1994. Princeton Survey Research Associates/*Newsweek* poll. April 1994. Roper Center accession no. 0215224.

Putnam, F. W. 1989. *Diagnosis and treatment of multiple personality disorder*. New York: Guilford Press.

Pynoos, R., and Eth, S. 1985. Developmental perspectives on psychic trauma. In *Trauma and its wake*, ed. C. R. Figley, pp. 36–52. New York: Brunner/Mazel.

Quiggle, N. L., Garber, J., Panak, W. F., and Dodge, K. A. 1992. Social information processing in aggressive and depressed children. *Child Development* 63: 1305–20.

Radelet, M. L., Bedau, H. A., and Putnam, C. E. 1992. *In spite of innocence: Erroneous convictions in capital cases*. Boston: Northeastern University Press.

Raden, D. 1981. Authoritarianism revisited: Evidence for an aggression factor. *Social Behavior and Personality* 9:147–53.

Rauterberg, A., and Jung, E. G. 1993. UV exposure, skin cancer and decrease in the ozone layer [in German]. *Ther Umsch*, 50:804–07.

Ray, D. L., and Guzzo, L. R. 1990. Trashing the planet: How science can help us deal with acid rain, depletion of the ozone, and nuclear waste (among other things). Washington, D.C. Regency Gateway.

Ray, D. L., and Guzzo, L. R. 1993. Environmental overkill: Whatever happened to common sense? Washington, D.C.: Regnery Gateway.

Rayner, R. 1996. What immigration crisis? *New York Times Magazine*, January 7, 1996, p. 26.

Reidy, C. 1996. Retailers post dismal holiday sales: More bankruptcies, store closings likely. *Boston Globe*, January 5, 1996, p. 29.

Reilly, P. M., Clark, H. W., Shopshire, M. S. Lewis, E. W., and Sovensen, D. J. 1994. Anger management and temper control: Critical components of post-traumatic stress disorder and substance abuse treatment. *Journal of Psychoactive Drugs* 26(4): 401–07.

Reuters, 1995. Mississippi House approves beatings for criminals. Reuters, February 7, 1995.

Richardson, R., and Evans, E. 1992. African American males: Endangered species and the most paddled. Paper presented at the Seventh Annual Conference of the Louisiana Association that is Multicultural, Baton Rouge, La.

Riley, V. 1981. Psychoneuroendocrine influences on immunocompetence and neoplasia. *Science* 212:1100–10.

Roan, S. 1989. *Ozone crisis: The 15-Year evolution of a sudden global emergency.* New York: Wiley.

Roberts, W. R., Penk, W. E., Gearing, M. L., Robinowitz, R., Dolan, M. P., & Patterson, E. T. 1982. Interpersonal problems of Vietnam combat veterans with symptoms of post-traumatic stress disorder. *Journal of Abnormal Psychology* 91:444–50.

Robinson, W. V. 1992. Buchanan says he'll prod Bush on foreign policy. *Boston Globe*, April 15, 1992, p. 21.

Rokeach, M. 1960. *The open and closed mind.* New York: Basic Books.

Rokeach, M. 1954. The nature and meaning of dogmatism. *Psychological Review* 61:194–204.

Roper Center. 1995. Women's equality poll. April 25, 1995. Roper Center accession no. 0237960.

Roper Center. 1987. *Parents Magazine* poll. January 14, 1987. Roper Center accession no. 0075545.

Rose, T. 1984. Current uses of corporal punishment in American public schools. *Journal of Educational Psychology* 76:427–41.

Rosengarten, T. 1975. *All God's dangers: The life of Nate Shaw.* New York: Knopf.

Rosenzweig, M. R., and Leiman, A. L. 1989. *Physiological psychology,* 2nd ed. New York: Random House.

Rowse, A. W. 1992. How to build support for war. *Columbia Journalism Review.* September/October, pp. 28–29.

Rush, G., and Molloy, J. 1995. Rep. Bob Dornan's family platitudes and attitudes. *New York Daily News,* April 19, 1995, p. 19.

Rust, J., and Kinnard, K. 1983. Personality characteristics of the users of corporal punishment. *Journal of School Psychology* 21:91–95.

Sales, S. 1972. Economic threat as a determinant of conversion rates in authoritarian and nonauthoritarian churches. *Journal of Personality and Social Psychology* 23:420–28.

Sales, S. 1973. Threat as a factor in authoritarianism: An analysis of archival data. *Journal of Personality and Social Psychology* 28:44–57.

Sandbach, F. 1978. Ecology and the "Limits to Growth" debate. *Antipode* 10: 22–32.

Sanford, N. 1971. The approach of "The Authoritarian Personality." In *A source book for the study of personality and politics,* ed. F. I. Greenstein and M. Lerner. Chicago, Ill.: Markham.

Sapp, G. L., and Jones, L. 1986. Religious orientations and moral judgment. *Journal for the Scientific Study of Religion* 25:208–14.

Scarpetti, W. L. 1973. The repression–sensitization dimension in relation to impending painful stimulation. *Journal of Consulting and Clinical Psychology* 40(3):377–82.

Schacter, J. 1957. Pain, fear, and anger in hypertensives and normotensives: A psychophysiologic study. *Psychosomatic Medicine* 19:17–29.

Scheier, M. F., and Carver, C. S. 1985. Optimism, coping, and health: Assessment and implications of generalized outcome expectancies. *Health Psychology* 4: 219–47.

Scheier, M. F., Weintraub, J. K., and Carver, C. S. 1986. Coping with stress: Divergent strategies of optimists and pessimists. *Journal of Personality and Social Psychology* 51(6):1257–64.

Scheier, M. F., Matthews, K. A., Owens, J. F., Magovern, G. J., Lefebvre, R. C., Abbott, R. A., and Carver, C. S. 1989. Dispositional optimism and recovery from coronary artery bypass surgery: The beneficial effects on physical and psychological well-being. *Journal of Personality and Social Psychology* 57:1024–40.

Schmookler, A. B. 1988. *Out of weakness: Healing the wounds that drive us to war.* New York: Bantam.

Schultz, P. W., and Stone, W. F. 1994. Authoritarianism and attitudes toward the environment. *Environment and Behavior* 26:25–37.

Science News. 1990. More groups address global warming. February 10, 1990, p. 95.

Scott, J. 1989. Conflicting beliefs about abortion: Legal approval and moral doubts. *Social Psychology Quarterly* 52(4):319–26.

Scotto, J., et al. 1988a. Global stratospheric ozone and UVB radiation. *Science,* February 12, 1988, p. 762.

Scotto, J., et al. 1988b. Response to letter from William B. Grant, *Science,* November 25, 1988, p. iiii.

Scurfield, R. M. 1992. The collusion of sanitization and silence about war: An aftermath of "Operation Desert Storm." *Journal of Traumatic Stress* 5(3):505–12.

Shabecoff, P. 1993. *A fierce green fire: The American environmental movement.* New York: Hill and Wang.

Shalev, A. Y., Orr, S. P., and Pitman, R. K. 1993. Psychophysiologic assessment of traumatic imagery in Israeli civilian patients with posttraumatic stress disorder. *American Journal of Psychiatry,* 150(4):620–24.

Shaw, R. E., Cogen, F., Doyle, B., and Palesky, J. 1985. The impact of denial and repressive style on information gain and rehabilitation outcomes in myocardial infarction patients. *Psychosomatic Medicine* 47:262–73.

Shedler, J., Mayman, M., and Manis, M. 1993. The illusion of mental health. *American Psychologist* 48:1117–31.

Sheehy, G. 1995. The inner quest of Newt Gingrich. *Vanity Fair,* September 1995, pp. 147–154, 217–222.

Simpson, J. 1987. Globalization, the New Religious Right, and the politics of the body. *Psychohistory Review* 15(2):59–75.

Simpson, J. H. 1994. The mood of America in the 1980s: Some further observations on sociomoral issues. *Sociology of Religion* 55(3):291–305.

Singer, F. 1989. Global climate change, human and natural influences. New York: Paragon House.

Sinha, R., Lovallo, W. R., and Parsons, O. A. 1992. Cardiovascular differentiation of emotions. *Psychosomatic Medicine* 54:422–35.

Smith, A. 1995. The jailing of America. *Boston Globe,* December 10, 1995, pp. 81, 82.

Smith, P. B., and Bond, M. H. 1994. *Social psychology across cultures: Analysis and perspectives.* Boston: Allyn and Bacon.

Smolowe, J. 1994. . . . and throw away the key. *Time,* February 7, 1994, p. 54.

Socolar, R. R. S., and Stein, E. K. 1995. Spanking infants and toddlers: Maternal belief and practice. *Pediatrics* 95:105–11.

Spiegel, D., and Cardena, E. 1990. Dissociative mechanisms in posttraumatic stress disorder. In *Posttraumatic stress disorder: Etiology, phenomenology, and treatment,* ed. M. E. Wolf and A. D. Mosnaim. Washington, D.C.: American Psychiatric Press.

Spielberger, C., Johnson, E. H., Russell, S. F., Crane, R. J., Jacobs, G. A., and Worden, T. J. 1985. The experience and expression of anger: Construction and validation of an anger expression scale. In *Anger and hostility in cardiovascular and behavioral disorders,* ed. M. A. Chesney and R. H. Rosenman. Washington: Hemisphere Publishing.

Spinney, D. H. 1991. How do fundamental Christians deal with depression? *Counseling and Values* 35:114–27.

Stack, S. 1987. Publicized executions and homicide, 1950–1980. *American Sociological Review* 52:532–40.

Staub, E. 1989. *The roots of evil: The origins of genocide and other group violence.* New York: Cambridge University Press.

Steele, C. M., and Aronson, J. 1995. Stereotype threat and the intellectual test performance of African Americans. *Journal of Personality and Social Psychology* 69:797.

Steiner, J. M. 1980. The SS yesterday and today: A sociopathological view. In *Survivors, victims, and perpetrators: Essays on the Nazi Holocaust,* ed. J. Dimsdale. New York: Hemisphere Publishing.

Stern, M. J., Pascale, L., and McLoone, J. B. 1976. Psychosocial adaptation following an acute myocardial infarction. *Journal of Chronic Disease* 29:513–26.

Stets, J. E., and Leik, R. K. 1993. Attitudes about abortion and varying attitude structures. *Social Science Research* 22:265–82.

Stevens, W. K. 1995. Trying to stem emissions: U.S. sees its goal fading. *New York Times,* November 28, 1995, p. A1.

Stone, W. F., Lederer, G., and Christie, R., eds. 1993. *Strength and weakness: The authoritarian personality today.* New York: Springer-Verlag.

Storfer, M. D. 1990. *Intelligence and giftedness: The contributions of heredity and early environment.* San Francisco: Jossey-Bass.

Straus, M. A., and Kantor, G. K. 1994. Corporal punishment of adolescents by parents: A risk factor in the epidemiology of depression, suicide, alcohol abuse, child abuse, and wife beating. *Adolescence* 29:543–61.

Strauss, M., Gelles, R., and Steinmetz, S. K. 1980. *Behind closed doors: A survey of family violence in America.* New York: Doubleday.

Styra, R., Sakinofsky, I., Mahoney, L., Colapinto, N. D., and Currie, D. J. 1993. Coping styles in identifiers and nonidentifiers of a breast lump as a problem. *Psychosomatics* 34(1):53–60.

Sullivan, R. 1993. An army of the faithful. *New York Times Magazine,* April 25, 1993.

Suls, J., and Fletcher, B. 1985. The relative efficacy of avoidant and non-avoidant coping strategies: A meta-analysis. *Health Psychology* 4:249–88.

Swomley, J. M. 1995. Neo-Fascism and the religious right. *The Humanist* 55(1):3–6.

Tamaroff, M. H., Festa, R. S., Adesman, A. R., and Walco, G. A. 1992. Therapeutic adherence to oral medication regimens by adolescents with cancer. II. Clinical and psychologic correlates. *The Journal of Pediatrics* 120(5):812–17.

Taubes, G. 1993. The ozone backlash: Critics of ozone depletion research. *Science* 260 (June 11, 1993): 1580.

Taylor, K. 1992. Book reviews. *Political Quarterly* 63:468–70.

Terr, L. 1994. *Unchained memories.* New York: Basic Books.

Tetlock, P. E. 1983. Cognitive style and political ideology. *Journal of Personality and Social psychology* 45:118–26.

Tetlock, P. E. 1984. Cognitive style and political belief systems in the British House of Commons. *Journal of Personality and Social psychology* 46:365–75.

Thomas, C. B., Duszynski, K. R., and Shaffer, J. W. 1979. Family attitudes reported in youth as potential predictors of cancer. *Psychosomatic Medicine* 41:287–302.

Thomson, D. J. 1995. The seasons, global temperature, and precession. *Science,* April 7, 1995, pp. 59–68.

Times Mirror poll. 1995. People and the press: Foreign policy poll. June 25, 1995. Roper Center accession nos. 0239893, 0239894, 0239895, and 0238281.

Tomkins, C. 1996. Children of a lesser country. *New Yorker,* January 15, 1996.

Tomkins, S. S. 1964. Left and right: A basic dimension of ideology and personality. In *The study of lives: Essays on personality in honor of Henry A. Murray*, ed. R. W. White. New York: Atherton.

Tomkins, S. S. 1965. Affect and the psychology of knowledge. In *Affect, cognition, and personality*, ed. S. S. Tomkins and C. E. Izzard. New York: Springer.

Tomkins, S. S. 1987. Script theory. In *The emergence of personality*, ed. J. Aronoff, A. I. Rabin, and R. A. Zucker. New York: Springer.

Tomkins, S. S. 1991. *Affect, imagery, consciousness. III. The negative affects: Anger and fear.* New York: Springer.

Tonry, M. H. 1995. *Malign neglect—Race, crime, and punishment in America.* New York: Oxford University Press.

Treaster, J. B. 1995. Drug therapy: Powerful tool reaching few inside prisons. *New York Times*, July 3, 1995, p. 1.

U.S. News and World Report poll. 1994. December 10, 1994. Roper Center accession no. 0225846.

Utility Environment Report. 1995. Report: Climate could cause more floods, droughts, health risks. October 27, 1995, p. 1.

Van Gestel, A. 1991. Why Massachusetts doesn't need the death penalty. *Boston Globe*, November 24, 1991, pp. A21, A23.

Van Stelle, K. R., Mauser, E., and Moberg, D. P. 1994. Recidivism to the criminal justice system of substance-abusing offenders diverted into treatment. *Crime and Delinquency* 40:175–96.

Victor, D. G., and Salt, J. E. 1995. Keeping the climate treaty relevant. *Nature* 373 (January 26, 1995): 280–82.

Vidmar, N. 1974. Retributive and utilitarian motives and other correlates of Canadian attitudes towards the death penalty. *Canadian Psychologist* 15:337–50.

Vissing, Y. M., Straus, M. A., Gelles, R. J., and Harrop, J. W. 1991. Verbal aggression by parents and psychosocial problems of children. *Child Abuse and Neglect* 15(3):223–38.

Volavka, J. 1995. *Neurobiology of violence.* Washington, D.C.: American Psychiatric Press.

Wagner-Pacifici, R. E. 1986. *The Moro morality play.* Chicago: The University of Chicago Press.

Wangh, M. 1989. The evolution of psychoanalytic thought on negation and denial. In *Denial: A clarification of concepts and research,* eds. E. L. Edelstein, D. L. Nathanson, and A. M. Stone, pp. 5–15. New York: Plenum Press.

Warr, M., and Stafford, M. 1984. Public goals of punishment and support for the death penalty. *Journal of Research in Crime and Delinquency* 21:95–111.

Weinberger, D. A., Schwartz, G. E., and Davidson, R. J. 1979. Low anxious, high anxious, and repressive coping styles: Psychometric patterns and behavioral and physiological responses to stress. *Journal of Abnormal Psychology* 88:369–80.

Weinberger, D. A. 1990. The construct validity of the repressive coping style. In *Repression and dissociation: Implications for personality theory, psychopathology, and health,* ed. J. L. Singer, pp. 337–86. Chicago: University of Chicago Press.

Weine, S. M., Becker, D. F., McGlashan, T. H., Laub, D., Lazrove, S., Vojvoda, D., and Human, L. 1995. Psychiatric consequences of "Ethnic Cleansing": Clinical assessments and trauma testimonies of newly resettled Bosnian refugees. *American Journal of Psychiatry* 152:536–42.

Weinstein, N. D. 1984. Why it won't happen to me: Perceptions of risk factors and susceptibility. *Health Psychology* 3:431–57.

Weisman, A. D., and Worden, J. W. 1975. Psychological analysis of cancer deaths. *Omega Journal of Death and Dying* 6(1):61–75.

Weiss, B., Dodge, K. A., Bates, J. E., and Pettit, G. S. 1992. Some consequences of early harsh discipline: Child aggression and maladaptive social information processing style. *Child Development* 63:1321–35.

West, L. J. 1967. Dissociative reaction. In *Comprehensive textbook of psychiatry,* ed. Freeman, A. M., and Kaplan, H. I. Baltimore: Williams & Wilkins.

White, B. L. 1994. Head Start: Too little and too late. *Principal* 73:13–14.

White, G., and Zimbardo, P. 1973. The Stanford prison experiment (slide and tape show). Stanford University.

Wiehe, V. R. 1990. Religious influence on parental attitudes toward the use of corporal punishment. *Journal of Family Violence* 5(2):173–86.

Wilcox, C. 1994. Premillennialists at the Millennium: Some reflections on the Christian Right in the twenty-first century. *Sociology of Religion* 55(3):243–61.

Wildavsky, A. 1995. *But is it true? A citizen's guide to environmental health and safety issues.* Cambridge: Harvard University Press.

Williams, J. P. 1969. *What Americans believe and how they worship,* 3rd ed. New York: Harper & Row.

Williams, R. B., Jr., Barefoot, J. C., and Shekelle, R. B. 1985. The health consequences of hostility. In *Anger and hostility in cardiovascular and behavioral medicine,* ed. Chesney, M. A., and Rosenman, R. H., pp. 173–85. Washington: Hemisphere Publishing.

Williams, R. B., Jr., Haney, T. L., Lee, K. L., Kong, V., and Blumenthal, J. A. 1980. Type A behavior, hostility, and coronary atherosclerosis. *Psychosomatic Medicine* 42:529–38.

Wolfgang, M. E., and Riedel, M. 1973. Race, judicial discretion, and the death penalty. *American Academy of Political and Social Science* 407:123.

Wood, C. 1986. The hostile heart. *Psychology Today* 20(September 1986):10–12.

Wool, M. S., and Goldberg, R. J. 1986. Assessment of denial in cancer patients: Implications for intervention. *Journal of Psychosocial Oncology* 4(3):1–14.

Woodward, W. E. 1936. *A new American history.* New York: Farrar & Rinehart.

Wright, R. 1995. Some like it hot. *New Republic,* October 9, 1995, p. 6.

Wuthnow, R., and Lawson, M. P. 1994. Sources of Christian fundamentalism in the United States. In *Accounting for fundamentalisms,* ed. M. E. Marty and R. S. Appleby, vol. 4, the Fundamentalism Project. Chicago: University of Chicago Press.

Wylie, L., and Forest, J. 1992. Religious fundamentalism, right-wing authoritarianism, and prejudice. *Psychological Reports* 71:12.

Yankelovich. 1994. *Time,* CNN, Yankelovich Partners poll. April 11, 1994. Roper Center accession no. 0214323.

Yeric, J. T., and Todd, J. R. 1989. *Public opinion: The visible politics,* 2nd ed. Itasca, Ill.: Peacock.

Young, R. L. 1992. Religious orientation, race and support for the death penalty. *Journal for the Scientific Study of Religion* 31(1):76–87.

Zeanah, C. H., and Zeanah, P. D. 1989. Intergenerational transmission of maltreatment: Insights from attachment theory and research. *Psychiatry* 52:177–96.

Zetzel, E. R. 1943. War neurosis: A clinical contribution. In his *The capacity for emotional growth,* pp. 12–32. New York: International Universities Press, 1970.

Zinn, H. 1995. *A people's history of the United States,* 2nd ed. New York: Harper Perennial.

Index